The
Power Pause

The Power Pause

How to Plan a Career Break
After Kids—and Come Back
Stronger Than Ever

Neha Ruch

G. P. PUTNAM'S SONS
NEW YORK

PUTNAM
— EST. 1838 —

G. P. PUTNAM'S SONS
Publishers Since 1838
An imprint of Penguin Random House LLC
penguinrandomhouse.com

Library of Congress Cataloging-in-Publication Data
Names: Ruch, Neha, author.
Title: The power pause: how to plan a career break after kids—and come
back stronger than ever / Neha Ruch.
Description: New York: G. P. Putnam's Sons, [2025] | Includes index. |
Identifiers: LCCN 2024003575 (print) | LCCN 2024003576 (ebook) |
ISBN 9780593716182 (hardcover) | ISBN 9780593716199 (epub)
Subjects: LCSH: Work-life balance. | Career development. |
Career changes. | Working mothers—Vocational guidance. |
Parents—Vocational guidance. | Family planning.
Classification: LCC HD4904.25 .R828 2025 (print) |
LCC HD4904.25 (ebook) | DDC 650.1—dc23/eng/20240307
LC record available at https://lccn.loc.gov/2024003575
LC ebook record available at https://lccn.loc.gov/2024003576

Printed in the United States of America
1st Printing

BOOK DESIGN BY KATY RIEGEL

Some names and identifying characteristics have been changed to protect
the privacy of the individuals involved.

For my father.

For always honoring my mother's impact in our home,

and for believing in me and this work, too.

Contents

PART THREE
Grow and Learn Through Your Pause

What Is a Power Pause?

DEFINITION: A phase of life in which a mother deliberately shifts her time, focus, and energy away from her career and toward her children and household. Through this process, she builds a robust community, develops a deeper understanding of her values, discovers new passions, and finds clarity on what she wants in the future. She comes out stronger—more herself—on the other side.

How to Use This Book

THE POWER PAUSE is for mothers who have the privilege to choose to stay home because it's what they want, and for mothers who stepped into stay-at-home life with reluctance, knowing it was the choice that best served their family. It's for mothers who face overwhelming burnout in the workplace and want to downshift, and for mothers whose children are struggling and need attention now more than ever. It's for expectant and postpartum mothers deciding what to do after maternity leave.

This book provides practical guidance on setting up a fulfilling life as a primary parent, but it also delivers a deeper understanding of what it means to be a stay-at-home mother in America today, along with a history of the cultural and political climate that led us here. The first section focuses on the most significant obstacles I've witnessed for women preparing to or trying to embark upon a career pause: reckoning with the identity shift, balancing a new budget, and making peace with the impact on your future career. The second section discusses settling into the season of life as a primary parent and prioritizing your fulfillment and support as you make more room for your family's needs. The third section is a reminder that even during this pause, you can evolve as a person and, yes, as a professional.

In short, this book follows the arc of a woman on pause: from the decision-making stage, to settling into the day-to-day, to unlocking your potential and embracing your next steps. Feel free to read straight through or jump to chapters that speak to where you are. *The Power Pause* offers personal stories, expert advice, and plenty of data, all of which I hope will help you journey through this stage of life with clarity, confidence, and even creativity. But like everything in motherhood, it's yours to make your own. Flag the reframes that work for you, and mark the practices that let you make the bold choices best suited to you and your family right now.

A Note About Language

THERE'S NO PERFECT term for referring to parents on pause. I don't love the phrase "stay-at-home mother," but for the sake of simplicity, I use it throughout this book. In my work with my platform Mother Untitled (and sometimes in these pages), I also use "career pause," "career break," "downshifted career," "gray area" (the in-between of stay-at-home and working mother), "lead parent," and "at-home parent." Language is powerful, and using it intentionally can help us rewrite the narrative about stay-at-home motherhood.

When I use the words "mom" or "mother," I am referring to any person who identifies as such. While this book specifically investigates the experience of mothers who pause their careers to stay at home, it's important to note that one in five stay-at-home parents today are men. This generation of fathers spends more time on parenting than any before, and much of the information in these pages is applicable to any parent who chooses to stay home. Still, men likely encounter their own unique hurdles to pausing, including external judgment for taking on a role traditionally assigned to women, and those challenges are not specifically covered here. The good news: as more women *and* men reexamine work and family, the time is ripe to rethink how our culture respects and supports parenthood—career pauses included.

The
Power Pause

Part One

Permission to Pause

1

Discover Who You Are
Without a Job Title

FALSE BELIEF

*My self-worth and identity are centered around my career,
so I'll be a "nobody" without it. Plus, parting with
my paid work means giving up on my ambition.*

NEW NARRATIVE

*I'm an ambitious and feminist woman embracing
motherhood, and that fact will help me discover
an identity even more remarkable than my job
title. There is no such thing as "just a mom."*

THE FIRST TIME I had to explain "what I do" after leaving my job,
I felt naked.

To my credit, I was close to it: wearing a bathing suit with a burp
cloth slung over my shoulder. My husband, Dan, and I were chatting with a couple who had camped out next to us at the pool club
we'd joined for the summer. Do you ever meet someone and immediately think, *Oh, she's exceptionally cool*? Well, the woman
holding her baby on the lounge chair next to mine exuded that
quality, from her gauzy coverup to her wide-brimmed hat (a look I

could never pull off). She seemed effortlessly comfortable, whereas I found the situation—it was my first time parenting in a bathing suit—sweaty and awkward. We chatted about the neighborhood and the ages of our kids. Then the dads took the kids to splash in the shallow end, and it was just us two on dry land.

"So, what do you do?" she asked.

It was an innocent question—the standard icebreaker of my life up to this point. Yet it caught me off guard because, for the first time, I couldn't give my usual answer: "I run brand strategy for a tech start-up." After business school, I'd come up with this response to instantly communicate a few impressive facts about myself. "Run" meant that I oversaw a department—shorthand for "I'm talented and was promoted to manager at a young age." In marketing, "brand strategy" also carries a panache and conveys creativity and analytical thinking. Finally, "tech start-up" implied I was plugged in and with the times.

When my first child, Bodie, was born, I'd downshifted my brand strategy work to two days per week. And now, six months later, I was hatching a plan to quit. Full stop. I'd done a lot of thinking about what that change would mean for my day-to-day life, but until that moment I hadn't really considered what it would mean for my identity and sense of self. Absent my job description, I realized I lacked a sentence to summarize my ambition and what made me unique. I had a hunch that this woman had a big career, and I wanted her to see that we were, in some way, the same.

I don't remember the exact stream of words that came out of my mouth as I attempted to answer her—probably phrases like "home with my son" and "used to be in marketing"—but I do recall that I spoke for a long time without actually *saying* anything. I felt the need to explain and defend my choice, so I talked about having lost interest in brand marketing and the shortage of resources allocated to my department and why I'd become disenchanted with my role. Basically, I offered a mouthful of business jargon without ever actually owning my decision to be home with my kid. In retrospect, I was justifying my choice not to this mom at the pool, who had done nothing but politely inquire about my work background, but to myself. Eventually I trailed off midsentence, redirecting the conversation to something about the babies, putting us both out of our awkward misery. It was clear I had work to do when it came to embracing my new identity as an at-home parent.

I was deep in thought as we loaded Bodie into his stroller and left the pool. Why couldn't I find the words to describe this new stage of life? Why did the most obvious answer—"stay-at-home mother"—feel wrong? And why did I care what a stranger thought of me, anyway?

Let Me Introduce Myself

My name is Neha Ruch, and I'm the mother to two wildly different kids—Bodie, age eight, and Lyla, age five. Our family resides on the Upper West Side of Manhattan, where we spend quite a bit of our free time shuttling between soccer practice and games, riding scooters in the park, doing craft projects at our dining table, and, like every other family, dealing with tantrums, picky eating, and ungodly early mornings. There are hard days, but I'm not ashamed to say that I love motherhood. This phase of my life has been my favorite so far.

That said, I never planned on leaving my job to raise my kids full-time.

For the decade I worked after college, I viewed my career as redemption for a few troubled teenage years when I underachieved academically (and overachieved socially) as an act of cultural rebellion and an attempt to fit into my predominantly white Massachusetts suburb. I immigrated to the United States from Mumbai at age four. Once I made it to college, I saw professional and educational accomplishment as a calling card, not to mention a way to honor my parents, who had risked a lot to give me opportunities I would not have had in India. I worked nights and weekends throughout my twenties, determined not to squander a single chance to rise up the ladder. My entrepreneur husband was attracted to my work ethic; we met at an industry conference and spent most of our courtship long-distance, venting about C-suite politics and my business school courses over FaceTime. But once I had Bodie, my world and my priorities changed. I knew in my soul that I wanted to be home.

On my first week of maternity leave, as I held Bodie in the white glider in his nursery, bottle feeding with one hand and reaching the ends of the Internet with the other, I felt a sense of calm and contentment that I'd been seeking since childhood—as if a lifetime of anxiety had been lifted from my shoulders. Don't get me wrong: I fretted over my infant like every new parent, worrying about breastfeeding (or lack thereof) and sleep (once again, lack thereof). But for the first time, I didn't worry about whether I belonged or where I stood. The prospect of exploring this new version of myself as a mother and letting this sense of peace and belonging transform me was too enticing to ignore.

But there was one wrinkle in my plan: leaving my career would make me a stay-at-home mother—and I knew just what my friends, colleagues, family, and corporate America thought of *those*.

Bodie was born in January 2016, just a few years after the publication of Sheryl Sandberg's bestselling book *Lean In*. This movement-spawning book bolstered countless women's careers but simultaneously (and much more quietly) fostered new shame around moving from paid work to full-time motherhood or even a part-time job. Everywhere I looked, someone was proclaiming that becoming a stay-at-home mother meant resigning yourself to an indefinite future of domesticity—and that if you didn't come back from maternity leave, you should forget your dreams of a big job. Even parent-centered media platforms gave little airtime to women committing most of their workweek to home life, instead favoring content focused on keeping women striving toward leadership roles. Women planning their families seemed to have two options: obsess over their careers and embrace full-fledged boss mode (like Sheryl Sandberg), or subject themselves to a selfless, dull existence at home as a stay-at-home mother.

I wanted to stay home but had no intention of being a martyr or giving up my friendships or interests. I also knew the best days of my career were still ahead of me, and I didn't see why pausing it should damage my prospects or change how others viewed me. I was determined to create a new motherhood narrative for myself and, soon enough, for the other women I met.

At the time, I lived in a fifty-story building just south of Midtown, with young families on almost every floor. Six of my neighbors gave birth to boys the year I did, and we convened in the building's playroom every afternoon. This unofficial mom group led me to other playgroups and music classes, where I met more women. On social media and in my text and WhatsApp groups, my community of fellow at-home moms grew even more. Each woman I encountered in those early days has been etched into my memory, from the merchandiser who wanted to go back to work but was laid off days after returning from leave, to the single mother who negotiated an extended maternity leave and a part-time schedule in her C-suite role. There was a seventh-grade teacher who transitioned to a part-time role as a math specialist, and a chemical engineer who switched to three days a week at home, then full-time motherhood, because she loved spending the days with her kids so much.

None of these women fit the caricature I'd been primed to expect. We had all established careers before deciding to shift focus to parenthood. Even though our babies were still, well, *babies*, we were already connecting to like-minded peers, percolating big ideas, and contemplating freelance or flex work opportunities down the line. Yet, just like me, every woman I met had been on the receiving end of some unwelcome commentary about her ambition, mental health, productivity, and contribution to the world. We all felt mislabeled and limited by the stereotype of a "stay-at-home mom."

Feeling fired up by this mismatch and eager to build my newfound mom group into a broader community, I let go of my part-time consulting work and slowly, in the fringe hours of motherhood, started Mother Untitled. The website is a first-of-its-kind digital community and resource for the ambitious woman leaning into family life. Today, Mother Untitled includes a website, a newsletter, an active Instagram account, and in-person events, and I employ a small team of moms who work for the brand part-time.

For me, Mother Untitled has provided an ongoing focus group to tease apart what I call "the gray area," the vast and varied space between stay-at-home motherhood and working motherhood, where women embrace part-time jobs, volunteerism, community engagement, and personal growth alongside parenthood. Through Mother Untitled, I've discovered that women leaving their careers for motherhood crave more guidance and insight into how to navigate their years at home. They've sacrificed *a lot* to be there and want to make the most of it, but they don't know how. Many of them feel caught off guard by challenges and wrestle with their new identity and the perception of being lazy and lacking in ambition. They want to return to the workforce someday and worry it will be all on them to figure it out. In running Mother Untitled, I've witnessed missteps and triumphs and noticed patterns. I've also learned how to minimize the downsides of a career pause and maximize enjoyment and peace of mind. This book is my chance to share all of that wisdom—and heaps of new research and advice—with you.

The Power Pause is a comprehensive guide to approaching stay-at-home motherhood—or a downshifted, part-time career—as an enriching chapter (essentially, the *opposite* of a death knell for your professional life). I'm not writing this book to argue that stay-at-home motherhood is superior to working motherhood. Children are just as likely to thrive with parents who work; there is ample evidence that high-quality daycare can be more developmentally enriching than a home environment. Staying home with your kids isn't a virtue, and neither is working.

Instead, this book is here to help you tune in to what feels right for you through each phase of parenthood. And if you feel that you must stay home, either because your children have intensive needs or because your salary is too low to justify the cost of full-time childcare, this book proves you can continue to feel empowered and professionally oriented.

My time away from the workforce occurred in fits and starts—with periods of part-time work and complete pausing, consulting for clients, and immersing myself in the mission-based passion project of Mother Untitled. Learning to regularly recalibrate your career and the time you commit to it—knowing your priorities will change repeatedly—is a big part of this book. So is dismantling the stereotypes of stay-at-home motherhood and creating a new authentic and multi-hyphenate identity. In your power pause, you can become more yourself than ever. You can discover what fills your cup and how to structure your days to feel good.

And the journey begins now.

ABOUT THE DATA IN THIS BOOK

This book references dozens of studies and surveys, and you can learn more about them in the endnotes starting on page 279. But I did want to call out one survey referenced more than any other. In 2023, eager to bring new research and well-deserved gravitas to the stay-at-home mom community, I partnered with Proof Insights, an independent research firm based in Maryland, to field a statistically significant survey to one thousand members of the general population and twelve hundred stay-at-home mothers. (All of these mothers had bachelor's degrees and children under 18 living at home.) My goal was to gather insight and data about the perception of stay-at-home motherhood in America and the lived experience of pausing an ambitious career for motherhood. I refer to this project throughout the book as the American Mothers on Pause survey, or the AMP survey for short. For more information on the survey or to read the full report, visit motheruntitled.com/americanmothersonpause.

Rewriting the Narrative

When I first embarked on a period of stay-at-home motherhood, I was determined to forge a new, empowered path. I wouldn't be a "traditional housewife" stuck at home in an apron, cut off from the professional world, meekly taking orders from my husband. I would be a feminist homemaker—eventually leading a generation of like-minded, well-educated moms who keep a hand in their careers and communities.

But as I began to dig deeper into the history of motherhood in America—reading books and interviewing historians and sociologists—one fact immediately became clear: the traditional portrait of stay-at-home motherhood, once idealized and now derided, has always been pure fiction. I'm not a historian, so I'm not going to deliver a detailed portrait of motherhood in America. (For that, I highly recommend a few history books that I reference throughout this chapter: *Modern Motherhood* by Jodi Vandenberg-Daves, *Mom* by Rebecca Jo Plant, and *The Way We Never Were* by Stephanie Coontz.) But I want to share a few insights here because once you see that your greatest fear is an invention—not a reality—it becomes much easier to sleep at night.

The archetype of the good woman and good mother as somebody domestically focused, family centered, selfless, and not as involved in the outside world began in the 1830s, says historian Jodi Vandenberg-Daves, the author of *Modern Motherhood*. But just because that model existed in literature and media doesn't mean it reflected the reality in American homes. "The majority of American mothers have always worked outside the home," says Andrea O'Reilly, a professor in the School of Gender, Sexuality and Women's Studies at York University in Canada, and the founder of the academic discipline of motherhood studies. "The idea that feminists of the 1960s invented working motherhood is wrong," she says. In the rural economy of the 1700s and 1800s, mothers were active economic producers on the family farm or in the family business. And with the rise of industrialization in the nineteenth century, mothers left their children at home alone or with childminders and worked in factories, just like men. Middle- and upper-class women didn't work for pay, but they also didn't care for their kids or clean. That work was left to governesses and housemaids, and mothers were expected to focus on entertaining and volunteer work, says O'Reilly.

Then, at the outset of World War II, women took on manufacturing and clerical jobs vacated by enlisted, wounded, and fallen soldiers. After the war, when surviving soldiers returned home, the media took on what O'Reilly calls "ideological warfare" to get women to vacate these positions. Historian Stephanie Coontz writes in her book *The Way We Never Were*, "Although 95 percent of the new women employees had expected when they were first hired to quit work at the end of the war, by 1945 almost an equally overwhelming majority did not want to give up their independence, responsibility, and income, and expressed the desire to continue working." To push women toward home, the nation invented new values, in which housekeeping was a virtue, not a chore to be outsourced or ignored. "Nineteenth-century middle-class women had cheerfully left housework to servants, yet 1950s women of all classes created makework in their homes and felt guilty when they did not do everything for themselves," writes Coontz. The amount of housework women performed increased in the 1950s, even with the rise of conveniences like boxed cake mixes, electric vacuums, and washing machines.

Because postwar America saw an unprecedented economic boom—with wages rising and the world's other industrial nations financially devastated—the American middle class widened, and some families could thrive on one salary. The circumstances were a "historical fluke," writes Coontz, and the family model it enabled sustained itself for only a short period. "The traditional nuclear family lasted maybe fifteen years for twenty percent of the population," says O'Reilly. "When I tell people that, they are shocked. Most people think that type of motherhood lasted for decades if not centuries."

Experts largely agree that the housewife ideal became cemented in the American mindset because it arose in lockstep with the invention of television. June Cleaver (from *Leave It to Beaver*), Lucy Ricardo (*I Love Lucy*), Laura Petrie (*The Dick Van Dyke Show*), and Samantha Stephens (*Bewitched*): these characters lit up TVs in just about every household in America in the 1950s and 1960s and played in reruns that still air today. When these shows debuted, they were pretty much the only entertainment available, and for that reason, they have become an inescapable, universal reference point.

The 1960s and 1970s brought the rise of second-wave feminism and Betty Friedan's seminal book *The Feminine Mystique* (1963), which critiqued stay-at-home motherhood to encourage women to step back into the workforce and vie for leadership roles. Feminists began looking at the careers of their brothers, husbands, and fathers. "They were thinking, *Why can't we have that? We have things to contribute.* And they were right," says Vandenberg-Daves. But the intensity of their frustrations and their fervent denigration of stay-at-home mothers fostered an unfortunate side effect: a distinction between "working" and "stay-at-home" mothers grew in the popular discourse. The mother at home was no longer someone others admired for her diligent care for her home and children. Instead, feminists came to view the stay-at-home mom as one to "defend tradition, not stay with the times, and potentially get duped by the patriarchy," says Vandenberg-Daves. "That was when we put the stay-at-home mom in a category." It's also when we saw the rise of horizontal hostility between mom groups (otherwise known as the origin story of the side-eye you got—or gave—at school drop-off).

In 1981, Friedan penned a new book—*The Second Stage*—in which she shared regret at the way the feminist movement had made female homemakers an enemy rather than an ally. "Our failure was our blind spot about the family. It was our own extreme reaction against the wife-mother role," she wrote. But as the image of a working mother with a briefcase and a power suit began to take hold, the archetype of the full-time stay-at-home mom remained saddled with a dated, antifeminist reputation, commanding less respect with each passing year. The stereotypical sitcom wife erased the contributions many "at home" mothers made beyond their homes. In reality, "many mothers at that time who were spending a lot of time at home with their kids were also becoming volunteers and community activists," says Vandenberg-Daves. Also missing from the history books and mainstream media: women working in the gray area in part-time roles or on side projects. Women, particularly women of color, have been at this practice for centuries.

By the 1990s, the mommy wars were in full force. In their book *The Mommy Myth*, authors Susan J. Douglas and Meredith W. Michaels describe the archetype of stay-at-home motherhood as "a boring, limited woman who had just said 'uncle' to patriarchy, spent too much time fondling Tupperware, and because she didn't work was a poor role model for her kids, especially her daughters." Thirty years later, America has yet to generate an appealing or authentic replacement for this extreme. Turn on the TV or scroll through social media and you'll see contemporary descendants of this stereotype. There's the "Real Housewife," the soccer mom, the dance mom, the PTA mom, the Queen Bee of the suburban clique, and a slew of Instagram and TikTok influencers who tend to specialize in certain subjects, from crafting to baking to organizing. Very few capture the layered existence of a modern mother.

Almost unbelievably, June Cleaver, the mother from *Leave It to Beaver*, is still the most likely persona to come to mind when people hear the phrase "stay-at-home mom." In the AMP survey, 22 percent of respondents wrote that name first when prompted to list famous stay-at-home mothers. The second and third most common responses were Carol Brady and Lucy Ricardo. By contrast, when asked to think of a working mother, the most popular responses were Michelle Obama, Hillary Clinton, and Beyoncé— real women who are deeply admired today.

The fallout from this is evident: ambitious, talented women who want to focus on family life for a chapter have few obvious role models. "Stay-at-home mothers are often looked down upon as if their education has been wasted," says Myra Strober, labor economist, former president of the International Association for Feminist Economics, and my professor in a favorite class at Stanford Graduate School of Business called Work and Family. "I hear a lot of 'Who do they think they are?' and 'They must have rich husbands,' and so on. Then, because of *Lean In*, we also got this notion that stay-at-home mothers are not only privileged but also lazy."

But if this mini history lesson teaches you anything, let it be this: stay-at-home mothers were never intended to be left out of the feminist movement, and if you pause your career, you have every right to keep your seat at the feminist table. "There's no one feminism," says Strober. "To me, the important thing in feminism is to figure out yourself what is it you want."

I genuinely believe that I became more feminist in motherhood than I was in my most traditionally ambitious work years, when I was employed at an ad agency and did whatever it took to get promoted. Feminism inspired me to start Mother Untitled, a community to support other women rerouting their paths. As for ambition? It's ambitious to direct your energy to childcare, home upkeep, and other personal and family needs for a time. This work is challenging and requires determination.

A power pause is an official invitation to untangle yourself from the archaic perceptions of stay-at-home motherhood and step into a collective of modern women. In post-pandemic America, remote work and side projects have become commonplace. Volunteering is respected. And you have access to digital learning, small business tools, and online communities that enable growth opportunities while your kids are asleep or at school.

If you leave your job for motherhood, you will not become June Cleaver. You will not become a Real Housewife. You will not be "traditional." And you don't have to say you're a stay-at-home mom if you don't want to. Instead, you will be a woman focused on family life for a chapter and a model of authentic ambition for your children and generations to come.

THE PROBLEM WITH THE TITLE "STAY-AT-HOME MOM"

One of the main reasons I found myself tongue-tied the first (second, third, . . . and twentieth) time I had to explain my profession in full-time motherhood is that I don't love the title "stay-at-home mom." (And yes, it's all over this book because there's no mainstream substitute in the English language.) On the whole, I agree with journalist Jessica Grose, who wrote in *Slate*, "[Stay-at-home mother] connotes 'shut in' . . . as if mothers who don't do paid work are too fragile to handle the outside world." I also concur with Jo Piazza, a mother of three who hosts a podcast about moms and social media called *Under the Influence*. When I asked her what the term means to her, she said, "The title 'stay-at-home mom' makes it sound like you do nothing—like you're a person who sits in the home, as opposed to being a person with agency."

The term replaced (and supposedly modernized) "housewife" and "homemaker" when it came into the vernacular in the 1990s, alongside the intensive parenting and helicopter parenting movements. *The New York Times* first used "stay-at-home mother" in 1992, and its rise in popularity marked a significant shift toward children's development as the top priority for the unpaid mom, writes historian Rebecca Jo Plant in her book *Mom: The Transformation of Motherhood in Modern America*. The "stay-at-home" part of the title is anything but fresh; that adjective has been around since the 1800s (it appears in the works of Charles Dickens and Jane Austen), when it was commonly used to describe people who barely left the house—not unlike hermits.

If it doesn't bother you to refer to yourself as a stay-at-home mom, more power to you. I readily admit that it's the easiest and quickest way to define yourself in this stage of life, and when you say it with joy, you are helping to infuse it with power. But if you find it borderline offensive, rest assured that your feelings have nothing to do with the reality of living as a full-time mom in the twenty-first century. And you're in good company.

I just ask one thing: no matter what title you land on, don't say—don't even think—"I'm *just* a mom." Motherhood is intellectual and emotional work that demands creativity, organization, communication, empathy, and more. There is nothing *just* (or, for that matter, *stay*) about it.

How to Create a New Identity
Bigger Than Your Work

Understanding what being a stay-at-home mother means to others and, more importantly, to yourself is just one part of the power pause identity equation. The second key component: grappling with what your job title and work mean to you, and what it will be like to move through the world without them.

We all self-identify with work in different ways and to varying degrees. In a 2023 Pew Research survey, forty percent of workers agreed that their job or career was "extremely or very important to their overall identity." Thirty-four percent said it was "somewhat important," while only about a quarter of those surveyed said it was "not too or not at all important." Those with a postgraduate degree were the most likely to associate their career with their identity (53 percent said it mattered a lot). These numbers reflect a decline from before the pandemic. The global lockdown spurred many to reevaluate how they spend their time and what they value.

"People are questioning the value of work, full stop, in a way that I have not seen in my lifetime," says Vandenberg-Daves. In 2023, *The Wall Street Journal* responded to the moment with the headline: "Stop Telling Everyone What You Do for a Living" in a story that encouraged professionals—employed or not—to make more space for interests beyond work in the identity they present to themselves and to others. Of course, following that advice isn't always easy. Parting with entrenched patterns takes time and practice.

I spoke with renowned gender equity researcher Amy Diehl, coauthor of *Glass Walls*, to better understand why titles mean so much to women in the workplace. The answer, she says, lies in the gender bias women face as they climb career ladders. "For women, a title conveys a level of authority. Women need that title to be perceived as credible and respected in a way that men don't," she says. "Men are often perceived to be an authority on account of one fact: they are men."

There's no question that job titles and professional titles are meaningful and important. But in a chapter at home, you'll discover that they are just one piece of your identity—and that it can be refreshing and joyful to cultivate a sense of yourself that includes your career but isn't consumed by it. A power pause is your chance to discover who you are for the long haul, and to build an even more robust, nuanced, and sustainable identity in which no single role—paid or unpaid—dominates. When you do this successfully, trust me, your confidence can soar far higher than it ever did in the workplace. This process isn't simple or quick, but approaching it strategically can help.

1. Let yourself grieve

"Grieving" might sound a little, well, *overwrought* to some. But losing (or at least changing) a big part of our self—our professional identity—can feel to many women like a profound loss. "We may think, 'Working part-time is better for my family and me; I do not regret the decision' and 'I miss the sense of purpose and accomplishment I had in the profession or job I left,'" says Emily Edlynn, a mother and psychologist who wrote for Mother Untitled about her downshift from full-time work. Many women report these same conflicting emotions, even when they are entering full-time motherhood with a lot of excitement and anticipation.

It's natural to feel grief in parting with the only adult version of yourself you've ever known. Becoming a mother is a mind-blowing transformation, and letting go of your career deepens its impact. If you're downshifting because you have no other choice, losing your job may feel particularly devastating, like a shocking breakup. Women I've met through Mother Untitled often share that their biggest challenge is answering the question, "What do you do?" after years of having a go-to response. (I'm not the only one tongue-tied at the pool.) And in the AMP survey, 23 percent of working mothers said that losing their work identity was a barrier to pausing their career, and 24 percent of stay-at-home mothers shared that they struggled with their identity once they lost their job title.

When you think about how and whether your job defines you, maybe you latch on to your skill set or your field—"I'm in tech recruiting," "I'm an anesthesiologist," or "I'm a writer." Or you might attach yourself to your employer. Ever heard someone call themselves a "Googler," or after leaving Google, a "Xoogler"? I'm guilty of that myself. In this book, you'll notice that I share the name of my fancy business school (Stanford) rather than referring to a generic MBA because I know, for better or worse, that "Stanford" adds to the perceived value. Others take pride in their title when it comes with an air of prestige (counsel, lead, director, president) or benevolence (nurse, teacher, social worker).

For Helen Ortiz, a mother of two in San Francisco, California, losing her title as a kindergarten teacher was the most significant mental stumbling block after becoming a stay-at-home mother. She had always liked the assumptions people made about her due to the role—namely, that she was kind, patient, fun, and devoted to work of meaning. "It was everything to me. It was fully my identity," she says. Helen's story reminds me of the broadcaster Audie Cornish, who held court at NPR's *All Things Considered* for ten years. She reflected on her decision to leave radio by noting, "This thing starts to feel like, 'Well, who am I without NPR?' And it took a long time to think that my own name meant anything."

Kate Terrill led a creative studio that developed marketing campaigns for a major sports retail brand, but in her heart, she wanted to be home with her kids, ages two and four. The primary block wasn't letting go of her work but her job title. Says Terrill, who resides in Portland, Oregon, "In my heart, I felt a desire to spend more time focused on family. But I was still hung up on the titles. I had done enough soul-searching to know that it was my ego talking, but I needed to do the work to be able to reconcile this."

The prestige associated with a title can be the hardest element to leave behind. Society is not likely to consistently acknowledge your value as a stay-at-home mom in any way that comes close to the cheerleading in the workforce. No one sends a community-wide email when you sleep-train your baby or manage to hold limits without yelling at your eight-year-old. But that doesn't mean you won't feel pride in your new role at home, or that the grief will haunt you for long.

There's no instant balm for grief, but acknowledging that the feeling is normal can make you less anxious about it. And remember: if pausing your career feels like a loss of identity, in some sense, that's a good thing. It means that your weekday life has mattered to you and that the career you picked was, in at least some respects, a good and meaningful match.

2.   Remind yourself that most careers aren't linear or singular

Although it may feel like our obsession with work was invented by LinkedIn, game shows, and the Mom Boss era, identifying ourselves by occupation is an age-old tradition. "People have defined themselves through their labor for centuries—think of surnames such as Baker, Brewer, Potter, and Weaver that spell out a person's profession," wrote journalist Maggie Mertens in *The Atlantic*. In the modern era, the habit typically takes shape in childhood, as we repeatedly come up with answers to the question, "What do you want to be when you grow up?" It's a bit of a strange question, given that an elementary schooler cannot fathom the options on the other side of college and graduate school. And it's also profoundly problematic—a question that assumes every person grows up to follow one career path and that depicts a career as a state of *being* rather than how a person earns a living. If you had a snappy response, and adults routinely validated it, you may have even pursued that path—developing a tunnel vision that made pivots, pauses, and plain old changing your mind feel like giving up or failing. In reality, swerves and pauses are not only normal but healthy.

As you adjust in the first weeks and months without your job, remind yourself that this is one of many influential segments of your story. "If you were to ask a sixty-year-old woman, 'Were you a stay-at-home mom or a career woman?' there's a good chance that when she looks back, there was a little bit of both, depending on her generation, race, and class," says Vandenberg-Daves. Remember that you haven't abandoned the identity of a working mom or your profession. Those are still part of your past and will also be part of your future.

While you may have stepped off a linear career path, pausing or downshifting creates an opportunity to build what organizational psychologist April Rinne calls a "career portfolio"—a theoretical envelope stuffed with all of your life experiences, jobs, volunteer positions, skills, and talents that can be interpreted and packaged in many different ways, to lead you in any number of directions. When you stop considering your career as following one trajectory, it becomes easier to see your pause as a new layer of your identity, not a gap.

3. Bring some of your work identity with you

When we start a new job, we can't help but remain attached to elements of our last one, whether it's a way of getting our work done, the panache of our title, or our place on the team. Sarah Wittman, assistant professor of management at George Mason University's business school and a mother of three, coined the term "lingering identity" to describe this common job-changing phenomenon. Sometimes, a lingering identity can be a strength—an unexpected superpower that makes you even better at your job or aligns well with your new workplace. But it can also be counterproductive, making it more challenging to feel at ease and accept the parameters of your new role. If a lingering identity lingers too large or too long, you may deem the new gig a bad fit, says Wittman. To circumvent the challenges of lingering identity, Wittman suggests that people select roles that cater to the elements of their identity they expect to have staying power. For example, if you take a lot of pride in managing people, don't seek out a role in which you have no direct reports. And if you tend to name-drop where you work in casual conversation, a company with a low-profile reputation may make the transition bumpy.

So how can you apply this advice to the transition from paid employment to stay-at-home motherhood? Some women assume that zero meaningful identifiers from their paid work will transfer to motherhood and that they'll be left with the nagging feeling that they're in the wrong place. One mother in the AMP survey wrote, "I didn't love telling people I was a stay-at-home mom. I felt like anyone could be that who chose it." The insecurity in these words nearly broke my heart when I first read them. The real work of motherhood demands intellectual labor and personal growth far greater than that found in most paid work.

To make motherhood a good job fit—one that feels like an honor—think of "mother" as the critical, elevated role it is, and take time to notice important elements of your paid work that will still be applicable. Focus less on the rote day-to-day tasks (cleaning, changing diapers, cooking) and more on the big- and small-picture thinking, planning, and self-regulation of purposeful, loving parenthood.

For example, the style of thinking and speaking that I developed working in an ad agency helped shape how I think and speak as a mother, both to my kids and the adults in their orbit. At work, I mastered the art of sharing big ideas with persuasive enthusiasm, and in motherhood, I've learned to harness that same skill in presenting new routines and projects to my kids. Other workplace skills that I'm continuing to develop at home: empathy, prioritization, and researching solutions to dilemmas both big and small.

Renee Manorat, a mother of two in Needham, Massachusetts, who held a leadership role at a global nonprofit, took comfort in the intellectual side of motherhood as she transitioned out of the workforce. "Contrary to the worst version of the stereotype of stay-at-home motherhood, parenting is such significant work that there are literally thousands of books written, and being written, on childhood development and parenting," she says.

4. Allow your sense of self to evolve

While there can be comfort in holding on to parts of your longstanding identity, there's also magic in letting yourself change and grow in motherhood. Try to stay open to the moments you learn something new about yourself or notice you've mastered an intimidating parenting task. Christine Hackett, of Brooklyn, has two children, one of whom has severe autism. Raising him, she says, has been like having a "flashlight" shined upon herself and her values. "He makes me question every assumption I had about life, and he helps me to have grace and compassion for myself when I struggle," she tells me. As for me: I used to shy away from singing and dancing, even in the shower, and now I'm the first to initiate an impromptu dance party during the witching hour. I reach for tickles and poop jokes when tantrums are looming. I've learned that I'm sillier and softer than I knew, and I love that about this new version of me.

5. Try not to worry about how your new identity is perceived

In her book *Quit*, Annie Duke, the famous poker player, explains that "the desire to maintain a positive self-image contributes to the problem with quitting." She also explains that we tend to assume people are judging us when the likelihood is far greater that they're not giving us a second thought. (In other words, that woman back at the pool was certainly much less concerned about my answer to her "What do you do?" question than I was.)

Dozens of women I've interviewed and befriended over the years have shared stories of friends, coworkers, loved ones, and strangers who questioned their ambition, mental health, productivity, and contribution to the world. They told me how those off-hand comments had instilled momentary or lingering insecurity. My friend Svenja Ostwald lives in New York City and paused a career in fashion for motherhood. (Before she moved to the United States and became a mother, she was a denim designer at Hugo Boss in Germany.) The two of us used to sit by a fountain in Madison Square Park and trade stories from our past lives in the workforce and our present lives caring for infants and, later, toddlers. She struck me as confident, energetic, and creative, and I loved to watch her and her daughter contentedly scribbling with chalk on the gray slabs of pavement between us. Svenja still remembers a comment a friend made casually when she was a few years into her career pause.

"She said, 'Wow, you have an old-school situation at home. You

raise the kids, and your husband works.'" Svenja had always pic-
tured herself as a career woman, but that comment made her examine how her pause reflected on her as a person. "I realized this
may look very 1950s, but it's also very forward. This is my choice—
and it's a conscious choice driven by my values," she says.

In the AMP survey, half the stay-at-home mothers reported
receiving negative feedback after leaving their jobs. (The most
common source of this dissent was peers and colleagues, followed
by extended family.) One thirty-seven-year-old mom wrote, "I
think people think I'm lucky that my family can afford for me to
stay home, and they think my life is easy." Another shared, "[I'm]
perceived as having nothing to do all day, perceived as unedu-
cated or unintelligent, perceived as unable to find work."

But these individual moments and experiences don't necessarily represent the larger perception. In the AMP survey, we
asked a thousand members of the general population to select
words that fit stay-at-home motherhood. Overwhelmingly, people
ranked positive traits the highest. The most resonant words (in
order) were "nurturing," "protective," "busy," "strong," "generous," and "patient," and the least resonant adjectives were "lazy,"
"selfish," "out-of-touch," "resentful," and "bored." Though un-
kind words tend to stick with us and leave us feeling unmoored,
remember that most people in America view your new job (and
title) as a net positive.

6. Create a new job title

Organizational psychologist Daniel M. Cable, a professor at London Business School and author of *Alive at Work*, has run studies
on how job titles impact employees and, through that research,

discovered that enabling workers to "retitle" themselves via a self-reflective process boosted their morale. For one paper, he studied employees at a chapter of the Make-a-Wish Foundation and a hospital chain. In both experiments, a group of employees was encouraged to "retitle" themselves, focusing on the highest purpose of their work. For example, an infectious disease specialist named himself "germ slayer," and an X-ray technician dubbed himself a "bone seeker." Cable and his research partners ultimately concluded that employees who retitled themselves had lower levels of exhaustion and felt more validated and better recognized for their work than those with traditional corporate titles. Rather than putting people into boxes, "titles can be vehicles for agency, creativity, and coping," Cable wrote.

In motherhood, you can create an energizing title that describes your strengths and powers more accurately than any rank manufactured by an HR department, and one that dignifies the intellectual labor that goes into this work. Mother Untitled members have crafted empowering (and accurate) titles including "domestic engineer," "family mastermind," and "chief family officer." Should you list this title on LinkedIn? Probably not. But you can write it down in your journal, post it on your refrigerator or bathroom mirror, or list it in your Instagram bio—and then see what magic transpires.

To write your own, follow Cable's suggested process: reflect on your job's purpose (what value is created and for whom), and then brainstorm titles, ideally getting input from colleagues or, in your case, respected friends and family. Cable contends that this process is likely more potent than the title it nets. "The exercise causes job incumbents to ask themselves, 'What is the purpose of the work, and what is my unique connection to it?'" Cable said in an article in the *Harvard Business Review*. "Most employees knew the answers to these questions at some point, but it is easy to forget them in the midst of day-to-day hassles." That truism applies to the workplace and motherhood in equal measure.

April Rinne views retitling yourself as critical to building a secure identity. "One of the things I like best about giving yourself your own title is that for as much change and uncertainty that exists in the workplace today, no one can ever take that away from you," she tells me. "You own it forever."

Being mostly at home has come to mean I am brave and free, and my values center on my family. Detaching myself from corporate organizations has allowed me to be myself, exactly as I am. I don't see any reason to shut myself into another box, and I hope that as you continue to read this book, you'll find the same freedom.

A Foolproof Formula for Answering "What Do You Do?"

When I think about the fraught nature of those four little words—"What do you do?"—I often remember a particularly moving passage from the 2001 book *The Price of Motherhood* by journalist Ann Crittenden. In it, she describes a moment at a cocktail party in DC when someone asked, "What do you do?" and she responded that she was a new mother. The person immediately walked away. "I had shed status like the skin off a snake," she wrote.

When I reflect on my poolside flub, I think a fear of that same reaction—losing this acquaintance's interest—led me to ramble nervously. With each sentence about my situation, the glow of my professional status, which was what I believed made me interesting, seemed to dim. So, after that day, I started to practice a response that made me feel like more of a bright light. Are you ready for it? "Right now, I get to be mostly with my kids." Occasionally, I toss in, "I used to work in branding" or "I'm working on a side project supporting other mothers."

While practicing might sound like overkill, preparation gave me peace of mind, and my confidence built on itself. I'm not a fan of avoiding the subject or steering clear of interactions where the topic of work might come up. Experts often suggest trying to drive conversations with alternative icebreakers like "What do you do for fun?" or "Where did you grow up?" but people *will* ask you what you do, so it's empowering to be armed with a response. After eight years of living in some version of this liminal, untitled space, I can honestly say that while answering "What do you do?" can be intimidating, it's worse not to get asked at all. Speaking with pride about your work at home—and your passions beyond it—signals that you are still part of the economy, that you still work, and that your kids are not a stand-in for your identity. You may not have a business card, but your weekdays are far from irrelevant to adults who work for pay. And as the years pass, your answer will evolve.

1. **Start with "right now."** I like to begin with the phrase "right now" to allude to the fact that a career is a long game, and this is one chapter. If people want to know what you did before or if you want to talk about it, this two-word phrase makes it clear that there is more to your story.

2. **Keep your answer succinct.** Avoid overexplaining. Most people don't need to hear your full résumé or your hopes and dreams; if they do, there will be time later to bring that up. Every interaction is not urgent, and it's not your job to make everyone understand precisely who you are.

3. **Pick your words carefully.** I like to say, "I *get* to be home with my kids," because downshifting was my choice, and there's positivity, empowerment, and gratitude in that phrasing. Had I not chosen this path, I would have started with, "Right now, I *am* home with my kids."

4. **Choose one specific secondary fact if you'd like.** Once I explain that motherhood is my main job, I sometimes share one side project, interest, or plan, just in case that tidbit resonates. Your instincts will typically tell you whether you're engaged in small talk or on the cusp of a networking opportunity. If you are with someone you want to connect with on a deeper level, give yourself more airtime to share your past, present, and future.

Here are a few responses you may want to borrow the next time you meet someone new:

- "Right now, I'm on a career pause. I'm taking a beat to focus on family, and I'm volunteering on the side."
- "I'm on a career pause right now. I'm focusing on motherhood and I'm networking to see what comes next."
- "I'm leaning into family life for this chapter. Right now, I want to be home with my kids, but I'm working on a few ideas alongside that work."

■ "I downshifted my career. I'm consulting part-time, which allows me to make more space for my kids and to work with some special teams."

Power Practice:
Craft a Modern, Feminist Portrait
of a Stay-at-Home Mom

This chapter addressed how a career pause for stay-at-home motherhood can affect your identity and laid out steps you can take to make the transition just a little bit easier. To get started on this work, complete the Mad Libs–style writing exercise below. I suggest going to your computer and typing all of the words out there, so you're left with a one-page document that you can tape up in your bedroom or keep in your bedside table, as a reminder of the dynamic person you are.

Directions: Imagine your best friend is about to tell a new acquaintance about you and your career pause. Your best friend is generous, complimentary, and admires you. Now, write what you think she would say. For some of the blanks, I've provided suggested words, but don't feel obligated to use them. Write a narrative that feels true to you.

My best friend just told me she is going to _____ (verb: pause, downshift) her work as a _____ (your former job) to focus on _____ (noun: family, her children, her own mental health).

I admire her _____ (noun: bravery, clarity, confidence, trust in

herself) for making this decision. Her ambition is clear because she is

aligning her choices and actions with her values, which include

_____ , _____ , and _____

(nouns: integrity, well-being, family, adventure, balance, change). I trust

that her career is still unfolding because she has _____ (number)

years of experience in _____ (industry) and she is _____ ,

_____ , and _____ (adjectives: creative,

optimistic, dedicated, motivated, dynamic, funny, likable, strategic, well-

connected). I know she is going to keep learning because she's also

using this time to _____ , _____ , and

_____ (activities: take online classes, participate in mom

groups, use social media strategically, find freelance opportunities, help

small businesses, volunteer, cultivate hobbies, read books, listen to

podcasts). She demonstrates her feminism every time that she

_____ (actions: advocates for her needs, is an ally to

others, negotiates, trusts her career journey). I can't wait to see how she

_____ (verb: grows, flourishes, evolves, thrives) in this

chapter!

2

Work Out the Finances and Feel Empowered

FALSE BELIEF

Giving up my salary means becoming financially dependent on my partner.

NEW NARRATIVE

My partner depends on me right now. My contribution to caregiving and family administration allows them to focus on paid work. We are an interdependent organization.

EVERY JANUARY, MY husband, Dan, takes off work for an afternoon and books a babysitter for the kids. The two of us then head out for a date that I've come to appreciate as much as any night at the movies: the annual budget forecast. It's a special New Year's version of our monthly money meeting, which usually takes place at the kitchen counter after we put the kids to bed, but before we're on the verge of passing out. On this particular January afternoon, we head to a restaurant and pore over a decidedly unsexy spreadsheet that Dan creates, which details our anticipated income and expenses. Back before we were married, Dan would plan absurdly intricate weekend-long dates for us, complete with picnic lunches and sunset hikes. These days he puts that energy toward this spreadsheet, and I have to say, I find it just as endearing. Since I shifted into at-home parenthood, my love language is respect, so I appreciate this ritual more than (most) gifts.

Our budgeting date isn't just about balancing our checkbook. We ask each other how we feel about our lives and what we want to experience and change this year. We share what worked and what didn't in the year that just passed. Then we look at the spreadsheet and try to optimize our resources. Together, we come to an agreement on every column.

No, we did not get married and turn into nerds overnight. When we were newlyweds, I knew little about finance beyond the basics of how much was coming in, how much was going out, and what was left over. But Dan ran operations at a start-up, and he immediately brought a businesslike approach to our saving and spending. When our credit card bill arrived each month, he would bring it to me with a highlighter and ask me to join him in flagging anything that stood out. At first, I balked. I wasn't used to talking about money with anyone or having someone review my taxi habit. But two years later, when I parted with my salary, I saw that going through this exercise forced us to discuss how we live, how hard we're working, and what we each need. These meetings, which started out awkward and even a little contentious, also gave us the space to talk through the financial ramifications of quitting my job—including the fact that I wanted us to identify as interdependent (a concept I hope you'll take with you by the end of this chapter) and to ban the word "dependent" from our marriage. Over the years, we've had more than seventy (and counting) money meetings, and I've become more involved in our financial planning than I ever thought I would be. I credit that growth and maturity to my career pause—and, yes, Dan's Excel skills.

Money Can Be the Biggest Hurdle

One of the most significant emotional and practical adjustments to stepping into at-home parenting or part-time work is how it changes your relationship with money. In the AMP survey, most stay-at-home mothers reported that staying home was worth the financial loss, but 44 percent also agreed or strongly agreed with the statement that they worry about money due to their decision. The most common concerns about pausing: having to rely on their partner for income (for those who were in a relationship), needing more money for leisure activities like travel and dining out, and needing more money for emergencies. The fourth most common worry was "losing my sense of self." Financial security and pride in our identity can often closely align.

When you look back on your career, I bet you can remember the first time you deposited a paycheck into your checking account; mine came from weekend morning shifts at a bakery in my hometown. You may also think back to hard-fought raises and big job offers that had you dialing your parents or partner with elation. When I landed a six-figure salary, I felt like I'd cracked a glass ceiling. I was on a digital strategy team with three male colleagues, and that raise made me the highest paid in the group. I was proud of this achievement. It felt like validation of my ambition. Like I'd made it.

But while money is crucial, it shouldn't be our measure of

whether we're living a meaningful or successful life. Feraud Calixte is a lawyer and certified financial planner in Burlington, North Carolina, and when I interviewed him, he shared the tagline of a company he once worked for: "Your net worth is not your self-worth," which is worth writing on a sticky note and putting on your mirror during this transition. He explained, "What that speaks to is that money is a terrible way to find dignity. Society does this to us. So many of us are hyper-consumers." But when Calixte counsels a couple through a financial life transition, he aims to help them identify values beyond acquiring and spending wealth. "I ask, 'What is important to you?'" he says. "And frankly, I can't think of a better use of someone's time than to care for their family. There is ultimate dignity in that."

Leaving your job, you might feel like you're no longer part of your family's financial equation or even the wider economy. I could write this whole book arguing that stay-at-home parents deserve (and need) a paycheck for their work. Stay-at-home mothers work an average of ninety-seven hours each week caring for their children and household. In 2021, economists posited that if these women were financially compensated for their duties, they would earn upward of $184,000 annually. Our work inside the home is critically important and valuable, yet few mothers I've met feel like a revered six-figure earner during their career pauses. Sadly, we live in a country with an infrastructure that devalues and deprioritizes caregiving in almost every way imaginable. It financially penalizes people who take on this task full-time or even part-time. The United States is the only wealthy nation without a federal paid family leave policy. As humans and mothers, we must fight for a better deal from our elected officials. (A few of my favorite advocacy organizations: Paid Leave for All, a project of the Hopewell Fund; Chamber of Mothers; Moms First; MomsRising.) And in the meantime, we owe it to ourselves to try to structure our home lives to be financially fair and respectful—and to preserve our autonomy as women.

I'm not here to sugarcoat the financial reality of stepping into primary parenthood; there are real economic risks that can have a ripple effect on your marriage. I also believe the only way to circumvent and minimize these dangers is to first understand them. Stay-at-home mothers often tell me that they worry about becoming "dependent" on their partner or that they've been told that they're making a dangerous financial decision. In some cases, the naysayers may be right. In the AMP survey, some mothers shared that the financial strain on their lives and marriage has overwhelmed them. I have heard the worst-case scenario: "[My] partner feels more pressure and stress as the sole financial provider. He takes this stress out on me," wrote one forty-one-year-old stay-at-home mom considering a shift back to the workforce. "He is controlling and financially bullying because 'it's all his money,'" wrote another, aged thirty-nine. But if you are in a modern and equitable relationship, and you develop a clear understanding of your shared values and the risks and rewards of your choice, I know these experiences do not have to be your reality. You can be a financially competent and confident stay-at-home mother.

Changing What It Means to Be "Dependent"

Women considering pausing their career for motherhood typically fall into two financial camps: a large group whose salary barely covers the cost of childcare and who decide working for pay isn't worth it, and a smaller group who are significant economic producers but very much want to stay home, even though they will deeply feel the monetary loss. (Just over half of opposite-sex marriages today have a husband who is the primary or sole breadwinner. In 30 percent of marriages, spouses earn roughly the same income; in 16 percent, wives earn more.)

Though Dan was on board with my choice to stay home, I don't think he initially understood the value of my work. He once called it a "luxury" to stay home, a common characterization of motherhood that leaves many women feeling like they lack value. But as I often say, conflating stay-at-home motherhood with luxury is flawed. There is nothing luxurious about changing diapers, soothing tantrums, and cleaning up toys, but there is economic privilege in getting to choose how you spend your time—whether you opt to work or stay home. Our marital dynamic shifted for the better in March 2020, when (as for so many people) our home suddenly became our office and Dan, who ran a technology start-up, had to work from our bedroom. With him upstairs focused on Zoom calls and me managing remote school, playtime, and meals downstairs, he saw the enormous career safety net I provided him. He could concentrate on his company (which was weathering a pandemic-fueled crisis) because I was caring for our kids. He depended on me just as much as the kids and I relied on his salary and health insurance.

In the AMP survey, 45 percent of mothers who paused or downshifted their careers cited spending less on childcare as a motivation. The annual cost of childcare in 2022 ranged from $5,357 for school-age home-based care in small counties to $17,171 for infant center-based care in very large counties, according to an analysis of the National Database of Childcare Prices by the U.S. Department of Labor. Stay-at-home mothers reported in the AMP survey that childcare would have cost their family, on average, more than 60 percent of their salary if they continued to work. Another poll by Harris, on behalf of *Fortune*, measured how much of their paycheck men and women are willing to dedicate to childcare. About half of the mothers with young children drew the line at 25 percent; if the cost of childcare rose above that threshold, they said they would opt to stay home.

Facing these statistics, it's easy to grasp why many mothers make a snap decision to leave their job once they calculate daycare costs. But even for those women, choosing this life should involve more than a simple calculation.

When you pause your career, remember that you part with the salary you make right now and the raises you would earn throughout your pause—a number that's impossible to quantify. When you eventually return to the workforce, you may face what economists call an "unemployment penalty," which is generally more pronounced for women than men. This penalty may make it more difficult to find a job. ("Employers view any 'voluntary' unemployment as a sign of unreliability," says Sarah Wittman, who has published research on career transitions and gaps.) Women who have paused their careers for more than twenty-four months tend to step into salaries earning 79 cents for every dollar a man who had *not* paused would earn, but the woman who stays in the market would only earn 84 cents of what a man would earn—so the pausing woman does risk a lower pay, but not quite to the extent commonly believed.

I share these details because I want you to go into your pause fully informed. But I also want to be clear that these statistics do not apply to every woman and shouldn't be considered your destiny. There isn't yet research measuring whether strategically planning your pause can help you skirt the unemployment penalty, but anecdotally, I've noticed that women who plan carefully tend to find success more easily on the other side. Plus, since the pandemic and the "Great Resignation" that followed, career breaks have become much more mainstream—which likely means the stigma is lessening. In early 2022, LinkedIn launched an option to list "career break" on its online profiles. The change was a response to customer feedback: when LinkedIn surveyed 23,000 workers and more than 4,000 hiring managers, 68 percent of women said they "wanted more ways to positively represent their career breaks by highlighting skills learned and experiences they had during a work pause." Carol Fishman Cohen, CEO of the career reentry company iRelaunch, summarized the trend in the *As We Work* podcast in 2022: "The pandemic made the career break more commonplace, made people recognize the range of professionals who take career breaks and what that might look like. So, we think there are going to be more career breaks in the future, not fewer career breaks."

But if you've read this far and are realizing that you're pausing mostly because you feel financially forced (as about 30 percent of mothers on career pauses in the AMP survey say they do), I suggest reopening the conversation with your partner. Together, think about childcare as a joint investment that comes from both your salaries and boosts your family's long-term financial health. "I see a lot of people making the calculation that their nanny or daycare will take their whole salary, and so based on that, they say, 'Oh, it just doesn't make sense for me to work.' But there is so much more cost associated with pausing than your salary. This is a choice you should make for many important reasons, and money can be one of them—but not the only one," says Ashley Feinstein Gerstley, a certified money coach in New Jersey who downshifted her career in banking to build in flexibility for eventual motherhood.

And if money is just one of many reasons you're pausing, don't forget to share your other motivations with the people close to you. This is a way to step fully into the power of this life stage. After she paused her career as a kindergarten teacher in the Bay Area, Helen Ortiz told people that her decision was purely financial. But when she thought more deeply about it, she realized that explanation was more socially acceptable than explaining that she longed to be with her son. In a way, by skipping that explanation, she missed an opportunity to bring more empowerment to stay-at-home motherhood. Plus, practically, if you tell your spouse that you're basing your decision only on childcare costs, it may become difficult to justify hiring any paid help—and every stay-at-home parent deserves that support.

Preparing to Live on One Income

There's no magic formula for removing one salary from your finances without feeling it. While it helps to hear from other women who have done it, the stumbling blocks, trade-offs, and lifestyle changes vary widely. For some couples, revamping the household budget may be so intimidating that they decide to skip the planning and wing it with a reduced income. Others may already be adept at living well below their means and manage the transition without much hassle. And, of course, there's another group for whom job loss has negligible economic impact. But for most mothers, pausing with power requires planning—a lot.

When asked about their considerations in deciding to stay home with their kids, less than half the mothers we surveyed spent a lot of time seriously contemplating "not having my income." Retirement planning received the least mental real estate: just a third of women gave it "a lot of thought," and almost 20 percent didn't consider the retirement ramifications at all. In the AMP survey, 40 percent of stay-at-home mothers said they left their jobs within one month of beginning to consider it. Just 15 percent spent six months or longer preparing for the shift.

If you've already paused without fully mapping out finances or you're considering going that route, let me offer some gentle advice: talking about money with your partner is necessary, and while it may be awkward or lead to arguing, it can also be eye-opening, empowering, and, as I experienced with Dan, can draw you closer together. "From a relationship standpoint, there's a lot of mixed messages in our society. We're taught to believe that when it comes to a partnership, money is unimportant and you're not a good person if you think about money—that it shouldn't influence a relationship," says Julia Kramer, a financial behavior and leadership consultant in Pittsburgh, who paused her career as an accountant for motherhood. "And yet, if you don't have these discussions before you pause, you're really asking for trouble."

It's normal to feel nervous approaching your partner to discuss how to make a pause work financially. Few of us grew up witnessing our parents discussing thorny dilemmas—and many of us don't have tremendous confidence in our financial acumen, which adds to the stress. "We take the labor course, we prepare the nursery, but we don't prepare our relationships for parenthood," says Tracy Dalgleish, a psychologist and couples therapist in Ottawa, Canada. "And I think culture is another piece in here. In some cultures, talking about money is just not what's done. It's pushed away, ignored, minimized, or kept secret."

But regardless of upbringing and etiquette, now is the time to speak openly so you can plan for the change with clarity. Even if your family is comfortable with your financial resources, as mine was, or manages to live without strict budgeting, these conversations will be medicine for your marriage, as they ensure that you and your spouse both understand the reasons you are pausing, what you each contribute, and why those contributions merit each other's respect. In addition, they force you to face what money (especially money earned through paid work) means to you both.

Just as important: even the most minor financial challenges can be difficult to conquer when you don't have a financial security net and budgeting system in place. Six years ago, in the final weeks of her maternity leave with her first child, Edil Cuepo decided to pause her career as a manager for a real estate firm. She loved her work but couldn't face the long commute and time away from her baby. She and her husband knew he made enough to cover their living expenses, but they didn't talk through the details. While they had a joint savings account covering basics, Cuepo had always maintained an individual bank account for her personal spending, so she carried on that way. "I had never wanted anyone dictating what I could or could not buy. I had always had my own money to buy myself things," she says. Then, about two years into her pause, she suddenly realized that she had spent more than 80 percent of her individual account—and felt uncomfortable and guilty having to ask her husband for money.

When it comes to finances, it's best to approach running your family the way you would a business. Both you and your partner are investors in it, and for the company to succeed, you must go into it with eyes wide open, a solid plan, and an understanding that risk is involved. Shifting into at-home motherhood does not require buy-in or understanding from everyone in your world, but you need all the key stakeholders to be on board. If you're in a relationship, that means your partner. And regardless of your marital status, it may mean talking to members of your extended family whom you rely on for support, whether financial, emotional, logistical, or all three. Together, take the following steps to prepare for your pause:

1. Build up your cash reserves

Calixte advises dual-income couples to have three months of cash in a high-yield savings account to cover their living expenses. That threshold grows to six months or more when one income is eliminated. Six months of reserves may not be necessary for everyone; the sum depends on your risk tolerance and whether you have an additional safety net (like a grandparent willing to help in an emergency).

Advanced planning also helps you prepare for the expected and sudden hardships that can happen to anyone—and it can assuage your anxiety. I've interviewed women who paused their careers only for their spouse to be laid off months later. Others have faced divorce. Having a plan prevents these scenarios from causing too much financial panic and allows you to focus on your family's emotional needs.

Finally, a practical to-do that goes a long way: before you pause, be sure to enroll in life insurance and get disability insurance for your partner.

2. Get clear on fixed and discretionary expenses

As you begin to save deliberately, take time to develop a complete understanding of your family's habits—an exercise that sounds anxiety-inducing (and boring), but actually reduces long-term stress. You can meet with a certified financial planner or sign up for commercial budgeting software and link it to your bank accounts and credit cards for three months. (One month typically won't give you a broad enough sense of your spending.) Erin Brown McAlister, who lives outside Philadelphia and worked in communications at a nonprofit, paused to escape an impossible pandemic treadmill of parenting without childcare. She said that the first thing she and her husband did was put every expense they could think of into a spreadsheet. "We included anything that could come up in the next twelve months—things we thought might need work in the house, things that we needed to plan for in terms of emergency expenses."

Another option: pretend you're already paused. Start putting your salary directly into savings and practice living on just one income. This allows you a trial run to track your expenses against your family's new income and be sure you're anticipating all the costs of daily life. Hannah Bryant, a mom of two and certified financial planner in Chicago who is currently on a career downshift, put as much of her salary as possible toward her 401(k) in the months leading up to leaving her job. This step allowed her to build her retirement savings and gave her and her husband practice at living off one salary.

3. Create a budget aligned with your values

Examining and committing to a budget is an exercise in defining what matters to you—and it can be pretty soulful. "Your values are essentially what is meaningful, what is important to you right now," says Dalgleish. "Values can be broad things like being connected with family, self-growth, physical health, emotional health, family, work career, education. When we start the budgeting with a conversation from a place of alignment with our values then we can start from a place of being more curious and open." Similarly, Kramer suggests that couples start by dreaming and brainstorming about what they want their life to look like. "They might decide that they still want to pay for some care or spend more on activities because their child won't be in daycare. They may envision that they'd like to take their kids out for lunch once a week," she says. (When you pause your career, some expenses like childcare and commuting will decrease, while others may increase.)

Once you have a list of priorities, examine your fixed costs— the expenses required to live. You may find that you can renegotiate a mortgage, find a cheaper cell phone carrier, or swap your car for a more affordable lease. Some couples also become open to a significant life change. To accommodate the career pause she had always wanted, one psychologist and mom of three decided with her husband to move from San Francisco to a more affordable suburb of Atlanta. They gave up easy access to their kids' grandparents and a community of friends and neighbors, but they were excited about a simpler, more sustainable life.

Next, review your discretionary expenses—shopping, "fun" groceries, dining out, travel, gifts, and more—and together, ask whether those expenditures align with what matters to you. Almost without fail, couples find they haven't been spending in accordance with their values, and it becomes clear where they should cut back (takeout) and where they may want to spend more (experiences). In the AMP survey, several mothers shared that shifting to stay-at-home motherhood has altered their shopping habits. Now they hunt for deals or drive farther to take advantage of sales or discount stores. "I am simply very frugal and see it as part of my job to save as much money as possible, so we don't have to struggle financially. I coupon, invest, and rarely spend on unnecessary purchases," wrote one mom.

Fair warning: this budgeting exercise may lead you to discover that a career break isn't feasible. Maybe you'll realize that you can't meet your fixed costs comfortably, or you'll decide that your values call for big purchases, like sending your kids to a private college or traveling internationally, and you need greater financial resources to live your dream. Complete career pauses aren't possible or helpful for everyone. If you reach an impasse as you create the budget, you may want to look into whether reduced hours or switching to consulting would make you happier *and* lessen the financial impact. It also helps to remember that your values and your lifestyle aren't permanent and will change as you and your kids get older. You can reevaluate your finances again in a year or two.

Assuming you decide to move forward with leaving your job, be careful to trim indulgences equitably. Often, the partner who downshifts their career ends up being the only one to downshift their lifestyle—a setup that breeds resentment. One mom in the AMP survey wrote, "I cut and dye my own hair. I don't buy myself any extras like coffee out. . . . I purchase things for my daughter for fun but no extra expenses for me." I share this experience because when we know how budgeting can go wrong, it's much easier to do it right. Try to think deeply about your family's favorite treats and why they make each of you happy. When you meet a friend for dinner, is it the restaurant that matters or the conversation? Also, try to create a list of what Feinstein Gerstley calls "frugal joys"—free or inexpensive things that make you happy, like taking a bath or watching a guilty-pleasure show. These are a great way to add happiness and enjoyment to your life without increasing the amount you spend.

Anytime you review your budget, sit together for no more than two hours at a time, Feinstein Gerstley advises. She calls these meetings "money parties" and suggests making them fun—either with a reward at the end or an upbeat playlist in the background. After a few sessions of talking, you'll eventually land on a budget that allows you to live off one income or that requires you to dip into savings each month.

As I've talked to women who have given up significant income to pause, one lovely theme has come up repeatedly: some find that they enjoy elements of the simpler lifestyle that come with their new budget. Godhuli Chatterjee Gupta left a career she never particularly liked to be home with her children. Now she has the mental bandwidth to write for pleasure, which has made the economic loss feel worth it. "My husband and I have the same philosophy: we have enough money to be comfortable, and there's nothing that we feel like we're lacking right now. We see people in our community who have extreme levels of wealth, and we've seen that sometimes it really is 'more money, more problems.' There's more competition. You're never satisfied," she says. For Bryant, it's helped to remember that when she and her husband first moved in together, their combined income was a fraction of what it is now, but they made it work. They plan to continue to do the things they love but in different ways. "We're going to have to scale back some of the luxuries—especially some of the ways we vacation. But when you think about parenting goals, it's probably a good thing that our baby won't stay in the nicest places," she says.

The financial sacrifice has been challenging for Lindsey, a mom in Liverpool, New York. "Sometimes we have to hurt people's feelings and say no," she says. Recently her husband declined an invitation to a close friend's bachelor party because a weekend trip to Florida wasn't in their budget. They also paused annual family vacations with grandparents because they were out of economic reach. "We continue to remind ourselves that our everyday life, with me at home, is what we want," she says.

LIFTING THE TABOO OF SPENDING DOWN YOUR SAVINGS

A career pause for motherhood is a valid time to spend your savings. (Yep, I said it.) This may not be traditional financial advice, but we're talking about what may be your only chance to be home with your kids. "I'm thirty-two years old right now," says Bryant. "When I'm doing retirement planning with clients, their goal is to wake up in the morning, feel energized, and spend their time the way they want. So, for me, I want that too. And if I take five to eight, even ten years to give more to my family, I don't think I will regret that." If you plan to use savings monthly, experts advise that you resist pulling that money from your six-month emergency fund. Instead, determine the projected length of your pause and save the amount you'll need before leaving your job. "For a two-year pause that requires one thousand a month in savings, you'll need to add twenty-four thousand dollars to the rainy-day fund," says Feinstein Gerstley. And take heart: you may not spend it all. As your values change and your kids grow, there may be levers you can push to increase your income or cut your spending. Your partner might also get a raise or a new job.

4. Write an informal agreement that defines your roles and the time frame

Writing a contract may sound like overkill (and if you feel this way, rest assured that this step is optional). But going through this exercise provides you with a set of commitments and a clear path to hold each other accountable to them. Dan and I didn't write an agreement when I paused my career, but in hindsight, I think it could have saved us from many growing pains. Stepping into stay-at-home motherhood is a lot like starting a new job, and in the working world, you'd never sign up for a new role without a clear job description and a rundown of your HR benefits.

There's no right way to write this agreement. It can be a basic enumeration of your roles and responsibilities that helps you validate each other's contributions or a more detailed document that establishes the monetary value of your work. (For many women, a fifty-fifty split of your partner's salary may make you feel most valued, but you can also come to this number based on what you would be paying outside providers, including daycare, a cleaning service, a "sick day" babysitter, even a house manager or personal assistant.) Once you set this number, you can determine the percentage of that "income" you'll each put toward your retirement. (Often, when a woman pauses her career for motherhood, her husband continues to fund his 401(k) while her retirement savings stall. By making this agreement, you can sidestep that unfair outcome.)

Next, set a date when you'll return to this conversation to reassess the decision. In her work mediating collaborative divorces, Kramer says she's met couples who weren't honest with each other at the outset about how long they wanted to operate off one income, which created a rift. You may feel a bit deflated as you put a preemptive pin in your pause, but a time frame that opens the door to negotiation is vital to financial and marital peace of mind. In short, this is the moment to write down, "I'm pausing my career for eighteen months, at which point we will reassess this decision together."

Finally, this agreement is the place to define your roles. Often, when a mother opts to earn less, her partner may feel compelled to shift into work overdrive. As he increases his dedication to earning, he may expect his wife to become master of everything inside the home—creating a traditional and somewhat claustrophobic structure. Dalgleish says that in her practice as a couples counselor, she routinely encounters men who "feel strongly that because they do the critical work of earning income for their family that they should be absolved of all responsibility in the home." Unfortunately, they rarely express this expectation out loud *before* their wife pauses her career, which is one factor that leads them toward counseling. Lindsey and her husband fell into this traditional setup soon after she paused. Her husband expected that she would be "the house executive"—that it was her job to delegate responsibilities to him, including telling him when it was time to take out the trash. Lindsey recently took it upon herself to redefine her role. Now he understands that it's her job to manage the day-to-day caregiving, not to clean the house. "All the other stuff is shared work between us," she tells me. "It's taken a lot of communication and conversations, and I'm grateful my husband is open to working on it."

5. Merge your finances and set a few rules

Although there's no single way to organize your money in marriage, financial advisors tend to agree that combining your funds and paying for expenses from a joint bank account is the most equitable option during a career break. Keeping a separate bank account and relying on your husband for a monthly deposit can quickly make you feel beholden to him (like a child receiving an allowance), stressed about going over budget, or worried there may be secrets in your finances. With a shared account, you can see all your resources and treat your partner's income as your asset too.

As you go about your lives, hold each other accountable to sticking to the budget (as best you can) and communicating before big purchases. But merging your money doesn't mean giving up all financial privacy. Within your family budget, set aside a certain amount for personal spending, and institute a "no judgment" rule about how that money is used. In our case, I tend to indulge in an occasional taxi, and Dan keeps ordering five of the exact same T-shirt. (Good for him!) Some couples find that putting these purchases on personal credit cards (paid from the joint account) creates a feeling of autonomy and ownership. As a bonus, it allows you to buy each other gifts without spoiling the surprise.

(Just be sure to set a separate gift budget so you don't deplete your self-care funds buying for others.)

6. Continue to meet about money regularly

Kramer suggests fifteen-minute weekly meetings. Feinstein Gerstley is a fan of one- to two-hour "money parties" monthly. For Dan and me, quick monthly check-ins combined with annual planning sessions have worked best. However often you hold them, regular check-ins are critical to maintaining a voice in your finances and building a team mentality in your marriage. "Couples need to learn to treat their marriage like the most important team that you are running," says Dalgleish. And when you make meetings a regular habit, you eliminate the need to say, "We need to talk"—four words that incite dread. As you sit together, you can work out the details of an upcoming purchase or restructure an investment, but more often, you'll talk through topics that may only seem tangentially related to money. *What do you appreciate about our relationship? How did you feel about the support I gave you last week? What's the biggest piece of your mental load right now?* "These are the questions that will strengthen your ability to communicate and be a team," says Dalgleish.

FIVE BUDGETING BASICS

For couples who live comfortably in dual-earner households, a career pause may be the first time they have had to monitor their spending closely. If you're creating a budget for the first time (or think you may be able to improve your process), here are a few helpful pointers from the experts:

1. Keep the categories simple. Unless you enjoy getting lost in detail, there's no need to make micro categories like snacks and hair care, says Feinstein Gerstley. Instead, start with catchall categories like food, clothing, personal care, travel, and so on.

2. Remember that there are 4.3 weeks in a month. Once you develop a weekly budget, multiply it by that number—not by four (a common mistake). Otherwise, you may end up at year's end short of funds by over a month.

3. Budget for the money that hits your checking account. This number tends to be much lower than your salary, which is subject to health care, 401(k), and tax deductions. If you freelance, estimate your earnings as best you can and then remove a sizable chunk for taxes. An accountant can help you determine the correct percentage based on your income and where you live.

4. Round up, not down. Most of us tend to be optimists when it comes to our spending, and when we're guesstimating, we tend to assume we'll be able to harness some newfound self-control or skip a year of buying ourselves clothes, says Feinstein Gerstley. But as one mom smartly said to me, "There's no magic money." Repeating that phrase has helped her look openly and honestly at her family's spending and match real funds to every purchase.

5. Expect to make mistakes. Try to avoid panic if you go over budget the first few months. Budgeting isn't an easy habit to adopt; just about everyone underestimates or forgets about expenses when they begin. Give yourself grace as you make errors and dip into savings. You and your partner will improve at this with time.

Pausing Your Career in a Rocky Marriage

While many mothers I've interviewed spoke about downshifting their careers in a solid, loving partnership with a deep-seated team mentality, others have shared a more complicated picture. "We need to normalize the idea of marital problems being in the background of this decision," says Dalgleish. Marriage is rarely easy, and marriage with babies and toddlers can be excruciatingly difficult. More than two-thirds of couples experience a significant decline in marital satisfaction in the first year after having a baby, and many continue to struggle for an additional three to seven years. Dalgleish says most of her new clients contact her when their kids are ages three to five and have been suffering without counseling for several years already. (Women are most likely to pause their careers for motherhood when their kids are toddlers, perhaps because that's when the dueling demands of work and parenthood become too much.) Though no one gets married expecting to divorce, the reality is that about half of first marriages end this way. Long story short: if you want to stay home with your kids but worry you'll end up in a financial crisis if your marriage ends, know that you're not alone and there is no shame in your situation. Many other women share these concerns, and it's wise to be prepared.

Before you take steps to leave your job, Dalgleish suggests honestly examining your partnership. "Ask yourself: Who is this person? Can I trust this person to support me if I give up my income to care for the kids? Are we a team? How do we negotiate power? And if you're not a team or your feel powerless, then the question becomes, How do we start being a team, and how do I take back some of my autonomy?"

It may help to "make deposits in your relationship bank"—ten minutes daily to connect and show gratitude for each other's contributions. Just as important: get help. Couples counseling could be life-changing, but it's not feasible for everyone. An online course or a workbook you complete together can also make a significant difference. Whatever you do, don't wait it out and assume that your connection will improve on its own. "The longer people wait to get help, the more entrenched these patterns become, and the harder it is to get out of it," Dalgleish says.

If your relationship is particularly unstable, take steps to pre-emptively protect yourself financially should you and your partner separate while you're unemployed. Consider setting up a personal (and secret) "walk away fund"—a reserve of cash (at least a few months of living expenses) that you can access if you need to leave a contentious partner before child support has been arranged. If you're concerned about your marriage, writing a contract (step 4 on page 51) is essential. You may even want to take it further and hire a mediator or attorney to transform this document into a legal postnuptial agreement. (A postnuptial agreement lays out the terms of a hypothetical separation, which allows you to stop worrying about the financial ramifications and focus solely on evaluating and shoring up your partnership.)

Finally, I encourage every parent on a career break to stay connected to her professional network and continue to hone marketable job skills. One of the gifts of stepping into this stage of life at this moment in time is that technology can help you continue to learn and grow. While this advice is intended to empower all women, it's especially crucial for women who lose their spouse's income. Kristi Rible is an executive leadership coach specializing in women and mothers, and she currently teaches a course at

Stanford called Motherhood and Work: Challenges and Opportunities for Positive Change. Years ago, when she left her demanding travel-centric job to care for her newborn, it never occurred to her that she and her husband would separate. But it happened. "At the time, I just thought, *I'm having this baby, I need to be present for this baby*. I didn't even think through how long I'd be out of the workforce," she said. Having endured a highly stressful period looking for work and getting set up as a single mom, Rible wishes she had stepped into her pause with a backup plan. While your partner may continue to support you after you separate, divorced mothers often need (and want) to return to work to fund their lives and receive their own health insurance and retirement benefits.

WHEN ONLY ONE OF YOU THINKS YOUR PAUSE IS A GOOD IDEA

You want to stop working and stay home with the kids, but your husband is adamant that your family can't afford it—and that the financial pressure will break him. Or you want to go back to work, but your salary won't come close to covering that much childcare. Your partner wants you to stay home until your youngest is in kindergarten. When you and your partner don't agree about the financial feasibility of a career pause, it can feel devastating for both of you. Feinstein Gerstley suggests getting to the root of each other's worries and desires. "A lot of conflict within couples boils down to their greatest fear, which usually formed in childhood. Your partner might say, I saw my parents struggle financially, and they were so stressed, and they never had enough savings. And you might say, I watched my mother work through my childhood, and I don't want that to happen to me. I want to take this time and really enjoy it."

Try to be open, listen to what your partner shares, and understand the other side. Once those concerns are out in the open, try again to agree in some way. "Couples often think that they should have the same opinions and level of excitement about a decision in order to move forward with it, but that's rarely the case in real life," says Dalgleish. "You must decide that you're a team and that you're going to support one another and navigate challenges together. That doesn't mean you're going to love every decision or agree with it."

If your partner doesn't relent or his anxiety outweighs yours, consider seeing a counselor or trying to compromise. Would he be more comfortable if you worked part-time or found a more flexible job with reduced responsibility? Now may also be a time to consider adjusting the time frame of your pause. Offer to try it for a short period (like six months) and to reassess afterward. Just be sure you're *both* willing to come back to the negotiation before you go this route.

Regardless of our financial means, a universal thread connects all power pausers: before kids, we took pride in responsibly funding our lives—and being independent—and we want to carry that feeling of worth and security into this stage with our kids. Fulfilling this desire starts with taking an active role in your family finances and speaking up about your economic needs for the present and future. When I realized that I valued time with my kids more than my time at work, I began to question how I spent another precious resource—money—and whether I was making the best decisions. You now have the tools and language to be an equal financial partner in your marriage, regardless of the income you bring home. Just as important, you have the beginnings of a road map to a life lived intentionally, including in the financial sense.

Power Practice: Define Your Money Values

This chapter explored the financial ramifications of pausing, how to determine whether you can afford it, and how to set up your finances so that you and your partner feel secure and empowered. Whether you're contemplating a pause or already in one, a financial tune-up—and meeting of the minds—is never a bad idea. Sit with your partner and take turns answering these questions. Conversations like these are the first step toward building an equitable, interdependent relationship in which you both feel financially empowered.

1. How was money handled in your family when you were a kid?
2. If someone gave you an extra week's pay right now, would you spend it or save it? And if you would spend it, what would you buy—things or an experience?
3. When you hear the word "finances," do you feel worried or confident?
4. What does financial success look like to you?
5. Do you think we are on the right path to "financial success," or do you feel overwhelmed by the challenge?
6. Do you feel aligned with me about our finances? If not, what could help us feel more aligned and like we're on the same team?
7. What do you want our children to understand about money and its importance in life?

3

———

Trust That Your Career Isn't Over
and Resign Strategically

———

FALSE BELIEF

*I'm leaving my job, and I may never be
able to find another one as good.*

NEW NARRATIVE

*I'm shifting my career temporarily, and I trust
I will learn about myself, develop skills, and
build connections that lead me to even more
meaningful paid work in the future.*

———

ONCE I DECIDED I wanted to leave the most prominent full-time job of my career, as the head of brand marketing at a hot e-commerce start-up, I resigned at the first opportunity. This was a year before I gave birth to my first child—but the mistakes I made then helped me figure out how to do it better years later, when I decided to pause my career (and the stakes were, arguably, even higher).

On paper, this position had been a dream job with a dream title, and I had just completed a dream project (a partnership with a major celebrity that would appear in an elite, glossy magazine).

Yet as we wrapped that long-awaited photo shoot, I kept ruminating on one question: *Am I good enough?*

I *thought* I was good at the job, but I was plagued by constant worries and doubts. My role and department seemed to be under constant scrutiny, and my budget was often slashed. This led me to feel ill at ease—convinced no one liked me and that my employment was tenuous. My day-to-day activities centered on maneuvering through internal politics and trying to find my place at a hectic, competitive company. But one worry plagued me most: that my successes wouldn't move the needle for the business.

With the benefit of hindsight, I now realize that much of the anxiety I felt was normal: a combination of daily life at a fast-paced start-up and a classic case of imposter syndrome. But at the time, I was completely unmoored by my insecurities. My goal had always been to be named chief marketing officer at a big company, but I realized that I was no longer motivated to stay the course required to get there. I wanted off at the next exit.

As my first anniversary in the role approached, the CEO of a smaller brand asked me to consider leaving to work with her. The offer felt like a life raft—immediate relief from a situation that kept me up at night and made it hard to be present during my downtime as a newlywed. I suggested joining her company as a full-time consultant, a setup I knew would help me distance myself from company culture. Once she agreed, I decided to resign immediately.

The next day, I arranged a meeting with the CEO and the chief design officer in the same brick-lined conference room where, just one week earlier, I had presented the end-of-year report on my team's accomplishments. As we engaged in a few minutes of small talk, I suddenly felt nervous and emotional. I blurted out a sanitized version of doubts I had harbored for months—I wasn't succeeding in this role, and I probably wasn't ever going to—and told them I was leaving to go into consulting. As I spoke, my eyes shifted between the two of them, and I registered disappointment, shock, and even sadness in their expressions.

"Is there anything I could have done that would have changed your experience?" the CEO asked quietly after an awkward pause.

"I just want you to know that you were never at risk of losing your job. We were never considering that," the CDO said. Somewhat shaken, I offered a quiet, "Thank you for understanding" in return.

After the meeting wrapped, I gathered my department in a smaller conference room and shared my news with them. Again, the response was not what I'd expected. One colleague who had often been critical of me welled up in tears. I had been sure she would be relieved.

Suddenly it hit me that my perception of the situation might not have been the reality. People there liked me, and they thought I belonged. They were looking forward to continuing to grow this start-up with me. Much of my insecurity had been in my head. A conversation with my manager back when my self-doubt first began could have made me a lot happier there—or at least have enabled me to resign with stronger relationships to carry forward. While I'm glad I left a role I didn't like, I wish I had known how to land my dismount.

About two years after I left that start-up, I resigned from the consulting job, this time to stay home with my son. A combination of more career experience and, perhaps, the insight of motherhood had made me wiser. My client and I began discussing my desire to be at home three months *before* I exited. Now, this long notice period won't work in every situation. (We'll talk more about this in the pages that follow.) But for me, sharing my truth helped us maintain our professional relationship, which was better for both of us. She was among the first people I profiled on Mother Untitled's website.

A Pause for Family Life Is Not a Career Dead-End

In chapter 1, we identified where the stigmas of stay-at-home motherhood come from, why they don't apply to our generation, and that staying home with your kids means joining a modern, ambitious group from which you can derive immense pride. In chapter 2, we examined the financial feasibility of a pause. But getting up the courage to quit requires one last reckoning: trusting that you can find an even better job when the time comes, and believing that your career will still have a robust trajectory.

When I speak to women contemplating resigning, they often fear losing a hard-fought place in their industry or organization. They dread watching others rise into positions they've coveted for years. And they imagine that when their kids are older, they'll be stereotyped as more oriented toward home than work—and struggle to get hired as a result.

Women aren't paranoid when they share these worries with me. It's a reality many have seen occur in their workplaces and community. Lisa Ziemba, a mother of two in Denver, left her job as the director of human resources at a construction company in 2021. "Before then, pretty much everyone I knew that had left the workplace for a pause was much older than me and had either never gone back to work or went back at a significantly lower level," she says. "I was concerned that I would never be able to return in the way I desired."

A 2023 survey of stay-at-home mothers by the job search website Indeed found that 93 percent had experienced or anticipated experiencing challenges reentering the workforce. In addition, 57 percent said they believe being a stay-at-home mother is seen by employers as a résumé gap, and 53 percent said they think potential employers will undervalue their skills because of their time as a stay-at-home parent. Similarly, for a 2018 study, sociologist Katherine Weisshaar found that résumés that listed a career pause for stay-at-home parenthood—whether male or female—were about half as likely to be selected for a follow-up interview as those of unemployed parents who had not stayed home with their children. Listing stay-at-home parenthood on a résumé "signals to employers that potential employees prioritize family over work," she wrote, adding that "the act of opting out violates the ideal worker expectations that are ubiquitous in modern workplaces." Think: long hours, responding to email on weekends, business travel, and more. Worry over this outcome seems to particularly affect women who've invested a great deal of money and time—also known as "sunk cost"—in their careers, such as those in finance, medicine, and academia.

"They are thinking, 'I have been well educated. I still have student debt. I have gone through so many steps to ensure that my career will be as successful as my husband's or my partner's—or anyone else's,'" says Sarah Wittman. In the AMP survey, 48 percent of stay-at-home mothers said they gave some or a lot of thought to how their pause would impact their career path. That number rose to 53 percent for women with graduate degrees.

Of course, in reality, when a stay-at-home parent decides to reenter the workforce, she has likely put a great deal of forethought into the decision and plans to commit to the work as much or even more than anyone else, says Wittman. And as career breaks become increasingly common, workplace experts predict that in the future employers will have no choice but to reconsider their views and eventually overcome their bias.

The Indeed survey also offered reasons to be hopeful. It found that mothers viewed their experience of stay-at-home parenthood as highly relevant to the commercial workforce, citing mastery of skills like negotiation, research and development, and people management while focusing on their kids. Moreover, the latest data on career returners—admittedly already somewhat dated (from 2010)—suggests that most women who pause their careers and seek to return to the paid workforce do so successfully. Some organizational psychologists have even begun to cite career breaks as a strategic tactic for building a career with longevity. In a 2023 opinion piece in the *Harvard Business Review,* author Dorie Clark wrote that "downshifting your ambitions doesn't necessarily mean you're throwing away your past or becoming a slacker. It may actually mean that you've finally recognized what it takes for achievement and ambition to be sustainable." Millennials expect to work for many more years than previous generations, and according to a survey by ManpowerGroup, 84 percent of them foresee taking a significant career break, with women citing the birth of their children (61 percent) and providing childcare (33 percent) as the top impetuses to do so.

Getting over the fear of future unemployability is as much about learning to package yourself for the job market as it is about developing a fervent belief in your abilities. "One of the most important things for women in this stage of their life—or really, any stage of their life—is to feel comfortable and confident and let go of any type of comparison with others," says Megan Martin Strickland, an executive leadership coach in Palo Alto, California, and a mother of three who left a career in finance to stay home with her firstborn son for a year.

Executive coach and HR executive Marlo Lyons was never able to afford a career break herself, and she only had four weeks of leave with her two children, now ten and twelve. (They were adopted, and Lyons didn't qualify for medical leave at her company.) Looking back, the Scottsdale, Arizona–based mom wishes she had had more time to soak up her kids' babyhood and avoid the chaotic treadmill of full-time work and parenting babies and toddlers. She adamantly believes it's possible to return to the workforce because she has helped dozens of women do so. "You will not be a statistic," Lyons tells me. "Once you know how to position yourself properly, you will be able to get back in."

And, of course, I share her view. I've encountered countless women who have built brilliant full-time careers that surpass their pre-kids jobs in flexibility, compensation, interest level, or all three. Yes, pausing affects your career, and worrying about the scope of that impact is legitimate. But the catastrophic, doomsday scenario is not fated and can be circumvented with strategic effort. (And in chapter 9 of this book, I will show you exactly how to do that.)

As you firm up your plans to resign and then pause, take a moment to look in the mirror and remind yourself of your capability and talent. Trust that your next job is out there and that many organizations would be lucky to have you. Stay true to your vision for your immediate future, knowing that you're leaving your job and not losing control of your career. It is possible to outsmart this unfair system on an individual level and to land a "comeback job" that pays what you deserve. Don't let *this* fear be the one that stops you from leaping.

What Comeback Careers Really Look Like

When discussing post-stay-at-home-motherhood careers, we often hear the phrase "go *back* to work." But few women I've met have wanted to return to the job or even the industry they left. Most seek out new sectors and insist on roles that allow for greater flexibility and the opportunity to do more meaningful work, says executive coach Kristi Rible.

Many of the most famous examples of women who built significant careers after stay-at-home motherhood did so in fields that were new to them. Zarna Garg, the stand-up comedian whose Amazon Prime special, *One in a Billion*, dropped in 2023, was an attorney before eighteen years of full-time motherhood. Once she had kids, she became the family comic—cracking everyone up at the dinner table and parties. Garg's teenage daughter encouraged her to leap to entertainment instead of returning to the law. Julie Aigner-Clark the founder of the infant entertainment company Baby Einstein, taught high school English before she resigned to become a stay-at-home mother. In her early years of parenthood, she shot the first Baby Einstein video in her basement with a borrowed camcorder and a few puppets. Eventually, she sold that video company to Disney for $25 million. And then there's Nancy Pelosi, who married Paul Pelosi right after graduation, gave birth to five children in six years, and then moved to San Francisco with her family. Said Pelosi, "Nothing prepared me for being Speaker of the House more than the values, discipline, diplomacy, interpersonal skills, the logistics, the quartermastering—all that you have to do to raise a family while never taking your eye off the children."

In Pamela Stone and Meg Lovejoy's seminal 2019 book *Opting Back In,* the authors interviewed mothers who had left the commercial workforce ten years earlier (and had been featured in Stone's first book, *Opting Out?*) to see how they had fared in their efforts to return. Overall, the women succeeded in returning to work, but many entered a new field—landing more gratifying and flexible roles that, frustratingly, also came with lower pay. But as Pelosi, Aigner-Clark, and Garg demonstrate, earning less doesn't have to be inevitable. Plus, *Opting Back In* was written before flexibility, remote work, and running meetings with children just off camera became mainstream. I do not doubt that a chapter of stay-at-home motherhood will forever cause women to reevaluate the kind of work that draws them in and to insist on flexibility for the future. But I'm optimistic that the salary penalty mothers experience will diminish as the years, and decades, pass.

Marlo Lyons credits the change in career priorities to the magic that happens when you get distance from the daily corporate grind. "When you're at work, all you can see is what's in front of you: the deadlines, pressure, frustration, exhaustion, and burnout," she says. "But our values change when we have children. And when you take time away from the commercial workforce, it allows you to clear your head and reassess what yours are. In time, you can translate those values into the next career you want to pursue. Taking a break can be incredibly important. It can launch you even further."

Without question, that's what my power pause did for me. When I left that consulting job after becoming a mother, I wasn't preoccupied with whether I'd get back into the workforce. I had a bachelor's degree, an MBA, and ten years of work experience, which landed me a strong industry reputation. But more than that, I knew I didn't want to return to the job I had vacated. In my time at home, I discovered what I wanted to do instead and developed the first valid answer to the question, "What do you want to be when you grow up?"

In 2022, after years of building Mother Untitled in just eight block-scheduled hours each week, I decided to give the platform more of my time and opted into flexible, close-to-full-time work as an entrepreneur. As the founder and CEO of Mother Untitled, I spend my days dedicated to a cause that matters, and I have the power to set my hours, choose my colleagues, and make it to school pickup when I want to. I don't make as much money as I did in that prominent director role at the start-up, but I have faith that I'll get there—and even surpass my prior earnings. More important to me than any amount of money: I feel fully alive and at ease when I go to the office (yes, "the office" is a closet attached to my kids' playroom). I would never have found this level of professional peace and purpose without my days fully at home.

You don't have to start a company to return to the workforce with gusto. More than two million women left the workforce in

2020 due to the pandemic, and by 2023, the number of working-age women in the workforce had returned to prepandemic levels. We don't hear these quotidian stories because most of us have been trained to hide the gaps on our résumés as a strategy for re-entering the workforce. But trust me: they are out there.

Danielle Knight, a mom of three in Seattle, had worked for more than a decade in recruitment for the federal government, juggling motherhood with extended hours. But in the rewarding days with her kids, she realized she could no longer commit to a job that entailed meaningless work. (In the role she left, she was often tasked with finding candidates for theoretical positions that would never be funded—a time-consuming project that helped no one.) At home, Knight marveled at her children growing up and discovered that she was particularly enamored with their preschool years. Today she teaches pre-K three days a week. "I don't have any interest in returning to what I was doing," says Knight. "The money's not what it was, but I'm happy to be in a place where I can take a job because I like it."

In contrast, Chinue Richardson left a grueling career as an attorney at a corporate firm in London and Washington, DC. But after a move to San Francisco and the birth of her second child, she and her husband realized that her pause was no longer financially sustainable, and she longed to be in the workplace again. She set out to find a new, lucrative position and ultimately landed an in-house role at a major tech company. At her new job, she can "parent out loud." As she explains, "It's not that I'm always talking about my kids, but I don't hide that I'm a parent. I don't make it small because it's such a big part of my life."

Lisa Ziemba, from Denver, already knows she won't try to

return to the job she vacated, even though she loved it at the time. "I took that HR department from quite literally running payroll to running a full talent program," she says with pride. But her time at home led to an epiphany about that work: "I have no interest in babysitting men old enough to be my dad anymore. I have my own kids to parent," she says with a laugh. Although she used to view herself on a straight path toward being chief human resources officer, her future now feels more open, and she has developed a more flexible vision of her résumé.

If you're worried about your future career prospects, I encourage you to take a cue from Lisa and the other women whose stories of career reinvention are told in this book. Remind yourself that they are several of *millions*. If these women all found new jobs that fit, so will you.

The Best Way to Resign

To write this chapter, I listened to dozens of resignation stories, including several false starts. Many women dreaded the resignation conversation and procrastinated about it until they reached complete burnout. A few shared that they tried to resign but were convinced to stay in part-time roles they hadn't wanted—and then had to work up the gumption to quit *again*. Others shared artful gradual exits, in which the door to their past employer remained open, and their connection with their manager continued long after they left.

There's loads of research on why people quit their jobs, but much less on how they do it and how that impacts their future career and mental health. Experts generally agree that at most organizations, resigning, or, in corporate lingo, "offboarding," is often an awkward endeavor that leaves both the employee and the employer feeling mildly unnerved.

Most of us have spent time practicing for job interviews, but we often rush our exits, desperate to get the tough conversations behind us. In our impromptu speeches, we pay a price: missed connections, an abandoned funnel for consulting work, and a lost chance to leave a positive last impression that does justice to all we contributed.

You can do little to reform your company's HR practices, but you *can* plan an elegant goodbye. Staying professionally connected—so that you can one day transition back to the workforce—starts with how you leave your job.

1. Develop final clarity on your decision

In the weeks and months before you give notice, you'll likely share your thinking with your inner circle—your partner, parents, siblings, and a few close friends. These conversations may help you follow your instinct but also make you second-guess your judgment. Your job is to receive these comments, process them, and determine if your desire to be home outweighs the doubts they bring up. Once you can decipher which worries and insecurities are yours and which stem from others' opinions and biases, you can move forward with conviction.

When I first told my husband that I was considering leaving my consulting job to spend most of my week with my infant son, he worried. His primary concern: "You won't feel fulfilled at the end of the day." The next objection came from my mother-in-law, who pondered how I could "give up" on a successful and growing career. My mom may have been the most against it. She didn't fully explain herself then, but recently she told me that most of her anxiety stemmed from whether I'd command respect. "I was scared that one day you would look back and feel that you didn't live up to your potential and that you would regret it," she told me. "And I worried about how you could have confidence without financial independence. I thought financially independent people tended to be more respected, and I wanted that for you." My mother's disapproval never bothered me, but the other comments (and yes, there were more) did. I've always been sensitive to criticism, and my pattern is to take people's words personally and lose sleep over them. On the bright side, the comments spurred me to seek out a therapist who helped me firm up my choice and determine what actually worried me.

In the months before she resigned, Simi Sapir, a mother in Boca Raton, Florida, consciously dedicated time daily to think through her options and "get quiet with herself." She took a walk around the neighborhood every night, letting her thoughts meander. Only in this quiet did she finally understand that she wanted more presence at home and no longer found the same fulfillment at her workplace. "If more people were willing and were brave enough to sit in a room by themselves alone, I just think they would make braver decisions, and they would be more aligned with who they are," she told me.

Melody L. is a child psychologist in private practice, and she's planning to pause her career when her third child is born. Her family members have already started chiming in with well-intentioned warnings. "I've heard, 'Oh, you're really going to throw away your career? You may never work again in your life!'" says Melody, who lives in a suburb of Atlanta. But she knows how to stop those opinions from echoing in her head for too long. "I come back to my husband. And I remember that we're together on this and that this is about what *we* value. I ask myself, Why are we doing this? Everyone else is not in our home. They're not in our day-to-day lives. We're the ones responsible for our family and our kids and how they grow up. As much as I love my friends and family, I know that we need to prioritize our family over what they might prefer."

If you feel particularly rattled by negative perceptions and doubt, know that it gets easier to ignore. As I developed greater certainty in choosing to be a primary parent, negative comments eventually bounced off me. In the meantime, if you're feeling emotionally down or stressed, I suggest meeting with a mental health professional who can help you through this significant life decision. When you bring your concerns to your boss, you'll want to feel sturdy in your reasoning. If not, you may easily get swayed to change your mind, even when your heart is at home.

2. Open the conversations months before you plan to quit . . .

If you read chapter 2, you already know how vital advanced planning is to a financially viable pause. The same rule applies to your long-term career health. Months before you resign, speak to your boss to share that you've been considering pausing or downshifting your career. This fits what organizational psychologists Anthony C. Klotz and Mark C. Bolino, who studied resignations for a paper in the *Journal of Applied Psychology,* call the "in the loop" resignation method—when employees confide in their manager that they are contemplating quitting before resigning. The pair studied the experiences of almost three hundred recently resigned employees and more than two hundred managers on the receiving end of resignations. They found that managers respond *least* negatively when this tactic is employed. Sarah, a mom of two in Phoenix, Arizona, had a fantastic boss open to testing and trying different arrangements to make a full-time job feasible for her. To enable Sarah to take her daughter to a weekly music class, her boss suggested she work extra hours Monday through Thursday and take off Fridays. But that model exhausted Sarah, so they tried another: half-days on Wednesdays and Fridays, with additional hours spread throughout the other three days. Even though that worked better, Sarah still wanted more time and mental presence with her kid and decided to pursue a different part-time job. The testing period helped her gain that understanding and helped her boss make peace with the outcome.

Keep in mind, of course, that this is not a one-size-fits-all solution. There are scenarios in which it may not make sense: if you work a retail job where they would sooner replace you than navigate a complicated (or simply untraditional) work schedule, for example, or you have a boss who would likely make moves to replace you if he got wind that you were considering asking for a schedule accommodation. Ultimately, you have to decide if this approach will go over well with your boss or in your industry. Look around to see if there are other parents in your organization who've had similar conversations with (or without) success so you can make an informed decision before moving forward.

3. . . . And before you're angry and bitter

"Often, we don't resign until we are at an absolute breaking point," says Wittman. "And the narrative is, 'I can't do this anymore. I have to leave. I have to choose my family.'" That message won't necessarily be well received by your boss, who may view your distress as a reflection of their shortcomings as a manager. Burned-out, resentful employees often treat resigning as a moment for justice, "the final chance to get even with their organization and their manager," write Klotz and Bolino in the *Harvard Business Review*. But while exciting and gratifying, resigning against "best practices" will not do you any favors when you set out to return to the workforce, Klotz and Bolino write. Anger can lead to "perfunctory" resignations, when you follow the protocol but don't explain why you're leaving; "avoidant" resignations, when your boss hears you're leaving through the grapevine; "bridge burning," when you seek to harm your organization or your boss; or "impulsive quitting," when you walk off the job without preparing anyone for your exit, leaving your entire team in the lurch. Even if you are polite, resentment may cause you to insist on a strict or compressed timeline. This can leave your team scrambling to redistribute your work, leading not just your former boss but also your former colleagues to start viewing you negatively. "If you open the conversation before you are stretched thin, then the off-ramp won't be traumatic for anyone," Wittman says.

SHOULD I TAKE MATERNITY LEAVE IF I DON'T PLAN TO RETURN TO WORK?

Yes! You have every right to benefit from your company's paid parental leave policy, and you should never leave benefits on the table. "Forgoing paid leave would be the same as canceling your 401(k) match because you're planning on leaving at some point," says Raena

Boston, cofounder of the nonprofit advocacy group the Chamber of Mothers and a human resources professional at Pricewaterhouse-Coopers in Tampa. There is nothing unethical about benefiting from a paid leave program, whether it's funded by the state or by your company. "Companies do not behave ethically when they pursue layoffs despite making record profits. These layoffs often include pregnant people and caregivers," she says. "As much as possible we need to remove ethics from the discussion."

So, what should you consider as you make this decision? First, make sure that giving notice won't have repercussions on your parental leave pay. Carefully review the policy at your workplace to understand if there is a "claw back," which would mean you're on the hook for repayment if you resign or leave. "Some companies or states may require that you return for a set amount of time before resigning to avoid repayment," says Boston.

You may also want to consider how exiting while on leave will impact your relationship with your manager and colleagues. Leaving without returning robs you of the chance for a slow goodbye full of networking. Also keep in mind that your manager will have to start at square one with hiring for your replacement once you resign, and if you've been absent for several months, they may also have to undo plans for your return. The most considerate way to leave without returning first: "Share your decision at least one month before your expected return date so that the company has time to start the hiring process," says Marlo Lyons. "You can say, I'm going to be resigning effective X date, which clarifies that your pay should continue until then." To ensure positive vibes between you and your manager, you could offer to come on board to consult to help with the transition and suggest candidates who could fill your shoes. You can also work with your manager to send a teamwide email with your contact details and use social media (liked LinkedIn) to stay connected.

4. Consider a part-time option

If you're interested in going part-time at your organization, these early conversations—before resigning—are the ideal time to discuss the topic and negotiate an arrangement. Working part-time will enable you to keep a foothold in your industry (helpful if it's work you enjoy) and earn some income. Wittman says it can also signal your commitment, making it easier to return to full-time employment later. Research also suggests that mothers who work part-time may fare best from a psychological standpoint. According to a study in the *Journal of Family Psychology*, these mothers were less likely to exhibit symptoms of depression in the early parenting years than mothers who stayed home full-time.

Dara Astmann was working in ad sales at Viacom when she came back from maternity leave and craved more flexibility to be home with her daughter. Instead of resigning outright, she connected with a colleague who'd had a baby around the same time and the pair pitched a solution: a job share that would enable each to work part-time and together do the work of one role. Dara and her counterpart would each work three days a week, with one day of overlap, which would offer each woman the time they wanted at home and in the workplace. The company agreed to try it out, and after a few years Dara and her counterpart got promoted together. Recently, they celebrated ten years in the job share.

Of course, part-time work can sometimes sound better than it is. With a part-time schedule, you won't fully relinquish the mental stress of your job, which means that even on days with the kids, you may find your mind wandering to your inbox. Before she resigned, Nichol Hibbard, of Spokane, Washington, watched other employees at her company scale back to part-time and she saw them take on more work than they wanted. "I was very protective of my time with my daughter and did not want part-time to creep into full-time, so I told my boss that part-time wouldn't work," she says.

5. Follow company protocol and offer as much advance notice as you can

If you don't know how resignations are supposed to work at your office, do a quick review of the employee handbook and follow the process to a tee. (Klotz and Bolino call this the "by the book" resignation style, and managers say it's a must if you want to leave a positive impression.) While your company may only require two weeks of notice and you may not *want* to stay any longer than that, being flexible about your final day of work (and offering an extended notice period) makes you look considerate and mature—and may help keep the door open to potential opportunities at your company later. (I cringe a little when I reflect on my quick exit from that start-up.) Lisa, the HR director in Denver, offered three months' notice when she resigned—a timeline she felt was necessary to leave on good terms. She had just returned from maternity leave two months earlier, and some team members she oversaw were new to the company. "Those people would not have known how to do their jobs if I left, and I wanted to give my manager time to figure out what to do," she says.

Similarly, Liz Mangino, a high school math teacher and department chair in Paducah, Kentucky, often spoke with her boss about the fact that she had doubts about whether she wanted to work or stay home. Then one winter day, when the two were discussing class schedules for the fall, Liz knew the time had come to resign. Her youngest daughter was three years old, and she'd only have two more years of a leisurely nursery school schedule. Liz gave eight months' notice. "It was difficult for me to work up the courage to tell him, but I just knew as we talked about the next year that I didn't want to come in months later and blindside him. I didn't want him to work hard to set the schedule and then have to redo it." When Liz left the school that spring, her boss told her a job would be waiting whenever she was ready to return. They've been in touch since, and he's repeated the offer, even though Liz expects her pause to last longer than the two years she initially planned. She loves being at home more than she ever expected.

6. Explain yourself (to a point)

A crucial part of the "in the loop" resignation method: sharing why you're leaving. You don't need to go into considerable detail, but you will likely find that authenticity strengthens your bond with your manager. Renee Manorat, in Needham, Massachusetts, had to resign from her job while on her first maternity leave because her mother suffered from a catastrophic fall that rendered her paralyzed. The news was deeply personal, and she wasn't looking for attention; still, Manorat knew that if she didn't explain what happened, there would be an air of mystery surrounding her exit. (In the absence of information, people often make unfair assumptions.) In the end, she says that telling her peers the sad story left her feeling more connected and supported. And a year after she departed, a former colleague invited her back for a part-time consulting project that she gladly took on.

7. Show gratitude, even if you don't actually feel it

Your resignation may be your last one-to-one meeting with your boss, so do what you can to leave a positive impression. "People don't remember what you say. They will remember how you make them feel," says Wittman. That means letting whatever has made you disgruntled fall away and gunning for brownie points. Tell your manager how much you have enjoyed working for her. Share specific attributes of hers that you appreciate. Write her a hand-written note and leave it on her desk on your last day. "You'd be surprised how many people bad-mouth their former employer or manager and don't realize that it reflects poorly upon them and burns the bridge to return in the future when the company may be a very different place," says Marlo Lyons. "End your time showing gratitude for all you've learned and use your time away from the office to heal the workforce trauma."

8. Network more than you've ever networked before

This may sound counterintuitive. After all, you're leaving and not looking for another job. Shouldn't you be excused from tedious lunches and coffee dates? But your last few months and weeks of work—the "lame duck period"—are the final impression you leave on your colleagues and the last truly "easy" chance to build your network. As Wittman puts it, "Before you take the off-ramp, take time to build your future on-ramp." To do this, have strategic conversations that fortify your reputation and work relationships.

List the people at your office who view you positively and could be an ally later. Think broadly as you invite colleagues (and yes, your manager) for one last lunch or even a first one-on-one Zoom. Consider people in other departments and in roles that differ from yours. When you're ready to return to the workforce, a current assistant may be the hiring manager, and you may have a new skill set to bring to the workforce. "Research shows that women often don't think strategically about where our best networking opportunities are," says Wittman. "Ask yourself: Who have been my champions? Who will be most saddened to see me go? Who believes in my potential to come back?"

Own the challenging nature of your decision when you get into these meetings rather than apologizing for your choice or slinking off quietly in embarrassment. Wittman suggests asking variations on these questions: *Knowing that leaving this job for motherhood can impact my career trajectory negatively, what strategic actions do you think I should take to help the door reopen when I'm ready? What would you like to see me do on my pause so that I can return to work in X years' time?* Through these conversations, you and your manager can shift your relationship from manager and employee to mentor and mentee, and your colleagues can become your confidantes and friends.

Don't worry about overstating your desire to return to your company when you chat. You are *not* committing to returning. These conversations are a way to actively change your colleagues' immediate perception of you from someone going off into the "void" of motherhood into someone taking a temporary break who still values their career. Believe it or not, gracefully exiting from your job can also ease your identity transition to a stay-at-home mother. As humans, we derive identity not just from what we do and what people call us but from the communities where we spend our time. Have you ever felt homesick for an old job in the first weeks at a new one? You might feel similarly in those first weeks with your kids. But when we exit gracefully, we can stay connected to colleagues. You might even be able to join them for a real lunch break occasionally. Even if you just connect with your team on LinkedIn and engage with their content, you will feel less at sea than if you cut off from your network cold turkey.

Some large, elite organizations like Google and Facebook have alumni societies for former employees and a referral program that funnels consulting work their way. These companies are eager to keep relationships healthy because they know that the value of their employees extends beyond their active tenure. While your organization's offboarding process may be a basic exit interview, your best bet professionally—and even from an identity standpoint—is to consider yourself a proud alum and to stay connected, as you would with your alma mater.

IF YOU'VE ALREADY paused your career, reading this chapter may have brought on little twinges of regret. Most of us have at least one exit that we wish we could do over. As I discovered all the best advice on this topic, I imagined a million new and improved versions of my resignations, from that first job as a teenager at a bakery to the hurried one at the trendy start-up. But rest assured: it's never too late to change the last impression you made. (Okay, fine: the high school job may be a lost cause.) After a few years in the cocoon of motherhood, I started posting my work on Mother Untitled on LinkedIn. In minutes my former start-up colleagues and classmates from business school were right there, liking my posts and commenting, seemingly curious about my interests and open to helping. I may have missed my chance to build a sturdy bridge back to working at that company, but I still have the power to strengthen the connections I made there.

Pausing After a Layoff

As challenging as it can be to work up the courage to resign, the process is also a gift—a chance to weigh the positives and negatives, come to your own decision, and bravely express that choice. On the surface, a layoff robs you of that process. But if you can take a little time to recover, grieve, and reflect after your dismissal, you may ultimately view this trauma as "happening for a reason." For several women I've met, it eventually served as the push they needed to pause their career and live the life they wanted (but might never have found the courage to claim).

"The week before I got laid off, I was wishing and hoping that I could just not work, not have a job that I had to check into and answer to," says Adrienne Farr, who is a single mother by choice to a six-year-old daughter and manages the care of her elderly mother, who has Alzheimer's and dementia. At the time, Adrienne was a senior editor at a major digital media company. "And then, one week later, I got laid off. So, at that point, I was like, okay, this is not by accident. I was like, *this is it*. I am going to take my time figuring out what I'm going to do now." When she filed for unemployment in New York State, she discovered a program—the Self-Employment Assistance Program—that would allow her to continue to collect unemployment as she started her own content company. Today she is a freelancer who writes on her own schedule and can focus more energy on raising her daughter.

In contrast, Bari, a mother of two in Westchester County, New York, was a director of product and innovation at a well-known beauty brand and loved her working mom "juggle." She describes it as "having an amazing career with amazing support and childcare help, making it all work and living that dream." But in 2020, she was laid off. Bari describes unplugging for a whole weekend to cry. "It surprised me how gutted I was and how it rocked me and shook my ego." But once she began to move past the initial shock, Bari realized she had an opportunity to test whether she wanted to stay home instead of returning to paid work. That phase of looking at potential job opportunities, taking time to understand her wants and needs, and evaluating her finances made it clear that she wanted a life at home, and she and her husband began to plan to move to a suburb. Though her exit from work wasn't her decision, in time, she reclaimed a feeling of agency and made a choice on her terms.

After her layoff from a tech company, mom of two Marissa Mast from Phoenix came to an important realization: "You have control of your career journey and your own career story and your own life story. A layoff doesn't rob you of that," she says. "For me, choosing to stay home was taking control of the narrative and deciding, this is what I want to do. I *want* to work part-time while I'm also doing pickup and drop-off. I also realized I could do less work and continue growing my skill set."

How Do I Announce My Pause on LinkedIn?

Once you've decided to take a career break, you get to decide whether and how to share the news beyond your workplace. Some women think of updating LinkedIn with their current status as a personal branding exercise—a chance to share with the world another dimension of who you are now and what you care about. In theory, I would love to suggest that you write a long, proud announcement about stepping into full-time motherhood. After all, it's past time the taboos around that decision crumbled, and when I see these kinds of posts on LinkedIn, my heart wells with joy. LinkedIn now even includes "stay-at-home parent" and "career break" as listable job titles.

But I will level with you here: research suggests that down the line, you'll be better served with a subtler explanation of your time rather than using these labels. If you're taking a part-time role, list that title. There's no need to mention how many hours you work at it. If you're stepping full-time into motherhood, close out the dates on your current job and create a new job title. If you find that you're still offering advice, even in only a casual capacity, to other professionals in your field, you might consider a "consultant" title. While you don't want to misrepresent yourself, you also shouldn't sell yourself short—whatever you're doing to keep your skills sharp should be accounted for.

"Consulting can be three minor, unpaid consultations you do in a year. Did you talk to friends about your expertise at a dinner party? That's a consultation," says Lyons. "Describe where you're using your skills and capabilities to consult, keeping in mind that it doesn't have to be a formal or paid engagement." If you aren't keeping a hand in your old industry, consider listing volunteer work or sharing steps to upgrade or maintain your skills, like classes or certifications. When you describe the volunteer work, write about it through the lens of the career you aspire to have one day so people can see how your skills are applicable.

Strategic or not, Simi Sapir wanted to announce her career pause on social media. She knew herself well enough to realize that being transparent and open would make it easier to forge genuine connections with contacts in her network when she was ready. "I remember saying to my husband, 'I'm going to make this a big deal. Because this is the biggest step forward I've ever taken—into something that has brought me more meaning in less than two years than my whole career.'" Her advice to those looking to do the same: focus on the lessons and accomplishments from your career thus far and share your enthusiasm to discover what comes next.

Power Practice:
Communicate Your Change to Your
Professional Circle—Starting with LinkedIn

This chapter explored how a career pause may impact your future job searches, and how to resign gracefully, keeping your best connections intact. The exercise that follows is optional and you can do it whenever you like. Some moms don't want to even think about sitting in front of a computer again, let alone updating LinkedIn, but many eventually write to me worried about how to account for what they're up to on the site. To enable you to fully unlock the following chapters and settle into the day-to-day, I suggest you address it now. It's important to think about for two reasons. First, you never know when opportunity will direct-message you. And second, and perhaps more importantly, this exercise can help you escape the limitations of your professional title and organization and begin to identify publicly with your strongest personal qualities, experiences, and interests.

This is an iterative exercise, meaning it's best to come back to it annually (or more often) to reassess how to describe your current moment and the ways you wish to spend your time now and in the future. Keep notes, maybe in your phone, about anything that might be relevant to your professional identity. Trust me, if you don't track your accomplishments, you will forget about how you helped a friend launch her business, tinkered with a creative project, or fundraised for a local charity. You'll be glad to have it documented when you're ready to revisit your résumé (more on this in chapter 9).

To come up with your headline, follow these steps:

1. Describe the industry or role in which you have the most experience. Using myself as an example, I would write "brand marketer" or "brand strategist."
2. Write a two- to three-word phrase that describes what makes you stand out. This could be a specific area of business, a character trait, a unique approach, or a particular achievement. For me, that phrase was "driven by women's consumer insights."
3. Finally, describe your current work or what you imagine wanting to do in the future. If you're drawing a blank and don't feel comfortable claiming the title "consultant," "advisor," or "volunteer," proudly list "parent" or "mother" in the

third spot. Alternatively, "aspiring" can be tacked onto any hobby or interest. Think aspiring writer or aspiring interior designer. Back when I was on a career pause, the third descriptor in my headline read: "advisor to female-founded businesses."

Here are some more strong examples to inspire you:

"Lawyer, passionate about M&A, community activist, and volunteer"

"Operations manager, small business advisor, and parent"

"Award-winning educator, reading specialist, and content creator"

"People operations leader, DE&I expert, and advisor"

"Sales professional, results-driven team player, and independent contractor"

"Marketing executive, 10 years of global experience, and open to new opportunities"

All of these headlines prove, without a doubt, that you don't need a job title or an employer to establish credibility and open yourself up to a bright future of work.

Part Two

Find Your Footing as
an At-Home Parent

4

Redefine Success for Right Now

FALSE BELIEF

A successful stay-at-home mother is a Supermom.

NEW NARRATIVE

*Success isn't doing everything or winning at
domestic labor. Success means focusing on the
areas of greatest value to me as an individual. I get
to determine what matters to my family and me.*

AT TWENTY-FOUR YEARS old, I was named the first digital strategist at one of the largest advertising agencies in Boston and moved from the open bullpen to a windowed corner on the thirty-fourth floor, with sweeping views of the harbor. Sitting there meant *everything* to me. It felt like the ultimate professional status symbol.

I barely noticed that the promotion had also come with sacrifices. I kept toiletries and a spare set of clothes in my filing cabinet for all-nighters—a signal to company leadership that I was more committed to our clients than anyone else. On most days, I managed to take a car service home sometime after nine p.m. and eke out a few hours of sleep in my bed. (Submitting receipts for after-hours taxis was another way to prove my value.)

Like many corporations in America, mine conducted annual employee performance appraisals capped with formal goal-setting exercises. Every spring, I would trot over to a row of modern orange swivel chairs at the opposite end of the thirty-fourth floor and chat with my boss. He and I would discuss professional benchmarks of success—clients I had won, skills I had learned—and what I could be doing to help even more. In truth, the whole endeavor felt like a charade. Every phrase I uttered was a disguised way of saying, "I'd like to keep my office, and I'm ready for a title bump, please." At work, goal setting is often a sycophantic exercise aimed at attaining surface-level rewards, most of which benefit the larger organization more than they benefit you.

In parenthood, I've found that the process is the exact opposite. Setting goals for motherhood is deep, complex, life-altering work. You must be your most authentic and honest self because that's who you report to now. Parenthood is a powerful opportunity to reacquaint yourself with how you derive joy and meaning from life, and to ask, One day, when I look back on this time, what do I hope to see and feel?

I've come to love the mental work involved in answering this question, even with its challenges. I think you will too.

Why Do Stay-at-Home Mothers Need Concrete Goals?

In my first year at home with my son, I didn't put pen to paper to crystallize my aspirations. Instead, as I observed myself through the ups and downs of nap times and diaper changes, outings, and early mornings, I casually mulled over what I wanted to get out of this period and how I wanted to grow. After I put my son to sleep and looked back on the photos and videos from each day, I'd smile at his images and stop to look at the ones of me. I noticed that I looked different—natural, playful, and a little messy. I didn't know what I wanted to do next. I could only articulate that I wanted more of that person in the videos.

Over the years, I've chatted with hundreds of successful career women about their transitions to stay-at-home motherhood. Most have shared a similar desire to discover themselves in the first months rather than actively focus on goals. Executive leadership coach Megan Martin Strickland explains that for many women leaving stressful jobs, the only choice at first is to recover from burnout. Plus, formulating a written goal may feel like corporate office work, which is probably the last thing you want to do. "When I quit to be with my first kid, I needed a few months just to *be*," she tells me.

You may be downshifting or pausing your career because your child needs more attention, and you just can't make the juggle work anymore. You may have been laid off and feel a sense of disappointment and shock. You may have stopped working to tend to an ill family member or process the loss of a loved one. You may have simply hit your breaking point, no longer able to smile through a toxic corporate climate or deal with a demanding boss. Psychologists and career coaches agree that recovery is an essential first step if you're entering this phase in a state of grief, exhaustion, or trauma. The trick is to notice when you start to feel better—and to change your mindset consciously. While many mothers have told me that they couldn't set goals initially, they have also said that they regret "floating" without meaningful goals for too long. In the end, most moms realize that they could have gotten over mental blocks faster, and moved with greater confidence and joy, had they done this inner work.

The benefits of goal setting extend far beyond productivity (though yes, writing your goals makes you 42 percent more likely to accomplish them). Early thought leaders in the field—Edwin Locke, an American psychologist and professor emeritus at the Robert H. Smith School of Business at the University of Maryland, College Park, and Gary Latham, former president of the Canadian Psychological Association (CPA) and professor of organizational behavior at the University of Toronto—spent decades proving a link between setting vivid goals and achieving "higher motivation, self-esteem, self-confidence, and autonomy." Time and again, studies have also suggested that during periods of anxiety, maintaining a purpose that transcends the stress of any given moment can reinstate a feeling of control. And making progress toward goals has been linked with increased feelings of hopefulness, accomplishment, excitement, and confidence. Although research is scarce on the impact of goal setting in stay-at-home motherhood, several studies suggest that personal goals—also known as "self-concordant goals" or "want-to goals"—tend to be more potent than goals that serve an external stakeholder, like an employer or a school. Even though want-to goals may require serious effort, we typically perceive them as having inherent ease, which makes us more likely to stick with the process.

Perhaps most importantly, when you deliberately set goals, you respect your choice and your time. Goals are a reminder that your growth at home is just as significant as your growth in your paid career, and that your family's future merits as much consideration as the future of your former organization. In the difficult days of motherhood—when your children ricochet from one tantrum to the next, messes pile up endlessly in your living room, and no one sleeps at night—you can return to your larger vision and put the struggles in perspective. Time is not evaporating as your kids do the vital work of growing up. This is your life too, and your goals can constantly remind you that you are not "stuck" in stay-at-home motherhood. Instead, you are evolving into the person you want to be.

Strickland says that you'll know it's time to be more intentional when you notice yourself questioning the legitimacy of how you're spending your time. Contrary to what many people think, a feeling of listlessness is not a sign that you've made a mistake in leaning into parenthood. Ambivalence is part of motherhood for just about everyone, and stepping into primary parenthood after a robust career often involves mixed emotions, even for those who choose it willingly. I like to think of that questioning feeling like ambition tapping you on the shoulder, asking, "No rush, but where to next?" Goals are guardrails to keep ambivalence from overwhelming you and to let intent take charge again. They enable you to repackage your worries about stagnation and accept the life choice you made with clarity. In the irreverent 2016 book *The Subtle Art of Not Giving a F*ck: A Counterintuitive Approach to Living a Good Life,* author Mark Manson explains that "giving up a value you've depended on for years is going to feel disorienting." Finding new metrics to guide your decision-making is the best and only way to combat that feeling.

Start by Identifying Your North Star

My moment to begin goal setting arrived around my son's first birthday. As I realized that the newborn milestones were in the rearview mirror and friends and family started to ask more questions about my plans, I felt scrutinized. I decided to restart a daily journal, a habit I'd given up years earlier, when I no longer needed to chronicle breakups and solo vacations. As a mom, I wrote with newfound optimism, exploring my daily motivations. Eventually, themes emerged, and one morning, I landed on an overarching objective: **I want to be present through each day with my family and be the calmest and most content version of myself that I can be.** Today, I consider that statement to be my North Star.

A "North Star" isn't just an ancient sailing navigation guide; it's a corporate organizational principle taught in business schools across the country. (I learned about it in at least two courses.) Put simply, the North Star is the singular vision that an entire company works toward, regardless of department, and it often serves as a filter for complex decision-making. Head to a bookstore or a library, or just google "goal setting," and you'll be flooded with options for frameworks and systems. Corporations often rely on SMART goals (Specific, Measurable, Achievable, Relevant, and Time-Bound). But there are also WOOP goals (Wish, Outcome, Obstacle, and Plan), HARD goals (Heartfelt, Animated, Required, Difficult), and the list goes on. While researching this book, I learned about many of these methods and tried to apply quite a few to the realities of a career pause. Most were created for employees at big corporations where productivity is king; some were engineered for individuals starting businesses. None are specifically intended for the mom settling into parenting. Out of all these systems, I think the North Star approach speaks best to our collective stage of life. In motherhood, your North Star is the one broad outcome that is non-negotiable to make you feel content; your focus, time, creativity, and energy should all align to reach it.

Just after we arrived in America, my family lived in a series of one-bedroom apartments in a transient side of a Boston suburb. Back then, and for many years afterward, my dad kept a drawing I made for him at around age eight folded in his wallet. On the back, I wrote, "To my wonderful father, from your only child." On the front, I drew a picture of a little girl in a tutu and the words, "There was once a little princess named Neha. She lived with a King and Queen. But they lived in a very, very, very small house." My dad never said it, but as he worked nights and weekends to build his career, I always knew that giving me a brighter future—and yes, a bigger home—was his North Star. In the day-to-day of motherhood, my North Star helped me decide when to wean my daughter from breastfeeding (a stressful public leaking situation was the final straw for my sanity), how to plan our family's social life (meeting friends at restaurants with our infant and toddler sent my calmness south, not north), and how to feed my kids (I have no issues with microwaved meals and baby food pouches).

Over the years, I've shared my North Star with friends and members of the Mother Untitled community, and many have said it resonates with them too. A few have even adopted it as their own. But while you are welcome to take a shortcut and borrow it, I encourage you to do the important work of figuring out your own.

To start, take time to reacquaint yourself with what makes you tick and to free yourself from the cultural conditioning that the best goals are big and impress others. Emily Pardy, a Nashville-based marriage and family therapist specializing in perinatal mental health, suggests setting aside a few minutes each day to flip through magazines and tear out images that light you up. (If you like, you can also do this digitally by saving posts on Flipboard or Pinterest.) In this same period, try to recall a few things about motherhood that you looked forward to before your child arrived. "We don't often admit that when we dreamed of having kids, we also thought about making cookies together or wearing matching outfits," says Orlesa Poole, a clinical social worker specializing in pre- and postpartum women in Bowie, Maryland. "These lighthearted, everyday experiences bring playfulness and fun into parenting. Lean into that as you set your vision."

Next, ask yourself a series of pointed questions, beginning with, "What do I want in life?" Then ask yourself *why* you want that. For each response, ask why again—three times in a row. "For example, if you want to quit smoking, ask, 'Why do you want to quit?' Then, if you want to quit for your health, ask, 'Why do you want good health?' Then, if your answer is to be alive long enough to meet your grandchildren, ask, 'Why do you want to meet your grandchildren?'" suggests Kelly McGonigal, a psychologist and the author of *The Upside of Stress*. "Through this process, you get to something that feels so obviously important to you." Other questions to which you can apply this line of inquiry: How do you want to grow? What do you want to be remembered for?

The Short-Term Goals That Can Make Your Vision a Reality

Your North Star is a powerful vision statement that can steer and comfort you for the long haul, but to achieve it, you'll need concrete goals. These should be timely, attainable, and to some extent measurable. Think of each as an attempt to move past a block or as a step in the right direction. As you age and your children's needs evolve, these goals will also morph.

In the goal-setting book *Designing Your Life*, authors Bill Burnett and Dave Evans describe determining short-term goals as "evaluating your life dashboard." They suggest setting goals in four areas: work, play, love, and health. But for our purposes, we can limit the dashboard to three categories: what you want as an individual (personal goals); what you want to achieve professionally, which can range from pursuing creative hobbies to engaging in paid work (career goals); and what you want to experience with your kids and, if applicable, your partner (family goals). This structure encourages you to keep your well-being and professional prospects in mind, even as your day-to-day revolves around caregiving. Within each category, commit to one measurable project. For example, if you set a career goal to stay connected to your professional network, your project could be to have coffee with someone in your network once every quarter. If your personal goal was self-care, you might set a goal to have dinner with a friend once a month or try a new exercise class. Keep the goalposts within reach. "In terms of numbers, take whatever number is in your head—say, working out six times a week—and cut it in half to three. Then, if you need to, halve it again," says Pardy.

Personal Goals

Typically, when I ask a mother if she has any goals for her chapter as a stay-at-home mom, she immediately starts talking about her children. "I want to raise confident kids," she might say. "I want to raise an athlete." "I want my baby to be bilingual." When I double down and ask, "And do you have any goals for *you*?" I'm usually met with a long pause—and what I assume is some panicked soul-searching.

If you feel guilty for thinking about your happiness before considering goals for your kids, remember: your children learn from your example. As you pursue your own rich life, you will show them how to be fulfilled and healthy. Any mother will tell you that parenthood is the ultimate leadership training ground, a period that forces you to look at yourself closely and recognize traits that you'd like to strengthen. As you set a goal for yourself, expect to think deeply about patterns from your past, and to experience healing as you work to achieve that goal.

As organizational psychologist Adam Grant so aptly put it, "How we define success is a source of happiness we can control.... Seeking fame, money, or beauty is a bottomless pit. Pursuing growth, kindness, trust, and health is a path to flourishing." This statement doesn't just sound good; it's backed by 105 studies on more than seventy thousand people across the globe.

My personal goals have changed from season to season. One that held for quite a while, starting when my firstborn entered toddlerhood: "I want to get help for my anxiety and feel more in control of my reactions." While I usually managed to appear serene out in public, my emotions were roiling under the surface—and at home, it was hard to hold myself together. Conflicts with my husband often ended with me yelling at him, and my worries over my kids routinely led me to spiral into tears. The root cause wasn't what you might expect. I wasn't triggered by mess, sensory overload, or resentment—the universal pet peeves of early motherhood. Ever since I was a little girl, I have struggled to develop a secure feeling of belonging in my community. In college and my twenties, I worked to get over that insecurity and feel confident in my skin, even if that skin was a different color than that of the people around me. But when I had children, my insecurities in this arena bubbled back up to the surface and transferred to my son and daughter. If my three-year-old son acted out against his little sister, I catastrophized his behavior—actively worrying that he would never fit in at school or that he'd be so aggressive he would never make friends. When my husband and I argued, even over small things, I worried that our cultural differences (I'm Indian, he is Jewish) were just too vast—and that we were destined for separation. Living in this heightened state of anxiety manifested in several ways, but the angry outbursts were the most overt.

Once I set an intention to be calm, I got to work. I found a therapist. I devoured podcasts and self-help books on anger and belonging. I tried dozens (yes, dozens) of mindfulness exercises, from tracing my hand to focusing on physical sensations that could pull me out of my head. Some of them helped for a moment, but not long term. Ultimately, I achieved my goal by engineering my own mindfulness exercise. One day, as my son was clinging to my leg rather than "presenting" as extroverted and independent at a birthday party, I looked up at the sky and focused on the clouds. I realized that what was happening—my son reacting in a particular way—was as normal as nature. In fact, not only was it expected, but it would also pass. Another mental hack that worked: thinking back on a challenging moment (a public tantrum, a fight with my husband) and realizing how insignificant and irrelevant it seemed now. Instantly, I could see that the present moment would one day amount to nothing—and that my reaction should be commensurate with that fact.

I also created a routine to support me in all this work on myself. To this day, I do my best to wake up forty-five minutes before my early rising kids to do a thirty-minute yoga and meditation practice, followed by a bullet journaling exercise in the Notes app on my phone. Sometimes it's more like thirty minutes in advance . . . or twenty. But the intention is there, and every little bit counts. This sequence isn't fancy or luxurious, but it allows me to enter the day with perspective on the overwhelming moments.

Margaret Brown, a mom of two girls from Montclair, New Jersey, set a personal goal when she noticed that she couldn't entirely focus on her daughter, even when they were one-on-one. "I was zoning out thinking about the things I needed to do while reading a book with her," she says. Brown was on a career pause from work as an executive coach, so she reached out to another coach in her community for help. "My coach told me to reflect on who in my life *is* intentional and present," says Brown. "I realized my children are the best teachers in just really living life, and my coach worked with me to observe them and emulate them." (Noticing when people embody an energy or trait you admire or envy can often give you a clue about your personal goal.)

To commit to "living with as much presence as her kids," Brown made a list of actions, including stepping away from social media. "I've found that social media can draw me into parts of myself that are not my whole self or my best self. I've had to shift my behaviors in what I'm consuming. I would go down rabbit holes if I saw all the comments, and it just would take me so far away from what I need to be."

PERSONAL GOALS TO CONSIDER

- I want to loosen up and feel sillier and more lighthearted.
- I want to feel connected to local culture and attend more events.
- I want to build a self-care practice that makes me feel stronger and healthier.
- I want to reevaluate my relationship with devices and create boundaries that protect my focus and headspace.
- I want to model kindness daily and incorporate more generosity into my life.
- I want to develop more acceptance of my whole self.
- I want to learn to let go of perfectionism.
- I want to work on standing up for myself, my beliefs, and my boundaries.

Career Goals

Kristi Rible, the executive leadership coach and mother who teaches a motherhood and work course at Stanford, paused a busy career filled with international travel after she had her first child. "I didn't pause with any professional goals or strategy," she tells me. "I didn't know what I know today about the impact on your career if you step out of the workforce without a plan. At the time, I just thought, *I'm having this baby, and I need to be present for this baby, and at some point—no idea when—I'll reenter the workforce.*" Rible's life did not play out as she expected—her marriage ended in divorce, and her need to return to work suddenly became urgent. These days, she has one big piece of advice for mothers pausing their careers: "When you're amid the excitement of bringing new life into the world, that's all you're likely to be thinking about. But it's equally important to hold on to the belief that you will get back to work that you love or work that is meaningful—and to live intentionally with that in mind."

A career goal does not need to be extensive or time-consuming. The main point is to avoid the urge to cut off from a professional identity entirely (a coping mechanism that bears a striking resemblance to blocking an ex-boyfriend on social media). Instead, frame this chapter as part of an ambitious trajectory and find a kernel of professional interest to keep in your purview. In stay-at-home motherhood, earning an income has taken a back seat; instead, get clear on what you like to do, and what you're good at, and explore tasks and projects you've never dared to try.

When I decided to pause my career for motherhood, I had already become disenchanted with the superficial elements of my field, which made the decision to leave easier. But there were also parts of marketing I enjoyed, like running focus groups and designing customer journey maps. Before I applied to business school, I had also been considering applying to journalism school. In my heart, I wanted to be in the media world, but I felt cowed by cultural pressure to enter a traditionally lucrative field, where success and financial security would be all but guaranteed. In my pause, I finally gave myself permission to explore the idea of turning my passion into my career. There's a famous quote by the writer Charles Bukowski: "Can you remember who you were before the world told you who you should be?" This moment is a rare opportunity to think back to when you had an *inner knowing* about your calling, and to listen once again.

Holly Blakey, a mother of three in Walnut Creek, California, always loved "doing anything to create a sense of calm in my surroundings—whether that was painting the walls, moving furniture, or decluttering." But she never contemplated turning this hobby into a career until she had her first child in 2014. When Holly parted with her career in public relations to be home with her newborn, she felt lost and missed the act of creating—in her case, press events for tech companies. Her first career goal was simply to connect with more people, as she felt lonely and missed office camaraderie. On one coffee catch-up, a longtime mentor asked her, "Holly, what would you do even if no one paid you?" Her answer was organizing—so for a year, she set a goal to simply research and read about what it would take to launch a business as a personal organizer. Six years later, Breathing Room Home routinely collaborates with major retail brands like the Container Store. Holly says knowing that her work is a form of self-care has helped her hang on to her dream even in the most exhausting phases of parenthood, when she was tempted to let it go.

Godhuli Chatterjee Gupta had always dreamed of being a writer, but for practical reasons, she opted for a career in corporate communications instead. A few years after she paused her career and settled into stay-at-home motherhood in the suburbs of Chicago, she became overwhelmed by the day-to-day grind of raising two young children. That's when she committed to a daily writing practice and began to post original poetry on Instagram. Chatterjee Gupta set measurable goals—submitting her work for publication once a month, posting something new once a week—and was gentle on herself whenever she faltered. "The goals were there to help motivate me and keep me continuing," she says. Recently she published her first book of poetry.

As someone accustomed to pursuing my career ambitiously, I struggled at first to set professional goals aligned with my North Star. Shortly after my son's first birthday, I had an idea for a business and immediately started planning how I'd execute it. My dad, who has decades of business experience, offered to help me figure this part out without losing sight of what mattered to me most.

We were taking my son for a walk in his stroller in Union Square in Manhattan, and I was passionately describing a new idea: opening a brick-and-mortar clubhouse where stay-at-home and part-time working mothers could take classes, have coffee, make friends, and grow their networks, skills, and confidence. "You're onto something," he said to me. "But there's no way you can build this *and* still be home in the way you are now." With his encouragement, I met with an acquaintance who opened a well-known frozen yogurt chain in California and asked her what it takes to raise capital for and then open a physical space. It quickly became clear that the stress and hours of the project, not to mention the massive financial investment required, would undermine my core goal, and that perhaps I had been thinking big because I didn't know any other way to think. After weeks of percolating on the idea, I opened my journal and wrote a new goal: "I want to create a space online for a conversation about the tension women feel between their ambition, their womanhood, and motherhood." I also wrote that I wanted to "keep my tools sharp" and continue "learning about technology, marketing, and culture." I purchased the domain name MotherUntitled.com, and, on January 10, 2017, I launched a blog for mothers in career pauses.

Of course, your work goal does not have to be entrepreneurial or based on passion. One of the wisest things you can do is stay connected to a skill you used at work. Many mothers fear that their knowledge will atrophy in motherhood, but that is far from inevitable. In truth, most people in nine-to-five jobs spend just a tiny fraction of their day improving their skills or learning new information about their industry. Just twenty minutes a day of reading newsletters, listening to podcasts or audiobooks, following relevant social media accounts, or watching an online webinar can teach you more than you might think.

"There's no cookie-cutter formula for every person," says Rible. "But I think homing in on what is meaningful to you outside of parenting and deciding how you will continue to do that meaningful work . . . that can be the thread that will keep you engaged during your time away from work." For example, let's say you worked in human resources and were particularly passionate about employee wellness. Then, says Rible, "tell yourself, 'I'm going to keep my finger in this area of wellness at work while I prioritize my family and my children. Maybe I write a paragraph now and then on the topic and post it online. Maybe I will take an hour a month to volunteer somewhere related to it.' The point is: strategically choose the thing that is meaningful to you, that you can tell a story about when you decide to return."

My knowledge of marketing has expanded dramatically since I left my job, and that's in large part because I read timely articles and listen to podcasts on the topic. I don't have plans to return to a traditional career in brand marketing, and you may not plan to return to what you were doing before you paused. But staying abreast of developments in my field is a simple and solid insurance policy for my future.

When Chinue Richardson left her nonstop job as an associate at a corporate law firm in London, one of the partners took her aside and gave her a key tip: don't forget to keep up your bar membership. (In order to maintain their licensure, lawyers must complete a certain number of continuing education credits annually.) Richardson followed his advice and decided to stay in touch with as many former colleagues as she could too. "I'm so glad he said that to me," she tells me, "because it turned out to be critical." After three and a half happy years at home, Richardson recently returned to a full-time job as an in-house counsel.

CAREER GOALS TO CONSIDER

- I want to take an online class to build my skills.
- I want to meet face-to-face with someone in a different industry each month.
- I want to read one new business book every quarter.
- I want to post regularly on LinkedIn to showcase my expertise and build up my community in my passion area.
- I want to find a new volunteer opportunity that taps into my professional interests.

Family Goals

This is *not* the part where I tell you that your children are the ultimate proof of your success in motherhood. "You can create the feeling in your home. You can create the values that you are embracing as a family. But you cannot create your kids as if they are little statues," says Rebecca Schrag Hershberg, a clinical psychologist and the author of *The Tantrum Survival Guide*. It may seem obvious, but still must be said: attaching your value to the way your children behave or perform will harm your relationship with your kids, and your own mental health. "You don't have full control," explains Hershberg. "One of the most dangerous aspects of parenthood right now is this idea that if I do X, Y, and Z, I can guarantee that my child won't have various problems. And therefore, if they do end up with those problems, it means I didn't parent them right."

Emily Pardy, the marriage and family therapist in Nashville, encourages mothers she counsels to think back on parenting plans—from birthing to breastfeeding to sleep—that have already taken unexpected turns and to reflect on their children's resilience and strength. "You can't parent your child into a specific outcome," she tells me, "And sometimes reflecting on these detours helps mom see that."

As instinctive as all this advice sounds, so many mothers, me included, fall into the "perfect kids" trap. I was personally convinced that my success as a mother directly correlated to my children's social skills. Hoping that my somewhat shy children would learn to greet people with gusto and confidence, I modeled big hellos and constant extroversion. Every time they refused to say hi to their aunts or their friends' parents, my heart would sink. *How could they do this to me? They are proving that I made the wrong choice by staying home with them. Would they have been better off in daycare?* My thoughts looped around these questions every evening when the lights went out and my family was asleep.

Another common pitfall in family goal setting: striving for success that fits the mold created by Instagram influencers—or that you think will elicit the most likes when you post it on so-cial media. In chapter 1, I shared the history of the stay-at-home mother stereotype, including the picture-perfect composite—beautiful house, innovative art projects, homemade meals, gentle parenting—generated on Instagram. As you set goals for your family, scrutinize whether you've come to idolize any social media accounts, and remind yourself that while there are crumbs of reality in your feed, the real story is off camera. "Striving for an Instagram-perfect life can create massive anxiety and depression in moms," says Jo Piazza, host of the *Under the Influence* podcast.

Women new to career pauses often write to tell me that they burned out trying to do "all the things" to earn their stripes as stay-at-home moms. "I wanted to do it so well that there would be no argument about my fitness to be my daughter's caregiver, as if taking a career pause was something to be earned with an invisi-ble grading structure by . . . whom? Family and friends? General society? The patriarchy? I'm sheepish to confess it now, but I was desperate to become my own version of Supermom," says Thao Thai, who lives in Columbus, Ohio, and paused her career as the executive director of a digital publication to be with her daughter and write occasionally.

When Edil Cuepo quit her job in real estate to care for her baby full-time, she lasered in on "take my daughter on outings all over the place" as her gold standard of outward success. "Every day, we had an activity. We're going to the aquarium. Now we're going to the library. Now I'm going to take you to a museum," says the mom of two in Rockaway Beach, Queens. "My daughter was bus-ier her first two years than she is now at age six. I had this urge to excel, to be this walking advertisement for a stay-at-home mom who wasn't just staying at home, who was giving her daughter something no one else could. I didn't need to put that pressure on myself," she says.

So, if there's no need to focus on superficial markers of success, what should your family goals be? One of the great advantages of limiting or pausing your career is that it gives you more mental space to think about the systems that guide you. This is your time to step into a leadership position and set the tone for your home environment, how you interact with your community, and your marriage (if you're partnered). You get to notice what parts of domestic life light you up and prioritize those. Family goal setting also gives you an opportunity to discuss the division of responsibilities and how you'll achieve the life you envision together. "Parents have four thousand things to do and setting aside time and effort to have a shared intention just takes you out of the weeds," says Hershberg. "Working together toward the same goal gives a feeling of connection and increases your compassion for the other person."

It can be tempting to set family goals on your own—and if your partner isn't on board with this process or isn't a true partner to you, then go it alone. But ideally, you can work on this project as a team. Whether you are in a two-parent household or a village that includes caregivers, grandparents, or friends, working together enables you to create a system that helps all the involved players and, ideally, allows you to circumvent the resentfulness that some say is intrinsic to motherhood.

As you've likely guessed, I eventually abandoned my goal to raise social butterflies, and together, my husband and I decided to set out to understand our children's development better. As they've grown, we've adjusted this goal to learn more about whatever may feel off in our family dynamic (too much rushing before school, unhappy mealtimes). We come together to learn about rituals or routines that could make everyday moments easier. After all, these moments fill our days, and those days will fill all the years of early parenthood. We have given ourselves permission to treat these small things as important things.

Of course, we don't do any of this work perfectly, and there have been periods when all we could do is hang on. Survival mode comes for all of us at some point, and certain circumstances may require it longer than anyone would like or expect. In those tough periods, keep in mind that even if all you do is *think* about family intentions occasionally, you're making a difference. Ashley Habib, a widowed mom in New York City, says that it was easy to feel like life was just about cooking and cleaning in the hectic milieu of running her household while grieving. "When you're a solo parent, it can be hard to enjoy your child," she says. Because she is often in survival mode, she has set a weekly goal to "build in times of joy and ease and fun."

Stacy Crocker, a mother of twin five-year-old boys in San Diego, wants to raise "empathetic children"—an outcome she knows can't be measured, which is why she focuses on the process. Crocker describes herself as the "driver" of family goal setting. "I write them down, but then I'll say to my husband, 'Would you want to add any, or do you have any ideas on how to do things?'" The pair completed an online parenting course as part of their shared work. "It was great because it was like, 'Okay, the kids are in bed, and we're going to go watch TV. But first, we're going to watch one little module of the course.'"

FAMILY GOALS TO CONSIDER

Remember, your goals can be big (raise independent thinkers) or small (Friday pizza nights that underscore togetherness). Neither type is better or more valid than the other. As you consider your goals, ask yourself, "When is my family at its best? What memories do I want my kids to have of their childhoods? And what are my family's ideals, and is anything in my life right now in conflict with them?" A few ideas to get the creativity flowing:

- I want to eat dinner at least once a week as a family.
- I want our days to end with a soothing bedtime routine emphasizing gratitude.
- I want to instill in my children that I value education and do my best to help them love to learn.
- I want our family to feel our healthiest—which means all of us exercising, sleeping, and eating well.
- I want to have more fun as a family.

Try It Yourself: Write Three Short-Term Goals

Step 1: Picture an ideal day in your life three years from now. Describe what you see, including where you are, how your relationships feel, what you spend your time doing, who you spend time with, and how you take care of yourself. Now look over what you wrote, and ask yourself:

- Does this day feel good to you, or just look good to others?
- Is this day aligned with your North Star? If not, which do you want to reevaluate—your North Star or how you're spending your time on your ideal day?

- What does this writing exercise tell you about . . .
  - What you'd like to spend more time on?
  - How you wish for your family to feel?
  - How you wish to feel?
  - What you'd like to change about how you spend your time now?
  - What you'd like to change about how you feel right now?

Step 2: Write one short-term goal for each category. Underneath each, list three realistic and enjoyable projects you can take on this year that will move you closer to the day-to-day life you described in step 1. Remember, you can come back here and rewrite your goals anytime.

Personal

My short-term goal is: _____

Project 1: _____

Project 2: _____

Project 3: _____

Career

My short-term goal is: _____

Project 1: _____

Project 2: _____

Project 3: _____

Family

My short-term goal is: _____

Project 1: _____

Project 2: _____

Project 3: _____

The Challenge of Striving Without Feedback

One big obstacle to transitioning to stay-at-home motherhood is that there are no external benchmarks to measure your progress. "There's no raise. There's no paycheck. Even if I have a bad day at work, I was doing it for the money. But if your baby screams all night, you're just alone, wondering, 'Am I a good mom?'" says Pardy.

When friends popped by to visit in the early months of my son's life, they often commented on his physical growth ("Oh, he's so big!") or the state of my home (yes, non-crawling babies make for tidy-ish homes). Neither comment felt like an assessment of whether I was good at stay-at-home motherhood. My husband was too tired and absorbed with running his own business to give out many accolades—and when he did pay me a compliment, it didn't exactly scratch my itch for validation. "I don't know how you do this. I could never do what you do," he'd say with incredulity as I moved from washing bottle parts to folding laundry to emptying the diaper pail. I've heard variations of this comment from men and women, friends, and acquaintances, and I've come to understand it as a "polite" way of saying, "I'm just too complex for at-home parenthood. I need the challenge of work to stay fulfilled."

However, I did receive meaningful feedback that I cherish to this day from my mother. (Yes, the same woman who was skeptical of my decision to stay home.) Watching me slow down and delight in just being present, she would often say something like, "I love watching you as a mom. It's the happiest I've ever seen you."

Her words made me feel seen for having found peace, purpose, and enjoyment in motherhood. My North Star was the biggest and most authentic goal I had ever set, and here I was, achieving it. Nothing I discussed in those orange swivel chairs on the thirty-fourth floor had ever come close.

While you may be lucky enough to have a parent, partner, sibling, or friend congratulate you or cheer you on as you evolve in motherhood, in truth, the only person you can rely on for motivation is yourself. And I'm not going to lie: it may feel impossible at times. In some phases of your children's lives, even the simplest tasks in pursuit of your North Star are unmanageable. (Ever vowed to take a five-minute mental health walk every day, and then discovered that your toddler has decided he now hates his stroller?) Family life is messy; keep that context top of mind as you set measurable benchmarks to reach.

Pardy suggests a loose and informal system: every three months, sit down and ask yourself, "Where do my time, money, and energy go?" If your answers don't align with your projects and North Star, try to recalibrate your schedule. My husband and I have found it's natural to check in at the beginning of the summer, back to school, and the start of the new year.

No matter what system you use to stay motivated, remember that these tools are here to help, not to punish or reward. There's no "winning" or "losing" in motherhood. The only true success is feeling at ease as you walk through the world.

Power Practice: Write a North Star Goal

This chapter looked at why you'll benefit from goals in your career break, how to identify those goals, and how to assess your progress. It starts with identifying the North Star—the one sentence that will act as a compass for all your more individualized objectives. Follow this two-step plan to identify a long-term North Star.

Step 1: Write a letter from your future self. Imagine you are twenty years older and have experienced a fulfilling two decades as a mom. Write a letter from that future you to present-day you. Describe all that you have accomplished personally and professionally. Write about your well-being, your community, your professional or creative pursuit, and your family. Share your regrets, your most significant accomplishments, and where you are now.

Next, evaluate the letter. Ask yourself:

- Why do these accomplishments make you proud?
- Is there anything in this reflection that focuses more on how you appear than how you feel? This is a time to check whether you are seeking outward approval or inner fulfillment.
- What does this letter tell you about . . .
  - Who you care about most?
  - Your three to five most important values?

- How you want to feel about yourself?
- What success truly feels like?

Step 2: Write a one-sentence North Star for the next decade or longer.

_____

_____

_____

5

Create a Daily Rhythm to Maximize Joy

FALSE BELIEF

*Stay-at-home parents become bored by
the monotony of housework and caregiving.*

NEW NARRATIVE

*I have the independence to structure a day
that allows me to find ease, flow, intellectual
stimulation, and fulfillment in parenting.*

DURING MY FIRST year of motherhood, I tried to do all the things. I was used to working a job where my daily calendar was packed with meetings and calls and blocks set aside for concentrated work time or business lunches, and I figured I should take the same approach to this new job of raising a small human. It's what kept me productive in the office, so I was sure the same would be true at home.

I researched the most popular baby classes in my neighborhood (and promptly signed up for the beloved creative movement classes with dancer Dionne Kamara that other moms raved about), organized playgroups, scheduled feedings and mealtimes, and was militant about my son's nap and sleep routines. I'll admit I was not always the most fun to be around—I had very little flexibility about things like nap time (as I would repeatedly tell my visiting parents, no, we cannot skip it or push it back *just this once*, only to catch the surreptitious eye rolls passed between them). While I don't want to use the words "drill sergeant," perhaps Dan would disagree.

In some ways, the plan worked out nicely—our family established some predictable rhythms, my kids were pretty good sleepers, and as they grew older I felt good about the mix of activities they were getting in their days. But as much as I wanted to model my scheduling approach on the pre-children, all-business Neha of years past, there were some key differences in my day-to-day that I forgot to account for.

The most important of which was: at the end of the work day, *you go home.*

Whether you are an elementary school teacher or a physical therapist or a marketing executive, there is a moment at the end of the day when you transition from work to life. And sure, you might answer some emails or tinker with a lesson plan from your kitchen table at night, but there is a delineation between the job and the home that reminds you to take a moment for yourself. During those earliest years with my kids, that moment of transition disappeared, and "take a moment for me" was the one thing I forgot to schedule into my day.

Another difference was that at the office, my scheduled blocks of work were usually bookended by a moment of downtime. I'd chat with a coworker or catch up on my favorite blog, *Cup of Jo.* At home, our scheduled blocks were bookended, or more often interrupted, by diaper explosions or temper tantrums or, on better days, stops at the ice cream truck or to watch a spider crawl across the sidewalk. I loved the fun of seeing Bodie eat his way through a Push Pop (and seeing the resulting Insta-worthy orange mess on his face), but the moments for me time were fewer and farther between. And I felt that loss—hard. I had figured out how to foster a rhythm for my son, but I clearly hadn't mastered how to do the same for myself.

Eventually, I began to schedule me-time blocks at home, too. Dan and I set up a standing date night, and we each set aside one evening a week to see friends (I took Tuesdays). He began taking wake-up duty so I could do a morning workout (though sometimes that "workout" turned into extra sleep). Even when I was with the kids, I was able to factor in my own desires when making the schedule—art time, my favorite shared activity with my children, came in the morning, so that I guaranteed myself a sense of accomplishment early in the day. There was nothing wrong with structuring our lives, I realized—in fact, I appreciated how our schedule allowed me to introduce some level of predictability into our weeks—but that structure needed to focus on the *entire* family, not just the kids. We all needed equal consideration.

Let Go of the Supermom Myth

Early in this book, we talked about the enduring image that has colored the overall perception of stay-at-home mothers: June Cleaver . . . shut in, bored, and endlessly housekeeping. But we've also referenced a newer, and perhaps more damaging, portrait that has weaseled its way into the minds of American parents. Rather than a singular picture, this one is more like a mosaic—a compilation of all the little squares we see on an Instagram grid or Pinterest board. In one afternoon scroll, you might be served a friend's adorable craft project and your cousin's spotless home and an influencer's homemade meatballs with hidden zucchini and carrots and a celebrity mom's jog with the stroller, and suddenly you've composed an ideal of all the things you think you should be doing in a single day to "succeed" as a primary parent. And, chances are, it's making you feel like crap. A 2022 study published in the journal *Computers in Human Behavior* notes that "social media has drastically increased the amount of parenting content that mothers encounter in their day-to-day lives," and much of this content is "idealized portrayals of motherhood," which the authors found can significantly increase levels of envy, anxiety, and comparison, and can be damaging to your mental health.

The problem: these idealized portrayals perform well. The "momfluencers" who make money by posting content aren't *trying* to make other parents feel bad or less than; they're just trying to publish images that generate engagement. "Photos on Instagram do the best when they're beautiful. That's just the truth," says Jo Piazza, who notes that this has been the case since the earliest days of influencing. "Everyone knows the algorithm promotes the photos that are the most beautiful, the cleanest lines, and the ones that look like magazine editorials. So from the beginning, when moms wanted their photos to be successful, they would post something beautiful. And that cycle is what generated this picture-perfect image of motherhood on Instagram. Suddenly we are seeing overly curated faux images of what being a stay-at-home mom looks like: it looks beautiful, you're juggling so many things so easily. And there was just none of the reality, the pain, the stress . . . it just doesn't come across in the picture."

It's very tempting to post the moments we are most proud of with our children. If I'd shared a photo on any given morning during my first five years of motherhood, I'd probably be sharing an image of me and my kids mid–splatter paint or microwaving Dove soap for an art-and-science experiment. Those were the hours I enjoyed the most with my kids, and I was happy to show them off, because I love art and I don't mind mess. It sounds Pinterest perfect, except what you wouldn't see was that I didn't pick up the paint-splattered mat or wipe the remnants of our activity off the wall until late in the evening. Or that I served chicken nuggets and hot dogs more nights than I care to put in print. I chose what I wanted to put energy into and what I didn't—but I wasn't about to widely share the places where I "fell short." No one parent can do it all, but the social media Supermom mosaic makes us think that we should (and that someone out there does).

One fact will always be true: there are only 24 hours in a day, and 168 in a week. We might want to do more for our kids and with our kids, but our time in which to do all that has not changed, and it never will. We're trying to cram even more activity into our days (specifically more activity devoted to serving others), which means that while our feelings of comparison are on the rise, so too are our feelings of *time poverty* and *burnout*.

Time poverty is the chronic feeling of having too many things to do and not enough time to do them, which many people consider unavoidable when you are home full-time with young children. This can be especially true in the early weeks and months of stay-at-home parenthood. In most paid jobs, workers encounter a straightforward schedule that requires little planning on their part. If you're in a corporate office, meetings get requested or put on your calendar. If you work in a school, there's a bell to start and a bell to end and the periods in between are predetermined. If you worked as a nurse before having kids or were employed in a doctor's office, the appointment calendar dictated how the day would go. Shifting to staying at home full-time can be a real jolt to the system, because these established schedules are no longer in place. As Stacy Crocker, who left her job in tax services and strategy at Intuit to stay at home, pointed out, "It wasn't like a slow transition: I worked fifty hours a week and had a full-time nanny, and then the next week I didn't."

Adjusting to such a radical shift can take a minute. "Times of transition leave people's heads kind of spinning, specifically when so much change is happening at once," says Anna Kornick, a mother, time management coach, and host of *It's About Time*, a podcast specifically geared toward overworked women. "It can be really difficult to find that solid footing in order to begin creating new routines that can support what you want your life to look like moving forward."

And because the time blocks in your new normal only exist if you create them (and doing so can feel like just *another* thing on an already endless list), it's easy to find yourself without a window to prepare or eat lunch—or worse, with a total inability to get to a doctor's appointment or care for yourself. In 2017, 24 percent of American women reported delaying or not obtaining health care because they couldn't find time, and 14 percent cited trouble finding childcare. According to a paper in the *Journal of Global Health*, these were just a few of the dire consequences of the rising issue of time poverty—and it is indeed a global problem. According to the U.K. census bureau, those living with children younger than fifteen had up to fourteen hours per week less free time than those living alone.

One common and unfortunate consequence of time poverty? **Burnout.** The concept, now understood as a general mental-health term, was originally introduced as a workplace phenomenon. In 2019, the World Health Organization (WHO) added the condition to the International Statistical Classification of Diseases and Related Health Problems, its official compendium of diseases. It was categorized as an "occupational phenomenon" (*not* a disease) and defined as a "syndrome conceptualized as resulting from chronic workplace stress that has not been successfully managed." Burnout, according to the WHO, is characterized by three factors: "feelings of energy depletion or exhaustion; increased mental distance from one's job, or feelings of negativism or cynicism related to one's job; and reduced professional efficacy." According to the Mayo Clinic, job burnout can lead to excessive stress, fatigue, insomnia, irritability, and high blood pressure, among other physical and mental conditions.

Given that being a primary parent is a job in itself, it's easy to extrapolate the original burnout definition to those with responsibilities outside the traditional workplace. Over the past few years, the term "caregiver burnout" has been used to describe these similar feelings in adults in the sandwich generation, those who are caring for both their parents and their children. In 2022, the motherhood lifestyle website Motherly released its annual State of Motherhood survey, in which 55 percent of the stay-at-home mothers polled stated that they "always" or "frequently" feel burned out (versus 49 percent of mothers who worked outside the home). And while time poverty can be one cause of this persistent feeling, it's certainly not the only factor. A study from the journal *Frontiers in Psychology* found that "feeling pressure to be a perfect mother was positively related to parental burnout." In other words: holding yourself to the standards of the mythical Supermom mosaic is not only unrealistic, it's also bad for your health.

There Are No Gold Stars

When I first transitioned to staying at home full-time, staring at a wide-open calendar felt, well, terrifying. The rigid family scheduling that followed was just as much for me as it was for my kids— I simply wasn't used to having a day where I wasn't trying to *accomplish* something. Plus, I was so defensive about the "What will you do all day?" or "Won't you get bored?" questions, and so insistent on fighting back against the stereotype of the overwhelmed mom who finds Cheerios in her hair because she can't find a moment to shower that I drastically overcorrected. Many mothers I've talked to had similar experiences.

"Those first weeks after I left my full-time job, I laid out intricate crafts, planning out our days down to the minute," shared novelist Thao Thai in an essay for Mother Untitled. "I set a schedule full of workbooks and outdoor activities and library visits. I zipped around doing as much housework as I could while my daughter was occupied with something else; no dish unwashed, no load of laundry unfolded. . . . I felt my day was only worth something if every second was accounted for and validated by some nebulous Good Parenting Committee."

But there are no gold stars for parenting, and while creating a strict schedule might give you an illusion of control over your time, if you try to pack it all in you may add an element of go-go-go to your day that is not particularly healthy for you *or* your kids. It's the other side of the time-poverty coin: you might fit in that doctor's appointment because you've got every single hour accounted for, but rushing from one thing to the next does not afford much time for fulfillment, which is likely what you were looking for when you made the choice to stay home in the first place. Parents who say they always feel rushed are more likely to say that parenting is tiring all the time and twice as likely to say that parenting is stressful all the time. And those feelings of stress—especially if you try to hide them—aren't just affecting you: they can be transmitted to your kids. A 2020 study found that kids can pick up on when their parents try to conceal stress, and that they actually have a physical reaction, feeling more stress themselves.

If the unscheduled day of a primary parent with no established time blocks can be described as "too soft," and the overbooked one as "too hard," then I promise there's a version of your day-to-day that will be just right. But it starts with considering the right pace for *you*. Your days can be built with the same intention you brought to choosing to pause in the first place. It will involve looking closely at what you want to focus on right now, as well as what you're willing to let go of, and knowing that none of it is set in stone.

Rhythms over Routines

Much has been made in the media about the benefit of daily routines. Headlines like "10 Things That Highly Successful People Do

Every Morning" or "9 Nighttime Routines of the Mega-Successful" can pretty much guarantee clicks. TikTok videos of teenagers' daily routines garner tens of millions of views. (My friend's eight-year-old daughter is constantly watching her favorite YouTubers' morning routine videos and adjusting her own accordingly—it starts young!) There's science to it—studies show that having regular routines can boost cognitive function, reduce stress, and improve productivity, among other benefits, and that kids with routines have higher social-emotional health—but there's also an aspirational element. The hope seems to be that if we can emulate another person's exact order of events, we will feel as productive and together as they seem to be. But the word "routine" might also suggest a level of rigidity that's unrealistic when you're home with young kids, and it can make you feel like a failure if you don't hit every mark.

This is why I suggest focusing on a *rhythm* rather than a routine. A rhythm can be as simple as determining a general time the family turns on for the day and the time they turn off, punctuated with meals and snacks or naps in between. In fact, the building blocks of any rhythm will begin with food and sleep, but they might establish a predictable pattern around when you enlist screens, and what time of day you usually go outside. Julie Morgenstern, author of *Time to Parent*, points to five daily "islands of predictability" for kids: when they wake up, when they leave the house in the morning (whether for school or with a parent), reuniting with family or winding down toward the end of the day, dinner, and bedtime. "Kids thrive on consistency," Morgenstern says. "In a child's world, everything is still fairly new and the world is unpredictable and full of surprises, both good and bad. So it's helpful to have several predictable anchors in each day. It allows kids to know that 'when I wake up, this is what will happen.'"

A rhythm doesn't account for each moment of the day in five-minute intervals, but it also doesn't let time stretch out endlessly before you with no structure in place, only for you to realize the day is over and you haven't changed out of your pajamas. Rhythms provide reliability, but also flexibility. "I like to have some structure in my day, because it helps me to accomplish the things I want to do and bring in the healthy habits I want my kids to see, but I don't want it ever to get overscheduled or like there is no wiggle room," says Olivia Metzger, a private-practice therapist currently on a career break with her four young boys in the Chicago suburbs. "A rhythm, to me, has malleability, and it's in tune with different phases of life or phases of the year. For example, we value sleep versus outdoor time differently in summer and winter because of the climate that we live in."

Rhythms also offer relief in moments that feel like they've gone off track. "The days I feel the least confident are the ones when I don't have a system in place," says Nicole Cole, a mother of two in Maryland who spent years as a supervisor of school quality for the DC Public Charter School Board. "Having a schedule helps me to know what's coming next, especially when we are having a bad day. With my two-year-old, I might feel like, 'Okay, playtime was a little rocky today, but we both know that an hour of quiet time is coming up and during that time we can both recharge.'" Rhythms help you feel in control of your day, rather than like your day is in control of you.

After our children were born, it took a little while for my husband to fully understand this. Before kids, he envisioned that we'd be what he considered a "go-with-the-flow family," two adults who changed their lives not at all when they had kids, and this was a source of friction between us during our first year of parenthood. That is, until Dan realized that predictable bedtimes and having a general flow to the day served him as well as it served the kids. He could throw himself into playing with the baby for a couple of hours after work if he knew that come seven p.m. we would start reading bedtime books and by seven forty-five we could relax in front of *This Is Us*.

The most important thing about establishing your daily rhythm is that you do so intentionally. This is your chance to design a day-to-day (or a week-to-week) that helps your family thrive and also supports your needs as well. Knowing that I need to be creative to feel fulfilled, I shaped our daily rhythm around morning play and art. It meant that every night for the years I had children at home I would scan a handful of go-to Instagram accounts for the easiest craft activity I could find, so that I could guarantee one chunk of time the next morning where I would feel hands-on and connected to my kids. Maybe your rhythm incorporates being outside because you grew up in the mountains and hate being cooped up indoors. Maybe it requires moving your body, because you're an athlete at heart. It could be that the most important part of your routine is giving yourself a break in the middle of the day. If you know that you function better if you have an afternoon rest hour, great. That doesn't mean you can suddenly leave your young kids home alone, obviously, but you *can* build your rhythm around an hour of independent play each day, so that your kids can relax and let their minds wander and you can be more hands-off.

If you are structuring your day to maximize your ability to get things done, you also want to take into account your internal rhythms. Recognize when you are most focused and when your attention span is weakest (a perfect time to RSVP to Paperless Post invitations or shop online). This also applies over the course of the week—if you're exhausted on Monday after the free-for-all of a weekend, maybe you schedule your big family adventures (or any activity that requires a high level of patience and energy) on Wednesdays or Thursdays. Yes, taking stock of all these tendencies and preferences, as well as those of your kids, might feel like a lot of work, but the return on investment is huge, says Lizzie Assa, a mother of three and founder of the Workspace for Children. "From the time we wake up until the time we go to sleep, yes, so much of it is intentional, and that sounds exhausting," she says. "But it's not exhausting if your life becomes easier, right?"

As you think through what your family schedule should look like, remember that your rhythms will change over time. "Our values are not necessarily a set-it-and-forget-it thing because we evolve as people, and the same goes for our routines and habits and how we envision our ideal day or our ideal life as our children get older," says Anna Kornick. "Our routines are going to age with them, and that relieves the pressure. When you go into it knowing, 'This is the routine for now, this is the best fit for my life now,' you're setting the expectation with yourself that hey, it's okay when the day comes that it doesn't work anymore."

THINK WEEK-TO-WEEK, NOT DAY-TO-DAY

Trying to plan the ideal day can be a recipe for disaster. Let's say you sleep 7 hours a night (which is probably not enough, but is slightly more than the average American's 6.8 hours)—that leaves you with 17 hours to fit in everything you want to do for yourself, your kids, your partner, your home, and on and on. Attempting to do that for just one day, without a single hiccup, is ambitious. Thinking you can plan your everyday rhythm around that, with no unexpected derailments, might be plain delusional.

"'What's everything that I want to feel or experience in a day? Okay, well, I want to do yoga and I want to meditate and I want to have time to cultivate my spirituality and I want to spend time with my husband and I want to work out.' . . . We become overwhelmed because there are so many things that we want to fit into this perfect day," says Kornick. But if you zoom out to a full week, well, now you have 168 hours to work with. Taking this broader view "gives you the opportunity to be consistent without doing something daily. We fall into the trap of thinking that consistency means every single day, but you can work out three times a week and still be consistent."

Optimize for What's Important

We live in a culture that prioritizes productivity, and one that generally defines productivity not by *what* you got done but *how much* you got done. But the reality is, you could cross twenty items off your to-do list in a single day and *still* feel like you didn't use your time wisely if you don't take a moment for something that matters to you. Morgenstern says this is a trap that moms in particular are susceptible to. "They lean on the to-do list because it feels like a way of taking control and taming the chaos. They say, 'Let me clean up or do the dishes because then I'll feel better,' but it's so transient," she says. "Of course, some tasks need to get done, but the kind of satisfaction that comes from hanging out with a friend or pursuing a hobby, it has a much richer and more lasting effect than crossing anything off a to-do list." If the important tasks—whether they're important because they're the most fun, the most aligned with your success metrics, or just the most immediately urgent—are left unchecked, you can still feel unfulfilled, and probably will.

The hard truth of parenting is that the to-do list is never done. There is always another lunch to pack, permission slip to sign, or next size up of clothing to buy. And even when your kids are bigger and more self-sufficient, there will be something new to worry about or one more thing to do to be helpful. I don't say this to be a downer—it's likely that one reason you chose to take this career pause was so that you could be available to do these things for your kids. But if you are waiting to get to the fun stuff once the more mundane tasks are done, you very well could be waiting forever.

Feeling productive is important to our mental health. Checking something off the to-do list releases a hit of dopamine, a neurotransmitter often referred to as the "happy hormone," and it got that nickname for a reason. It makes us feel good. Productivity also signals growth—it says we've been working toward a goal and have made progress. It's when we feel stagnant that mental health suffers. But what if you redefined productivity as getting the *important* things done, rather than the *most* things? If rather than optimizing for doing *more* as a parent, you optimized for doing what *matters*? If feeling productive meant feeling fulfilled, or at least like you're moving forward rather than merely staying afloat, you might find your daily or weekly schedule would change pretty significantly.

In chapter 4, we talked about redefining success, identifying your North Star, and establishing the short-term goals that can help you feel successful on a weekly or monthly basis. For you, what's important might be community, or cultivating a sense of adventure for your family, or maybe, like me, it is about growing more patient. Keep those intentions in mind as you think through your days or weeks—if you consider your schedule a vehicle to help propel you toward your goals, it might crystallize what you actually want to pencil in and what you can leave out.

What's important, or what qualifies as productive, can be a moving target, one that changes from season to season. Reading-together time might give way to outdoor time in the summer months, for example. I often think of those back-to-school weeks in early September as a seasonal exception to our usual rhythms. The world thinks of this time as an uber-productive period where everyone gets back into the groove of a regular schedule. What the world often forgets is that these weeks are also fraught with nerves for the kids—*Will my teacher like me? Will I be able to keep up? Will my friends from last year still be my friends this year?*—and too many get-to-know-you gatherings for the parents. If you have really little ones, you might also be required to attend school for an hour in the morning, or pick them up at a different time each day, as the young kids learn to phase in to their school day. For this reason, every September I reset my priorities for what is important that month, and what will qualify as productivity. I lighten my expectations of my Mother Untitled work and accept that I'll see my friends less, and instead I focus on maintaining my mental health and trying to keep life at home feeling predictable for the kids while our outside world is in a state of transition.

Lower Your Standards for Tasks You Dread

The only way to prioritize your schedule for what you really want to get done is to let go of what you can't get done . . . or, better yet, what you simply don't want to do. "Don't just do what you think you're supposed to do to enrich your kids," says Assa. "If you hate the zoo, don't go there! Your kids will eventually go to the zoo on a field trip or with their grandma, and if they don't, it's fine. If you love the beach, figure out a rhythm to get your kids to the beach and get them really good at going to the beach, because that's good for everyone."

How's this for a confession? I'm a stay-at-home parent who hates the playground. I was never that mom who got to sit on the bench and watch happily while her kids ran free. Mine were always trying to pull me into the sandbox, which wasn't fun for me, or sit with me on the sidelines, which wasn't fun for them. I felt guilty at first—what kind of mom hates the playground? Well, it turns out, this kind. And I've accepted it. Sometimes Dan will take them on weekends, or they go with a playdate or a babysitter. My children are not deprived of monkey bars or slides, but I don't have to suffer, either.

Keeping your North Star in mind might also help you give yourself permission to let go of those things you *think* you should do, but, deep down, you know that you shouldn't. Once I realized that my North Star was maintaining my sense of calm, I actively let go of the big to-dos that would definitely cause me stress. So long, big birthday parties and family photo shoots. I won't say it doesn't have consequences—every year around the holidays, when the cards featuring family and friends in matching outfits start arriving in my mailbox, I momentarily regret not having my own, featuring my adorable kids or that year's family vacation. But then I remember the twenty-four hours (minimum) of my life that I gained back by bypassing this tradition, and I envision the stress I would feel from agonizing over which outfit and which picture and who to send it to and what to say in the note, and I feel good about my choice.

Because this is real life, we can't simply drop every painful task and fill our schedules with only the fun stuff. There will be chores that must get done, whether they are important to you or not. Dirty clothes and dishes need cleaning. Food needs to get on the table at dinner. But none of these tasks must be done perfectly, whatever that even means. By actively lowering your standards for the household tasks you dread, you free up time for the activities that are meaningful to you. If straightening up grates on your nerves, perhaps you keep one room in the house presentable for company, and the rest can stay a bit messy. As Liz Greene, a mother of three in Andover, Massachusetts, explains, "I cook chicken nuggets more nights than I care to admit, enjoying laughter and lots of ketchup instead of negotiations over broccoli."

Monotonous household tasks are also great opportunities for kids to get some experience with chores. "If emptying the dishwasher and folding the laundry feels good to you, by all means, do it yourself," Assa says. But if it doesn't, incorporate the kids. In her house, Assa says she makes an informal chart of the household tasks that need to get done each day, alongside the fun activities her kids really want to do. "Then in the morning, I sit down and say, 'Here are the things we want to do this morning, and here are the tasks that have to happen. How can we work as a team to get it done? How can we divvy that up?'" Sure, the laundry might go back in the drawers unfolded, but it'll just get grass stains and wrinkles again soon anyway. It's a small price to pay for peace of mind.

An added bonus? Research says kids who are assigned chores as kids are happier and more professionally successful as adults. Julie Lythcott-Haims, author of *How to Raise an Adult,* spoke to this connection in her popular TED Talk, "How to Raise Successful Kids—Without Over-Parenting." Citing the longitudinal Harvard Study of Adult Development, which started in 1938, she noted that "professional success in life . . . comes from having done chores as a kid, and the earlier you started, the better. . . . A roll-up-your-sleeves-and-pitch-in mindset, a mindset that says, there's some unpleasant work, someone's got to do it, it might as well be me, a mindset that says, I will contribute my effort to the betterment of the whole, that's what gets you ahead in the workplace." Give the tasks you're willing to relinquish to your kids. You'll have less to do, they'll get to experience ownership and accomplishment of a task, and you'll all be able to get to the fun stuff sooner. Everybody wins.

EMBRACE THE OFF HOURS

There are plenty of perks to being on a career pause, and a major one is being free from the traditional nine-to-five (or, who are we kidding, eight-to-six) schedule. In the early years of parenting, before your kids are in school, allow yourself to embrace the off-hours and think creatively about when you want to do various activities with your kids. There's no need to navigate crowded spaces in the afternoon and on weekends just because that's what you're used to. "I really appreciate that I can go to the zoo or the Discovery Museum or the park during the week in the middle of the day," says mom-of-two Helen Ortiz. "It's not all after work or on the weekend, shoving in swim classes at the same time as everyone else. There's a pace now that feels much more comfortable, that I never felt when work was my identity. It always felt very rushed."

Schedule Time to Yourself

Just as any professional in a working environment needs time away from the office, every parent who stays at home will need time away from their kids. When you find yourself being referred to as "Bodie's mom" just as often (if not more) than your actual first name, it's important—to your happiness and your confidence and your sanity—to take time to remember and reconnect with who you are individually, not in the context of who you are in relation to someone else.

As if your happiness and sanity aren't enough, your physical health is also buoyed by time to yourself. Leslie Forde, CEO and founder of Mom's Hierarchy of Needs, focuses her work on helping mothers make space for self-care and surfacing the link between that self-care and a mother's well-being. She notes that carving out me time is about more than just treating yourself to an occasional night out or a face mask. "Even if you weren't interested in your own happiness—and you should be—women are at greater risk for most stress-related illnesses," she says. "We disproportionately suffer from anxiety and depression. If you look at conditions like hypertension and heart disease, there's a pretty strong case on the medical side that not caring for your mental and physical health isn't sustainable. If you're a caregiver and you have this responsibility for your kids, and possibly also your aging parents or other loved ones, you're taking on more strain—more physical strain, more cognitive strain—and you're probably not getting as much sleep."

Claiming this time, however, will take some work. A 2018 survey of two thousand parents (from the recipe website Munchery), found that parents only get thirty-two minutes of me time a day, and that they "hide" from their kids about four times a week just to get a moment to themselves. And leisure time is harder to come by for women than men—dads have three hours more of it per week than moms. You might be gifted a night to yourself for Valentine's Day, or get a Mother's Day coupon book with a voucher for "one kid-free hour," but to incorporate time to yourself consistently, as part of your daily or weekly rhythm, you may need to advocate for it and proactively take it. As we know, free time will never magically appear—which is why at Mom's Hierarchy of Needs, they don't call it the "to-do list" but the "never-done list." "There's no pot of time at the end of the rainbow," says Forde. "You are going to need to do something to make the time. You are going to have to ruthlessly prioritize it and viciously defend it and you're going to have to explain one hundred times to the people in your life that you need it."

I've talked to enough primary parents to know that I don't really need to convince them of the importance of time to themselves. They believe it, and they want it. *Getting it* is the hurdle that's tough to clear. In our AMP survey, we found that, on average, four in ten women develop at least one new hobby after becoming a stay-at-home mom. For the most part, moms said they work on those hobbies after the kids are asleep or when they're at school. A smaller number do it before the kids wake up. This is when it becomes critical to observe and cater to your own internal rhythms—if you're a night owl, trying to force yourself to wake up early to fit in hobbies isn't going to work long term. Same if you're an early bird trying to stay up late. Hobbies are not fun if you're trying to strong-arm yourself into enjoying them.

There will, of course, be times when none of these options work. If your kids are not yet school age and you need to go to the doctor, you probably can't do that after bedtime. Or maybe your particular hobby is a middle-of-the-afternoon activity. This is when that ruthless prioritizing and vicious defending will come in. You may need to hire help, or negotiate with your partner so that they come home an hour earlier once a week, or put them in charge for a chunk of time on the weekends. Perhaps you trade one morning a week with another stay-at-home parent. When my daughter was six months old, I hired a mother's helper to come by a few afternoons each week (less expensive than a babysitter, since I was still home) so that I could get some time to myself.

In comedian Ali Wong's stand-up special *Hard Knock Wife*, she does a bit about how she finds the time to perform while parenting a small kid at home. "It's so sexist when people ask me, well, if you're here, then who's taking care of the baby?" she says. "Who the f*ck do you think is taking care of the baby? The TV is taking care of the baby, okay?" Like all successful jokes, there's a kernel of truth in there. When used intentionally, screen time can be a great way to steal a few moments alone. But intentionality is key. If I'm at my wit's end and I plop my kids in front of the television because I can't take another second of parenting, I will feel immensely guilty. I'll be mad at myself for seemingly losing control or giving up. But if I actively plan for it—scheduling two half-hour windows, one in the morning and one in the evening, so that I can take a breather—then I feel like I've made a good choice for everyone. And it's not about the amount of time the kids spend on the screen (the American Academy of Child and Adolescent Psychiatry recommends limiting screen time to one hour per weekday—and three hours per weekend day—for kids between two and five, after which there is no set recommended time limit), but rather having made the decision on my own. The feeling of exasperation, like I can't handle this job I've signed up for, is what makes me feel guilty. Not the thirty minutes or hour in front of *Bluey*.

Once you've navigated how you will schedule your me time, what you do with it is up to you. If you're stuck, and I've talked to plenty of parents who say that time to themselves feels so foreign that when it happens they're almost paralyzed with indecision, I will say first and foremost: skip the errands. There will be other moments for the tasks that are in service of your dependents—this time is about *you*. If you're still unsure, think about prioritizing your health. It's a pretty all-encompassing directive, but as you consider what "prioritize your health" means to you, the best use of your time might become clear. "Self-care—or caring for your mental, physical, and emotional health—does involve things like movement, and sleep, and stress management, but it also involves connecting with other adults and having healthy relationships, and learning and growing and having fun," Forde says. "It's multiple things. It's not just one thing." Napping, exercising, meditating, seeing a friend or talking to one on the phone, engaging in your hobby, even just sitting down for a quiet moment with a cup of coffee . . . all of these will help you slow down, refocus on your-self, and will benefit your health.

You might even create a physical space that's just for you, so that the clutter of toys or looming household chores are not star-ing you in the face when you're trying to step aside. We've all heard of the man cave. The female equivalent, sometimes re-ferred to as the "she shed," hasn't quite made its way into com-mon vernacular. Still, the underlying intention has merit. One mom in the Mother Untitled community was so overwhelmed with the piles of family *stuff* that she craved a room (even a small one) of her own. Because she had left her full-time job, and thus didn't need a whole office wardrobe anymore, she was happy to convert the section of her closet that once housed business-casual shoes and dresses into an office nook with dark moody wallpaper, a small desk, and an IKEA shelf.

There will inevitably be seasons when solo time is harder to come by. Your kids are out of school, or your partner is on a work deadline, or your go-to babysitter is on vacation. If a thirty- or sixty-minute window feels completely unrealistic, focus on the smaller pockets of time. There are a lot of in-between moments in parenting—time spent waiting in the pickup line or in the lobby during a dance class—as well as "dead time" when you are, say, emptying the dishwasher or folding laundry. I'm not usually a proponent of multitasking (studies show that trying to do so de-creases efficiency and increases distraction), but these are the perfect times to call a friend or relative, or listen to a podcast or audiobook. Rochelle Knowles, a certified life and health coach and founder of Mindful Eyes Limited, notes that mothers need a "brain break," and when time is tight, we need to take what we can get.

WHEN SPECIAL CIRCUMSTANCES
THROW A WRENCH INTO THE SCHEDULE

Rhythms, routines, time alone . . . if you're a single parent or the parent of a neurodivergent kid, all of this may sound great in theory and impossible in practice. There will be times when the goal really is just to get through the day by any means possible. But it's in these circumstances, which likely require more concentrated chunks of hyperfocus from you, when self-care is even more critical. Christine Hackett, a mother of two children, one with special needs, creates space for herself by "radically letting go." Rather than centering schedules around what must happen, she frees up her schedule—and mental load—by accepting what doesn't need to happen.

"When my son comes home after school, I just let him do whatever he needs to do. In the past I would have been like, 'Oh, there's this expectation you need to come home and do your homework and eat a snack' and instead I say, 'Whatever you need to do to decompress, this is your time,'" she says. "My oldest, he hates singing at birthday parties. When we go to a birthday party on the weekend, I tell him, 'They're going to sing now, you can go away.' And that's just how our daily life is—if this is something that's too hard for you, you don't have to do it. I'm not going to engage in a power struggle over something that's not really that important." This frees her up to do the stuff that *is* important, but difficult for her son, on her own schedule—while still giving herself an occasional break. Remember, there are no rules of the rhythm. It's about giving yourself permission to create a schedule that works for you.

SAMPLE SCHEDULES

Everyone's daily schedule is going to look different, based on factors including how many kids you have, how old they are, where you live, your childcare situation, your partner's job and whether they work from home, your personal interests, and your current priorities. The schedules that follow are specific to the women who live them. Consider them inspiration for what your rhythm *could* look like, but don't limit yourself to the time chunks or activities listed here. The only thing that's necessary for your schedule is that it's manageable on a consistent basis and that it takes into account your kids' needs and also your own.

Schedule 1

Mom of: Three boys, ages two, four, and six
Lives in: Boston suburbs
Mom is primarily focused on family, some freelance writing and editing on the side
Dad works remotely from home

6:15 a.m.: Middle child wakes up (he watches a show in bed with parents as they slowly wake up)

6:45: Mom wakes and gets dressed, does hair and makeup. Every other morning, shower and blow out hair. "I sleep with my hair up in a bun, with a silk scrunchie to keep it nice on day two, making fifty percent of my mornings easier."

7:15: Mom wakes up oldest son and sends him downstairs (older two boys prepare their own cereal) as dad makes toast and waffles for the youngest

7:30: Youngest child wakes up. Kids eat breakfast/parents put lunches in backpacks, etc.

8:15: Dad leaves to drop middle child off at preschool, Mom escorts oldest down the street to the bus stop with youngest in tow. Husband returns home and parents finish coffee and discuss the logistics of the day ahead.

8:45: Tidy up house, do laundry, stroller walk around the neighborhood with the youngest child while listening to a podcast

10:00: Storytime at the library with youngest, run an errand or two

11:30: Lunchtime. "As I make lunch for my youngest, I do the same for my older kiddos and place them in the next day's bento boxes. This removes the dreaded 'still need to pack lunches' moment at the end of the day, and there's no way I could make them the morning of—too much going on!"

12:00–2:30 p.m.: Nap time for youngest. Housework on pause while mom solely works on freelance writing assignments and family admin/paperwork.

2:30: Youngest is awake and needs a snack. Fold laundry, other household chores, regroup for the rest of afternoon.

3:15: One parent leaves to pick up preschooler

3:45: One parent walks to bus stop to get oldest child off the bus

4:00–5:00: Boys empty backpacks and lunches, then play. "We limit after school activities since our boys aren't home from school until close to four p.m. and they're still on the younger side. Family dinnertime and quiet time during the week is essential to the health of our family. The oldest has soccer practice once a week from five to six p.m., and games on the weekend, and the

middle child has an art class once a week at four p.m. Other than that, they're home after school."

5:00: Baths/showers for boys as Dad preps dinner. When each boy is done with his bath, they return downstairs to watch a TV show until dinner. Mom lays out school outfits for the next day and preps bedrooms for sleep (blinds, noise machines, etc.).

6:00: Family dinner

6:30: One parent cleans up, the other assists with teeth brushing, light play

7:00: Reading time or another quiet show (depends on parents' energy levels)

7:30: Dad does bedtime routine with youngest, Mom with older boys

8:00–9:00: Dad typically returns to work at his desk, Mom does skincare routine and tidies up house, addresses any remaining work and family admin priorities for the day

9:00: Goal time for Mom to be in bed and reading a book

10:00: Goal time for lights out for Mom

10:30: Realistic lights out for Mom and Dad

Schedule 2

Mom of: Two girls, ages five and seven
Lives in: New York City
Mom is fully at home, recently starting a health-coaching business on the side
Dad works from an office, out of the home

6:00 a.m.: Wake up

6:00–6:45: Business hour—answer emails, etc.

6:45: Get ready—brush teeth, wash face, brush hair

7:00: Kids wake up

7:00–8:00: Make breakfast, pack kids' and husband's lunch, and calm down tired and cranky kids. Drink green juice while getting kids to dress and brush their teeth.

8:00: Kids put shoes on while Mom does a quick cleanup of kitchen and living room

8:10: Leave for school on bike

8:20: School drop-off

9:00: Work out twice a week

9:45: Quick grocery stop

10:15: Home, shower, dress, quick breakfast (smoothie or oatmeal)

11:00 a.m.–2:30 p.m.: Work—emails, review recipes, work on cookbook, create content, phone calls with clients, business partners

2:30: Leave house for pickup

2:45: School pickup

3:00–5:00: Time with the kids (occasional work email thrown in)

5:00: Dinner prep

5:30: Dinner

6:30: Playtime for kids, Mom cleans up

7:00: Kids bath, brush teeth, etc. Dad comes home.

7:30: Kids' reading time (occasional iPad)

8:00: Kids in bed

8:00–10:00: Couch with Dad—watch a movie, scroll Instagram, fall asleep on couch

10:00–10:30: Go to bed

Boredom Happens (to All of Us!)

I love my children very much. Just as I know you most certainly do too. And yet, there are afternoons when my son asks me to sit on the carpet and play with him and I just cannot stand the thought of building another LEGO-vehicle-turned-dinosaur. On those days, the schedule is so monotonous, and the time seems to crawl so slowly, that I feel bored out of my mind. And then I feel guilty for feeling bored. And *then* I start to wonder if I made the wrong choices for this stage of my life. Would my children be better off in an after-school program, with other kids who never tire of LEGOs? It's an easy spiral to fall into.

Momentary blips of boredom happen, even in a rhythm that's optimized for joy. When they do, you're allowed to say it out loud without guilt. "Just because you feel bored doesn't mean you're doing [motherhood] wrong," explains marriage and family therapist Emily Pardy. After all, these feelings of tedium come up no matter your line of work. The media loves to portray the stay-at-home parent as bored out of her mind, so much so that sometimes I think the world has forgotten that *every* job can be dull. A survey from the staffing firm OfficeTeam found that employees spend 10.5 hours per week, on average, feeling bored in the office. More generally, more than 60 percent of U.S. adults report feeling bored at least once a week, according to the Mayo Clinic.

Put simply: feeling bored from time to time doesn't make you a bad parent or an uninvested one. It makes you *human*.

Annoyance and frustration are also part and parcel of paid work, and it would be unrealistic to expect a life devoid of those. In these moments, and especially in moments of boredom,

Morgenstern suggests that parents focus less on their own enjoyment of the activity and more on studying why their child is so engaged in it. "If they want to ready this story for the forty-seventh time or go to that park for the twenty-second time, watch them with an eye towards: What is it about this story that delights them? What choices are they making at the playground? How determined are they? How do they interact with other kids? Studying how another human being thinks or operates or connects the dots is endlessly fascinating."

I try to pay attention to the words my daughter uses or how my son moves. I study how they play, what gets them excited, what gets them down. When I ground myself in the notion that I'm here not just as an unpaid supervisor but to get to know my child in a way that only I can, the stretches of time that might otherwise feel like a waste start to feel purposeful instead.

On the days when even *that* feels boring (studying is important, but as we learned in school, study breaks are as well), I simply try to mix it up—a change of scenery, an unexpected visitor, a new playlist blasting through the speakers. The nice thing about having a reliable rhythm is that you can interrupt it and go off script without your day going topsy-turvy. You can bill this change of pace, to yourself and your child, as a special treat and then get back to your regularly scheduled programming the next day. Routine is so important, but occasional breaks in routine can be invigorating, too. It's the balance that keeps us satisfied.

It's All About Systems

In business school, they teach a lot about systems and the importance of having them in place in order for an organization to function efficiently and reliably. People know their roles, there is a general standard of care, and there is a structure in place to prevent chaos. Your household is an organization in itself, and it too benefits from systems. As Eve Rodsky explains in her book *Fair Play*, there are those who shudder at instituting systems in the home because they worry that "a regimented approach to our domestic life will kill our spontaneity." But to those who would rather go with the flow, Rodsky has a reminder: "Chaos isn't fun.... Systemization allows for fun and fulfillment."

All the rhythms and schedules we've been talking about in this chapter? These are systems. They aren't about hard-and-fast rules, they are about managing expectations so everyone is aligned on what the schedule will usually look like. Every day is not a new scramble. "The systems you put in place will have a lot to do with your life, the age and independence of your children, your health, the health of the people around you, and what kind of support you have," says Forde. "They help reduce your mental load but know that they'll continue to evolve."

And, of course, things will go wrong. This is real life. Children are not robots. They aren't employees. Unexpected challenges come up all the time, from the small-but-annoying spit-up just as you're leaving the house, to the bigger and more long-term obstacles like a sick family member who needs your care or a child who suddenly has night terrors. When you have a system in place, you're usually better able to handle those challenges because you've got an otherwise reliable schedule. And when you're not, you change the system. But being able to look at your family rhythm as a whole, not as daily individual one-offs, will help you cope in hard times and, perhaps more importantly, relish the good ones.

Power Practice: Audit Your Time

This chapter explored the unrealistic expectations we set for our days, the importance of establishing daily (or weekly) rhythms, and how to schedule days that maximize joy for everyone. But it's impossible to implement a new or improved schedule until you understand your current one. How are you spending your time? When is it serving you? When is it not? Anna Kornick has her clients engage in an "eye-opening" time audit exercise where they track their time in fifteen-minute intervals for an entire week. "We only have one hundred and sixty-eight hours every single week. We don't have an unlimited amount of time to work with," she says. "When you really sit down and put pen to paper, you begin to realize that gosh, on one hand our time is limited, but on the other hand it's abundant."

Keep a time tracker for one week of everything you're spending your time on. Try for fifteen-minute intervals; do thirty minutes if you must. Include a description about how you felt in the morning, afternoon, and evening, and note if you have any especially pronounced feelings after completing a specific activity. Reflect on it at the end of the week.

1. Which activities reflect your values and goals for this chapter of your life?

2. Are you spending enough time on those?
3. Is there a way to make the time more fulfilling if you can't increase the hours?
4. How can you simplify or eliminate tasks that are draining your time?

6

Get Help Without Guilt

FALSE BELIEF
I don't deserve help if I don't make money.

NEW NARRATIVE
*My work as a parent is 24/7 and I need
breaks and support to be strong.*

I'M STILL HAUNTED by the first time I truly yelled at my son. He was newly three, his sister five months, and I was home alone with them on a bright winter day. I desperately wanted to take Bodie outside to enjoy the sunshine and get some fresh air, but Lyla needed her afternoon nap, so I had to make a choice: I could let her sleep in the stroller and take my son outside, or I could keep him indoors so she could get some decent rest. I was still militant about sleep schedules, and I knew what the fallout looked like when nap time got cut short—which it usually did when she didn't sleep in her crib—so I opted to keep us inside. I sat Bodie on the couch in front of *Peppa Pig* while I took Lyla to her room, but I was wracked with guilt. I hated having to choose between what I knew was best for my two kids.

As I sat feeding Lyla in her glider, I could hear Mummy Pig

talking to her little piglets on the other side of the wall. When Bodie was a baby I would rock him to sleep for his afternoon nap, and I wanted to do the same for his sister, but now I wondered if I should just put her down and go play with my son so at least he got some quality time with his actual mom rather than a bonding session with a hog in an orange dress. (Don't get me wrong, I love Mummy Pig. But still, between the two of us, I hope I'm the better company.) As I was contemplating, Lyla's eyelids started to droop. She was on the edge of sleep, drifting off . . . and then Bodie opened the door to ask me if I could change the episode. Lyla's eyes burst open and I lost it on my sweet boy, raising my voice and kicking him out of the room. He'd done nothing that any three-year-old wouldn't do, but I let my guilt and frustration get the better of me, and Bodie was on the receiving end. He was in tears, Lyla was in tears, and I was pretty damn close.

Lyla eventually settled down and went to sleep, and Bodie found his place back in front of the TV, but my regret and guilt about my behavior stuck with me throughout the afternoon. Not much feels worse than knowing we've yelled at our kids when it's not warranted. I followed all the scripts I'd learned from parenting experts to apologize to my young son. But the fact that I feel compelled to declare, five years later and in print, that my child was not irreparably traumatized from this outburst is probably a sign that I didn't entirely come to terms with my own actions. We've all been there, but have I truly forgiven myself? I'm not sure. But I do know that I was in the trenches of postpartum anxiety—underslept and overwhelmed—and that my kids didn't deserve my outburst. And neither did I.

Despite my regret about that moment (and yes, I've shouted at my kids since—even when we know better, we don't always do better), it crystallized something important for me as a mother: my kids and I are both better off when I have more support. I'd had babysitters from time to time before that moment, but I wanted something steadier.

"Mom, I think I need more help," I told my mother on the phone the next evening. If I'd had a babysitter for even a couple of hours that afternoon, they could have taken Bodie outside while I rocked Lyla to sleep, or vice versa. My mother was a stay-at-home mom who never once paid for childcare. My parents immigrated to the United States from India when I was young and they were still finding their footing financially and culturally when I was a little kid, so sourcing and funding childcare was off the table. But ever since I decided to pause work, my mom had been a broken record about the fact that she would have enjoyed motherhood more if she'd taken breaks. Now that I was on the other end of the line, bemoaning my lack of support and inability to take time off, it was all she could do not to say "I told you so." She also reminded me that as my kids got older, and needed shuttling to various activities, it would only get harder, so we'd all be better off if we got used to having extra people around . . . sooner rather than later.

I shouldn't have needed her permission, but it was a huge comfort all the same.

Why Do We Resist?

When you're a full-time working parent, you need full-time childcare. When you work part-time, you need part-time childcare. But these two truths often lead parents to a third, less accurate, conclusion: when you stop paid work, you don't need any childcare at all. That one is just plain false, and it's holding back count-less women from stepping into the full power of stay-at-home motherhood. Still, it's a misconception that's ingrained in a belief system that starts at a national level.

The United States is one of very few high-income countries that does not offer parents affordable childcare options. You've probably read about our nation's unimpressive maternity leave offerings: we are the only rich country without "nationwide, stat-utory, paid maternity leave, paternity leave, or paternal leave," according to a 2021 UNICEF report. But the problem of gov-ernment support, or lack thereof, extends into toddlerhood. In its ranking of forty-one rich countries on their parental leave and childcare policies (rich countries are defined as "high-income countries that are part of the Organisation for Economic Co-operation and Development [OECD] or the European Union [EU]"), the United States took the second-to-last spot, followed only by Slovakia. Rich countries across the globe contribute an average of $14,000 a year toward a toddler's childcare, according to a *New York Times* article on how our nation stacks up to other countries. The United States, on the other hand, contributes $500 per year.

When it comes to affordable childcare, different countries have different models. Belgium, Denmark, Lithuania, Norway, and Slo-venia all provide free access to childcare for kids under the age of three, according to UNICEF. In France, parents have the option of putting their preschool-aged children in daycare centers known as *crèches*, or hiring "childminders" at home, for which they re-ceive tax credits of up to 85 percent of the cost. As the UNICEF report points out about the United States: "Weak investments in leave and childcare appear to indicate that childcare is seen more as a private rather than a public responsibility." I would take it a step further. Since childcare is not supported at a systemic level, the message parents receive is that it's not a necessity for all families. And because our culture has not assigned value to care, parents who step into a chapter of staying at home internalize the message that they are "not contributing" or "not working." In countries where there is a childcare stipend, there is an acknowledgement that caring for children is valued work that benefits the economy. In the United States, it's largely seen as a luxury for those who stay home with their children, and thus carries undue shame and stigma for those who "indulge" or, worse, "can't handle their kids on their own."

In our AMP survey, we found that 29 percent of stay-at-home mothers didn't use any childcare at all. Of those that do, close to 40 percent use grandparents or relatives—usually a cost-effective option, though it comes with its own drawbacks. (It's a lot easier to be clear with a babysitter about your family rules than it is with grandma or grandpa who, first, are often working for free and, second, may not always defer to your authority. Anyone who's ever heard a parent say, "I think I know what I'm doing. I raised you, didn't I?" can probably relate.) Only 17 percent of stay-at-home parents use in-home childcare, while another 16 percent use daycare.

But the reason stay-at-home parents aren't using childcare isn't because they don't need it or want it. In fact, in Motherly's 2022 Annual State of Motherhood survey, 42 percent of stay-at-home moms reported being "dissatisfied" or "very dissatisfied" with their childcare arrangement. That's a big chunk of dissatisfied parents!

So what's holding us back? Cost, to be sure. Childcare in the

United States is expensive and only getting more so—the average cost of a sitter for two kids in 2023 was just north of twenty-five dollars an hour. In New York City, the average family spends more than a quarter of their income on childcare, according to data from the Department of Labor. That's more than three times the amount that the U.S. government would deem affordable. One Mother Untitled member told me cost was absolutely prohibitive when it came to hiring babysitting help. "We live on one income— my husband is an engineer—and the reality is that it has pushed us to take on debt," she said. "I would love consistent once- or twice-a-week help, but right now that is not financially possible. It's a choice between debt or sanity sometimes."

But what we found in our survey was that these high prices weren't the biggest barrier to entry for parents resisting non-family or paid childcare. Stay-at-home moms cited quality concerns more than cost (73 percent versus 59 percent), voicing a skepticism that they could find someone they trust to stay with their kids. Guilt also plays a giant role, whether moms feel guilty for leaving their kids with someone else (49 percent) or they feel guilty paying for someone to watch their kids when they don't earn a salary (37 percent).

IT *WILL* COST YOU

There's no denying that cost is a factor when considering childcare. In the United States in 2024, babysitters ran parents an average of $26.57 per hour for two kids, and $23.61 per hour for one, according to UrbanSitter's babysitting rates survey. That's up from $25.37 per hour and $22.68 per hour, respectively, in the previous year—a 4.5

percent increase. The rate of inflation, by comparison, was only about 3.4 percent. The cost of your sitter may vary based on several factors—age or experience, for example—but the biggest variable is location. In San Francisco, the market rate for sitters is the highest in the country. A whopping $29.67 per hour for two kids, $26.75 for one. San Antonio, on the other hand, has the lowest going rate: $18.43 per hour for two kids, and $16.14 for one.

There's no sugarcoating the fact that hiring outside help may require some financial juggling. "There was a time where I had to choose between having a therapy session or having a babysitter," says Ortiz. "And for me, the cost of my therapy session would allow me six to eight hours of babysitting. I was like, 'Oh my gosh, I can exercise, I can get time to see friends again.'" Ortiz chose the sitter. Not every mom would make the same choice, and for some moms, a therapist is the exact outside help they need. But each of these decisions comes at a price, and it's imperative to plan accordingly.

Grappling with Guilt

When it comes to bringing in childcare help, the guilt piece feels tricky and pervasive, and the takeaway seems to be that no mom is immune. I can still summon the guilt I felt when I snapped at my son because I *didn't* have any childcare, and thus had become a version of myself that I didn't entirely recognize. But I'll admit that now, even after establishing a childcare routine that works for our family, I wrestle with a different kind of guilt, this time at having childcare when I don't really "need" it. Of course, the misconception of "need" is what this whole chapter is about. Even in championing this movement of career pauses and parental empowerment, I still occasionally succumb to the idea that we only "need" childcare if we are doing work for other people. When I did part-time paid consulting work a couple of days a week, I got childcare for those days. After I shifted to working on Mother Untitled, a passion project I launched while watching my kids full-time, I felt less comfortable with the idea of spending money on outside babysitters. I wasn't getting paid, so did I really deserve help? Had I earned it? Was I really about to put my family in the red, so to speak, so that I could work on something that was still mostly a vision inside my head? I was much more aware of the toll that shouldering all the childcare was taking on me, and the rational part of me knew I made a good decision when we brought in some outside support, but there was a deeper, more vulnerable part of me that wondered if I'd failed.

Godhuli Chatterjee Gupta, a mom of two in Chicago, struggled with a similar guilt when she took time away from her kids to work on her writing, a creative pursuit that didn't bring in any income. "I feel like I can only justify the help if it's for something that's paid, so I find myself usually writing when the kids are asleep or at school," she says. On the rare days when she does ask someone to watch the kids so she can have some creative space, she tries to remember that she's making an investment in herself. "It's for everyone's mental health. I am a very introverted person— I really need time to myself to be a happier, more energetic mother to my children. Writing is therapeutic for me, it's my way of processing things. And I need that time for myself."

For Chatterjee Gupta, writing is a form of self-care, and despite the increased attention to self-care over the past decade or so, her ambivalence about carving time out for it is all too common. An independent study funded by the cosmetic company Birchbox found that 39 percent of parents feel guilty when they take time for self-care; among those without kids, only 26 percent feel guilty. There are moments when I still must ask myself, "Am I really choosing to spend time away from my kids rather than with them? Didn't I elect to live this life, where I stay home rather than leave for work?"

Julie Morgenstern notes that many stay-at-home mothers she works with are under the impression that anything they *can* do at home, they should. "What I usually coach is that if you are choosing to stay at home to raise your kids for any period of time, you should identify the things that only you can do," she says. "That is usually the relating piece—getting to know your kids for the unique individuals they are—and the relationship cultivation, which takes time, energy, focus, and self-care. That is stuff you can't delegate. Most of the other stuff on your to-do list you can delegate, and just because you *can* do them doesn't mean you should. You need to prioritize the right things."

It doesn't help that social media is rife with images of moms supposedly doing all the things with zero help. And not because that's the case, necessarily, but because, as journalist Lauren Smith Brody wrote in her *Harper's Bazaar* article "The Invisible Nannies of Instagram," when you're a momfluencer, or even just a regular mom posting on social, you often "don't acknowledge there's a caregiver in [your life] at all." There are logical reasons that a mother posting on social media might omit images of babysitters or nannies—privacy chief among them—but the by-product of not acknowledging a caregiver's existence is that your followers don't know they're there. Out of sight, out of mind. No wonder stay-at-home moms feel guilty bringing in help. Scrolling the feeds of other primary parents will inevitably beg the question, If she can do it all by herself, why can't I?

Some moms I've spoken to also voice an element of pride bundled with their guilt—they appreciate being able to say they are present for their children close to full-time, or they know they're bordering on burnout, but they still *want* to be in the room where it happens . . . whatever their kid's "it" might be. After all, 83 percent of moms in the AMP survey said they were pausing or downshifting in order to spend more time with their kids, so "going back on that" only amplifies the guilt—any time spent away from the child makes them feel like a hypocrite. Edil Cuepo, a mother of two in Rockaway Beach, New York, says this was how she felt during her first two years at home. "I was clutching on to my first child, like, 'I'm a stay-at-home mom, I have to be the one who does everything. If I'm home and my work is tied to taking care of my kid, then I shouldn't have to ask anyone for help,'" she says. "I feel like so many stay-at-home moms drive themselves to the edge with this false belief until you kind of just can't take it anymore."

Childcare Is Self-Care

Every job deserves support. Back when you worked outside the home, you probably didn't do it all solo. It doesn't matter whether you were in a corner office and had an executive assistant or you *were* the executive assistant, you probably had colleagues you could tag in if you needed a vacation day. You likely performed better, managed your time more wisely, and protected yourself from getting overextended by relying on other people.

Unpaid labor should be no different. You can't do your best

work if you don't have a team you can count on when necessary. Yes, you may have a spouse or partner who shares the workload, but assuming that person works for pay, there may be times when you need more help than they can give.

After all, parenting is *hard*. It seems like such an obvious statement, but it's one we too often overlook. For plenty of parents, it also comes as a surprise. In fact, 62 percent of parents polled in a 2022 Pew Research Center study said being a parent was at least somewhat harder than they expected—a quarter of parents said it was a lot harder. And for mothers, that number bumped up to 30 percent. If you made the decision not to return to work when you were still expecting, and you assumed you wouldn't need any childcare, hiring or enlisting outside help can feel like admitting defeat. It shouldn't, but it can.

And yet, for all the reasons we talked about in the last chapter, you need support: to avoid burnout, to get to the doctor's office, to carve out time alone or with friends or your partner. You might need it because you have two kids with two different activities at the same time, on opposite sides of town. Or because you need someone to stay in the house while your daughter naps so you can bring your son outside on a beautiful day.

"It all goes back to those questions of how do you want to feel, how do you want to show up as a parent, and what do you need to get yourself there," says Lizzie Assa, founder of the Workspace for Children. "What you need to get yourself there is *time*, right? And relaxation and filling your own needs. A babysitter is a tool that you should use." In other words, rather than thinking of childcare as a financial drain you haven't earned, think of it as an investment in your family dynamic.

But let's say you simply can't get past the income piece. Would it help if I reminded you that in 2021, Salary.com valued the work of a stay-at-home mother at $184,820 per year? In their annual Mom Salary Survey, the company looks at all the jobs performed by mothers—including everything from CEO to van driver to facilities manager to nutritionist—and estimates the value of the position based on real-time market prices. The survey also found that stay-at-home moms put in an average of 106 work hours per week, or seven 15-hour days. While we shouldn't need a price tag to justify getting help, I hope this number offers some perspective on the magnitude of work you are doing. For so many stay-at-home moms, the true hurdle to childcare—the devil on your shoulder that is driving the guilt—is perspective: I want you to see yourself as holding a big job, and like any executive, you need to strategically assemble the right support team. If a friend was working fifteen-hour days in an office job with barely any days off, and making what would probably amount to $200,000 a year after bonuses or overtime pay, you'd expect that they'd have not just one support person but an entire department.

And if that friend didn't get any help? They'd probably begin to resent the work or feel bitter toward the colleague who's supposed to be helping but isn't. Primary parents run this resentment risk as well, but the colleague in question is likely your partner. You may have made the decision to stay at home and take on the bulk of the parenting duties, but if you're working around the clock at a job that requires more than you expected and you don't feel like your partner is doing their fair share (not the *equal* share, to be clear, just the *fair* share), you'll probably notice the resentment building inside you.

Couples therapist Tracy Dalgleish says bringing in outside support can help relieve this toxic intruder before it begins to erode your relationship. "What are some reasons for resentment? Sometimes it's about envy. Sometimes it's that things don't feel fair, or you're not getting your needs met, either because you're not communicating them or because your partner is not meeting them," Dalgleish explains. "Here's an example: I choose to sort my kids' clothes on a Saturday night, while my partner is sitting and watching the hockey game. In that moment, I *could* choose to sit down and rest and enjoy a show, but I choose not to. And that's when resentment shows up. So when I talk to clients about offloading resentment, I invite them to ask themselves, 'What am I doing in this moment? Is this what I need? And if I'm overwhelmed, how can we redistribute the load?'" Some of that might mean looking internally at your relationship to redistribute the household labor, but it might also require bringing in an extra set of hands. If you can offload even a small percentage of what's on your plate, you may not find the Saturday-night hockey game so irritating.

A Family Investment

Parents on a career pause often don't contribute financially to the household income, and those who get paid for part-time work likely contribute less than they once did. Moms who struggled with the financial aspect of the stay-at-home decision often take solace in the belief that while they may not be bringing money in, they are saving it—because they're not working, the family doesn't need to spend on childcare, or housekeeping, or takeout . . . you name it. That, in itself, is a monetary contribution and gives plenty of stay-at-home parents the sense that they're pulling their weight.

If this sounds familiar, you might not be the only one who looks at the family budget this way. As noted in chapter 2, finances are a big part of the discussion when one parent decides to down-shift their career. Perhaps you wanted to take a pause and had to convince your partner that it was financially feasible for your family. Maybe your previous salary barely covered the cost of childcare, and that was the impetus for reevaluating your work status while you had young kids. In either case, spending on child-care can feel like you're going back on an agreement, or simply not holding up your end of the bargain. Your job is to save money, not spend it, right?

Not really. As a stay-home parent, you are more than a piggy bank or a cost cutter. You are running a household and doing the lion's share of the day-to-day caregiving and housekeeping, as well as ensuring that your children are raised in accordance with your family's values. You are building a community for yourself and your family, pursuing passions, and hopefully making it a little bit easier for each individual in your household (including you!) to realize and step into their full selves. To do all that, you may need extra support along the way, so take that support for what it is: an investment that benefits your entire family. Instead of looking at every childcare spend or investment in household help as a with-drawal from your column of the family budget, it's important to reframe this expense as a shared line item. Childcare should come out of the joint family budget because it supports the collaborative family organization. It's an allocation that helps keep each indi-vidual healthy, and it also serves the various relationships: child-care can improve marriage quality and benefit the kids directly.

Dalgleish says she's seen plenty of couples where one partner—usually the higher earner—resists paying for childcare. "If your partner says, 'No, I don't see the need for that,' then this might be an indication that they don't understand what's going on with you. It can't just be a 'No, that's not possible'; it has to be a conversation," she says. When couples are on the couch across from her, Dalgleish reminds the resistant party of all the reasons why everyone will be better off with some help. "I offer the picture that when your partner is less stressed, and when they have more support, it offers freedom, space, and time for other things. When women get to nurture intimacy with themselves—maybe she goes to the gym, maybe she works on a side project that fills her up, or maybe she's reading a book—she comes back to the relationship with renewed energy and a deeper ability to give to her family."

But some partners need to see it to believe it. In Helen Ortiz's household, there was a bit of a push-pull when it came to hiring childcare because her husband was concerned about the spending. "Finally we started allowing ourselves to have a babysitter, not just for when we had an event or a date night or some pre-scheduled thing, but just to come over for four hours on a Tuesday afternoon," she says. "It took this pressure off me that my children were happily engaged with someone else, and I could get things done without worry. I could run out the door and do what I needed to do. My husband told me that he, in turn, feels so much more supported because I can show up better [for all of us]. He actually said to me, 'Helen, I realize how important this is, it just took some time.'"

I can attest firsthand to the benefit of childcare for the kids who receive it. I mentioned earlier that my parents never brought in any babysitters or nannies when I was a kid. I spent the better part of my elementary school years terrified that something was going to happen to my mom or dad because I didn't trust my teachers, as loving and present as they were, to take care of me. In fact, I didn't trust that anyone aside from my parents could handle me. Tovah Klein, director of the Barnard College Center for Toddler Development and author of *Raising Resilience: How to Help Our Children Thrive in Times of Uncertainty,* notes that bringing in caregivers does indeed help a child feel more safe rather than less. "Loving caregivers feed into a child's ability to trust others. They see that there are different ways of being cared for and kept safe," she says. "The aim is for a child to know they are loved and not alone. Caregivers, whether family members or a nanny or a babysitter, show a child *more* ways of being loved and taken care of." Outside caregivers might also expose children to different cultures, languages, and food, Klein points out, which is a big added bonus.

Ortiz says that for a long time, her son had the same fear I did, because she didn't bring in any babysitters until she had her second kid, a daughter. "I felt this weight before having help, like I was the only one who could ever meet my kids' needs, which was not a service to any of us," she says. "My daughter has grown up with a much different outlook because she was just turning one when we finally got support. She's grown up with different faces around and she is fully trusting and enjoys other people. She's sad when I leave sometimes but it's different—it's not panic. And I think that's because she learned from a young age that other people can meet her needs."

Now, whenever I spend a whole day apart from my son and daughter—thanks to a mix of school and an afternoon babysitter— I remember that I'm giving them the gift of feeling supported and loved by an entire village. I come home at the end of the day with the kind of energy, contentment, and patience that I wish I'd seen in my parents, and I hope my kids will never forget.

A True Partnership

I'm not willing to call your partner or co-parent the babysitter or childcare. I'll admit it really irks me when I hear parents, mostly moms, tell people that they were able to go out at night or get away for a day because "dad is babysitting." A babysitter is, by definition, someone who looks after a child when the parents are out. If you're the parent, you're not the babysitter.

That said, if you're the primary parent and you need a break or a little extra help at a low cost, turning to your partner is an obvious place to start. Hopefully, this person is already involved in your children's life, but to ensure that you get the support you need, you may need to formalize the setup, choosing specific times or places where your partner is entirely on duty. Every partnership has different dynamics and strengths, and when one parent is primarily at home, fifty-fifty is rarely the goal. But if there is some wiggle room in your partner's schedule, perhaps it's time for them to do more or to contribute in a new or different way. Neeti Narula, a yoga instructor and mom of two in Brooklyn, New York, with limited babysitting hours, has a deal with her husband: he takes over in the mornings and for bedtime every night. Leah Fink and her husband have school-aged children, so they block and tackle after-school care, and they each take an allotted number of days a year to travel with friends. Maya Uppaluru, a mom of two in Washington, DC, divvied up the household tasks on a spreadsheet and went down the list with her husband, so she felt more supported day-to-day with the household tasks.

This kind of formalized shared childcare system is contingent on an acceptance and understanding that both partners, working for pay or not, are contributing value to the household. And it will require communication—your partner likely won't know you need or even want the help unless you ask for it. In a conversation for the Mother Untitled community, Erin Erenberg, founder of Chamber of Mothers, a nonprofit that advocates for mothers' rights (specifically paid leave, maternal health, and affordable childcare), admitted that she resisted this conversation for a long time because she didn't feel entitled to her partner's help and didn't feel she could impose on him. "The belief I held that I didn't deserve help, especially from my husband, unless I was making lots of money, was really imprisoning me," she said. Erenberg told me she found freedom in communication and suggests that any moms in a similar bind share what's eating at them and ask for support as honestly and vulnerably as possible. When it comes to how to best argue for yourself and your needs, Erenberg says she takes her lead from all-time-great women's advocate Ruth Bader Ginsburg. To quote RBG herself: "Reacting in anger or annoyance will not advance one's ability to persuade."

Not all partners have the flexibility in their jobs to participate in even close-to-equal caregiving, so if sharing the load equitably isn't possible, expectation setting needs to be. My husband has consistently owned grocery shopping, meal planning, and cooking responsibilities. During periods when he must focus more on work and those tasks are left to me, we lower the standards by relying on a fair number of frozen foods. We also invested in a once-a-week cleaning service to handle laundry and deep cleaning and assembled a plan for tidying in the morning before he leaves for work and again after the kids' bedtime. I leveled with him that the house was going to be toy-ridden when he got home, and we would need to make resetting the house a team effort before the two of us ate dinner.

No matter your distribution of labor, rather than leading with bitterness that your partner isn't doing more, or shame that you're asking them to, approach a conversation about this aspect of your lives with curiosity. Ask yourselves, "Are we each owning our responsibilities? Are we valuing each other's contributions? Are we both getting the support and space we need to thrive?"

Help Comes in Many Forms

There is no one way to tackle childcare. There were years I had a babysitter two days a week, and years I had no paid childcare but instead leaned on both sets of grandparents and my husband to share hours on the weekends so I could have time to myself. Before my kids were in school full-time, Dan took the first morning shift at home so I could have twenty minutes to myself before entering the kitchen and starting my "work day." After the whole fiasco with Bodie, Lyla, and Peppa Pig, I invested in a mother's helper four days a week who did a mix of cooking, laundry, and helping with childcare when I wanted to be with one kid and needed eyes on the other. That saw us through one year of a transition period where I needed the extra support. Now that both my children are in school, we have an afternoon babysitter a couple of days a week.

Fortunately, as the world of work grows more flexible and varied, so does the pool of childcare options. For you, help might look like enrolling your kid in after-school or daycare a couple of days a week or trading playdate-hosting duties with a friend so you each get one afternoon free. For nearly half of the respondents to Care.com's *2023 Cost of Care Report*, bringing in help involved relying on relatives. As for those who didn't have family nearby, about a third said they enlisted friends or neighbors.

I've been blown away by the various ways members of the Mother Untitled community have created childcare solutions. One member described to me a date-night childcare swap among her group of mom friends: one parent heads to another one's house after bedtime to babysit, so the couple who live there can go out for a date night. It works as a rotation, so that the next week a different parent is babysitting, and a different couple gets to go out. I think it's genius: the babysitter gets to sit and watch Netflix in a quiet household of sleeping children, and the parents get time away without the added cost of childcare. A win-win.

Other parents have told me about babysitting trades with siblings, so that the parents get free childcare and the kids get cousin time. Or group babysitting activities, where a few different kids go to one sitter to diffuse the cost to any one family. (For more creative solutions, see the box on pages 177–178.)

Building a support team doesn't have to involve childcare at all. Maybe you're in the early stages of motherhood, beholden to the nap schedule and housebound for each two-hour stint, but you have a dog that needs walking so she doesn't pee in the house. Enter pet care. If you simply want to claw your eyes out at the thought of cleaning toilets or doing yet another load of laundry, maybe your ideal help is in the form of a housecleaner rather than a babysitter. For some, the thought of getting dinner on the table every night sounds less like a culinary adventure and more like a *Groundhog Day* situation. If that's you, have you considered a meal delivery service? There is no right choice, no help that is better than others.

Even within the category of your chosen support, there is no universal job description—only the one that is best for your family. Some parents resist babysitters because there are aspects of parenting or moments with their kids they don't want to give up. If you love cooking dinner and sitting down to a meal with your family, or it's important that you're the one to handle bedtime or afternoon homework help, you can mold your sitter's responsibilities around those tasks. What you do or don't want to outsource is completely up to you, and Lizzie Assa says having a clear understanding of your wishes will make it easier for you to find the right help. "I often sit down with parents and say, 'If nothing else existed—if no one was going to judge you and money wasn't a thing—what would you have your babysitter do?'" she explains. "'What would your relationship with them look like? What would their relationship with your kids look like? And now, how can we use that as a guide for what you really want and need?'"

DRAFTING A JOB DESCRIPTION

Putting together a clear job description for whatever help you need benefits everyone. The simple act of sitting down and spelling out what you're looking for can give you clarity on what you want in a caregiver, more than just "Help!" It will also give a potential babysitter or nanny or mother's helper a sense of what to expect in terms of hours, duties, engagement with kids, housework, and other logistics. The more specific you can be, the more likely you are to find someone who meets your particular requirements. As you draft your job description, focus on the following four areas:

Qualities: What qualities are you looking for in this person? This can include personality traits—gentle or authoritative, for example—or more objective traits, like being comfortable with a mom who is present in the home or being bilingual.

Experience: Do you want someone with a background in childhood education or nutrition? Do you want someone with a certain number of years under their belt, or, say, a history of watching twins? If so, say so directly.

Duties expected: Here is where you can go over everything that you expect this person will assist with. If it's a long list, give a general sense of the breakdown in workload. For example, when I wrote a job description for our mother's helper, I explained that childcare would make up 50 percent of the role, with housekeeping, grocery shopping, cooking, and errands making up the other half.

Bonus items: Every family has their own specific needs and wants. A babysitter who drives or is willing to travel. A housecleaner who is comfortable with pets. Someone who can work nights or weekends. Whatever it is, include it here.

Where to Find Help

You know you need help, you're on board with hiring, and you've got a job description in hand. Great! Now what? Where will you find this magical Mary Poppins? (Kidding, kidding. We're all human, and if you're expecting Julie Andrews to appear at your door, you may find yourself disappointed when a perfectly capable and qualified individual shows up without a flying umbrella or bottomless purse.) I'm a big believer in word of mouth, and the first thing I did when I was looking for a mother's helper was to blast out the job description to local family and friends. You might be surprised how many people know someone who knows someone who's looking for babysitting hours, once you actually start asking around. But the online opportunities for finding help seem to be growing every day. Depending on what you're looking for, some of these options may be better than others:

Facebook groups: Your local neighborhood parents' group and local interest groups, like a baby-wearing group or breastfeeding support group, might have recommendations of sitters who are local and can offer firsthand referrals.

Care.com: The largest babysitting platform in the United States, Care.com allows users to post job listings, view the profiles of those who apply, and browse profiles of caregivers in your area. For a membership fee, you can also contact applicants directly to schedule interviews and get access to background checks. But because it's a big platform, you could get hundreds of responses to your post. To narrow it down, home in on your local area and be tight with your filters.

(Similar caregiving websites and apps include UrbanSitter, Curated Care, Hello Sitter, and The Sitter Club.)

Local colleges: Schools in your area might have babysitting boards or Facebook groups for students looking for part-time caregiver jobs.

Nanny placement agencies: If you're looking for something more long-term, most major cities have placement agencies that can help narrow down your prospects based on your specific requirements. While they specialize in full-time nannies, many can place part-time help or nanny shares.

CREATIVE CHILDCARE SOLUTIONS

Childcare isn't just babysitter or bust. If you don't want to pay an hourly rate for a sitter, and you don't have family or friends you can count on nearby, never fear. Gyms, play spaces, churches or temples or other places of worship, community centers—these gathering spaces (and many more) often offer various forms of childcare, including either a few hours on-site for members, or a monthly parent's night out where you can drop your kids and take some time for yourself.

When we polled our Mother Untitled community members, one pair of moms shared that they cowork in each other's homes—the kids play together, and the moms take turns interacting with the kids when they need help. Another group of four moms with part-time jobs banded together to trade childcare, each one signing up for one weekday to host all the kids in their home. "It can be a circus sometimes, but doing this gives each of us three workdays to focus in a quiet house," says Genoveva La Placa, a mom in San Francisco who left her job as a CFO at a hedge fund to be a stay-at-home mother, and then transitioned back to part-time consulting. You might even be able to find a local babysitting co-op, where a group of parents trade babysitting duties in a formalized system where you "earn" babysitting hours by watching other kids.

Common Pitfalls

Once you've landed on a childcare solution, making it work is a two-way street. Whoever you've hired needs to fulfill the job description and do good work, but you, as the parent and employer, should do your part to set them up for success—both out of fairness to the person you've hired and because the only way *you'll* benefit is if *they* succeed. This can be harder than it seems. If you've never let anyone else be in charge, letting go, even for just an hour or two, can be hard. "There are a lot of people who will finally give in and get the help they need, but then they don't know how to delegate or they micromanage," Assa says. "As a result, they're not getting anything out of it." If you're standing over your sitter correcting their every move, or you can't get yourself to trust them, you may find yourself in the "it's just easier if I do it myself" mindset, which will ultimately put you back at square one. I can promise you, it's *not* easier to do everything alone. It will take time and energy at the outset to teach your sitter or other outside help how you like things done, but the return on investment will be huge.

Like any boss, once you train your employee—showing them the nap time routine or what snacks are acceptable for after school or how you like the laundry folded—you have to trust them to do their job. "Letting go was hard because I've always had a vision for how I want motherhood to run, and nannies bring their own personality and their own background into the childcare situation," says Olivia Metzger, who admits she had to adjust to bringing in a sitter for her four kids. "I don't want to be overly controlling of a nanny because I want them to be happy in their work environment and to be themselves. I schedule myself to be out of the house during that time, so that they have the house under their wing and they know they're trusted to do a great job, and it's always worked." If you've hired a sitter so that you can have some time to yourself in the house—to work in your home office, to exercise, whatever—talk to the babysitter about this ahead of time, setting clear expectations for what it will look like when you're sharing the space. Discuss this with your kids, too. If their habit is to run to mom for every little thing, that will be their default. If you want all questions and concerns directed toward the sitter when that person is on duty, that needs to be clearly established and enforced.

As problematic as micromanaging can be, there's an opposite end of the spectrum that can be equally detrimental to the childcare setup. American women commonly self-identify as people pleasers or exhibit people-pleasing behaviors, but this is not the time to walk on eggshells or fear advocating for yourself. Sure, you will want to make your caregiver feel comfortable in your home, but not at the expense of your own comfort or your children's. Being an employer requires direct communication about expectations and problems. If you have concerns with any aspect of your caregiver's behavior or performance, be reasonable but clear. Giving feedback is important; it's the only way this employee can learn and improve. Even a nanny with decades of experience will have a learning curve. She may be able to change a diaper with her eyes closed, but adjusting to a new family's expectations is about so much more than potty training or cooking mac and cheese. Every family lives differently, so what a previous employer wanted won't necessarily be what you want. Don't be scared to have a straightforward conversation about what you'd like done differently. This relationship is based on mutual respect and professionalism first and foremost; friendship with your kids' babysitter is a bonus second.

More than anything, remember that every new job has an adjustment period, for employee and employer. Hiring help requires a certain amount of self-awareness. Take stock of where you may struggle with adding someone new into your family dynamic. Simply being aware of your resistance can help you overcome it—at the very least it can help you differentiate between an actual problem and your own personal hang-ups. Once you've brought someone into your home and your children's lives, and given them the lay of the land, let yourself enjoy the benefit. Don't spend the whole hour they're in your home watching on the nanny cam! The point of a support system is to give you time and space to fill your cup, so even if you were reluctant, give this setup a chance to work. You may be surprised at how much it allows your whole family to blossom.

Interviews and References

Different types of childcare will likely involve different hiring processes. You may want to conduct multiple interviews and reference checks for a full-time nanny, while a recommendation from a friend might be enough for a Friday-night sitter. But it's different for everyone—if you know you won't be comfortable leaving your kids until you've seen them interact in person with the caregiver, that's just fine. But I recommend having an adults-only conversation first, so you can each be candid about your kids and what you expect from whoever fills the role. Here are some essential topics to discuss:

- **The job description:** Sure, they probably already read it, but here's an opportunity to elaborate or clarify any aspects of the gig, or emphasize which pieces, if any, take priority.
- **Babysitter's preferred activities:** What does this caregiver enjoy doing with children? (Active sports, arts and crafts, cooking/baking, reading, etc.) Also use this time to ask if there's anything this caregiver prefers *not* to do.
- **Discipline style and approach:** It's important to know if your babysitter has strong feelings about how to discipline; it's equally, if not more, important to let them know how you would like any disciplinary problems handled.
- **The typical day/afternoon:** Ask if they have any preference or perspective on routine or structure with children. If it were entirely up to them, what would their typical day with your kids look like?

- **Logistics:** It's important to be aligned on values, but if this caregiver isn't available when you need them, or isn't willing to accept your pay rate, the whole conversation might be moot.
- **Previous conflict:** Ask about any issues that have arisen with previous families or children, and how they managed. Even in a dream babysitting gig, stuff will happen. You can tell a lot about a person from this conversation, including how they manage conflict and what constitutes an issue for them.

Once you've found someone you like and are interested in hiring, it's time to check references. Do not discount the importance of this step, no matter how much you adore the candidate or how quickly you need some help in the home. Reference checks might feel time-consuming, but they go a long way in building your trust. In the AMP survey, 73 percent of respondents said they struggle to find someone they trust to stay with their children. A quick call with a previous employer can be very telling. Make sure to ask not only what worked well but what didn't. One way to delicately do so is to inquire what you can do to set your relationship with this caregiver up for success.

When reviewing referrals, make sure to keep in mind the setup of the household that's providing the recommendation, as well as the scheduling and unique style of that individual family. One of the very first caregivers I hired received a wonderful referral from her previous employers, but I failed to consider that the family in question had two parents who worked long hours due to demanding careers, so they needed a full-time caregiver for their children. This woman had managed everything for those children and that home, so while she was an amazing asset for families willing to hand over the reins completely, it didn't end up working in my household, where I wanted to work collaboratively with our caregiver and maintain control over routines.

IF IT'S NOT WORKING OUT

It's possible that the first person you hire may not be the right fit. If something about your new caregiver feels off to you—even if it's just that they don't vibe with your kid—go with your gut. "If there's something that is just making you uncomfortable about a provider, you don't have to continue with that provider," says Sara Mauskopf, founder and CEO of Winnie, an online marketplace for childcare. "Your child will be fine to switch childcare options. Kids are really flexible and adaptable, so if you tried something that didn't work out, you can try something else. Parents sometimes feel like when they find a daycare or sitter, they have to stick with that option forever. But your needs may outgrow that situation, and you should feel open to exploring other options." Still, just because this one person didn't work out doesn't mean nobody will work out. In any job there will be people who don't work out—don't let this turn you off to childcare forever.

Power Practice: What Help Do You Need?

This chapter addressed why families with a stay-at-home parent resist bringing in childcare, how to get comfortable with building a robust support system, and how to find a caregiver who will fit with your family. That last piece begins by identifying the type of help that will most benefit your family and then considering who will make the most sense from a logistical and financial perspective.

Step 1: Think about the care tasks that you least enjoy. This could be because they are time-consuming and drain your energy, because they are a source of friction in your family or marriage, or because they limit your ability to invest in activities that help you stay whole. In the following list, circle the three that you dislike the most.

- Laundry
- Tidying
- Deep cleaning
- Transportation
- Meal prep
- Cooking
- Groceries
- Family admin (paperwork, scheduling)
- Home organization
- Morning childcare
- After-school childcare
- Evening childcare
- Party or holiday planning
- Miscellaneous errands

Step 2: Consider the type of help that seems feasible to you for the tasks you identified in step 1. Feasibility can be based on a number of factors, including your schedule, finances, and personal comfort level. Work your way down this list and circle at least three options that might be available to you, or could be compensated for supporting you with the care load.

- Partner
- Retired caregivers or teachers
- Taskrabbit
- Instacart or grocery service
- Local grandparents
- Teenage neighbors
- Meal delivery services
- Laundry services
- Cleaning service
- School parent carpool
- Nanny share
- Flexible daycare or drop-off playgroups
- Church, temple, or library drop-off program
- After-school programming
- After-school college babysitters
- Local parents (rotation where one parent takes kids for set hours on one day, and the other parent does the same on another day)
- Family helper (part-time option)
- Nanny (part-time option)

Step 3: Identify a time period—the school year, the summer months—during which you can test a new system of outsourcing care tasks. Now that you know the what, who, and when, here's a sample script for broaching the conversation with your partner:

I'm noticing that I [or we, or our family] am feeling overwhelmed. It's important to me that we all feel supported so that we all benefit from a calmer [or more fun/positive/healthy] home environment. I spent some time thinking about areas where our family could benefit from extra

support. Are any of these things you can help out with more, or can you

help me think through who we can ask or hire to support us for this school

year [or alternative period of time]?

Part Three

Grow and Learn Through Your Pause

7

Discover the Limitless Value of Mom Friends

FALSE BELIEF
My network will dry up when I stop working.

NEW NARRATIVE
*Motherhood is an invisible thread that allows
me to connect quickly and deeply, and I'm going
to build relationships that serve me
personally and professionally.*

SITTING ON THE dusty linoleum floor, I exchanged a knowing glance with the mothers on either side of me. We were gathered in a basement room of the Union Square Babies"R"Us, following our baby movement instructor's directions to tap tap tap on our babies' calves. I didn't know these women, but I wanted to. One had an almost regal demeanor, polished despite the flurry of burp cloths on her lap and shoulders; the other was all smiles, and she exuded the warmth I would come to learn was the hallmark of her personality. Our eye contact and stifled laughs acknowledged that there was something ridiculous but also joyful in what we were doing. It clued me in to the notion that we were all still rookies at this motherhood thing, but were opening ourselves up to a new, less serious side of ourselves.

Toward the end of the class, our teacher instructed us to let our babies "be free," which meant the adults in the room could talk amongst ourselves. I learned that Suzi, the regal mom to my left, had worked in banking. Her job required a lot of travel, so she wanted to take a couple of years off and return to the office once frequent trips felt more palatable. Caroline, the bubbly and warm mother to my right, had been laid off six months after returning from maternity leave and was taking it as a sign to stay home for a stretch. Other mothers in the class, which was intended for babies six months and up, had extended their maternity leaves or were working part-time. We talked about our kids' development, comparing sleep and feeding schedules, and traded suggestions of favorite parks or play spaces. To an outsider, our circle of moms might have looked stereotypical—there were topknots and athleisure wear, and multiple tumblers full of coffee—but we represented different careers, family structures, and cultures of origin. The group of us, sitting in a circle, were physical proof that there was no one way to make room for motherhood.

As I returned to baby movement class each week, I felt validated. Not that the choices I'd made were "right," necessarily, but that being a mom could feel expansive and ambitious, just like any other stage of life. And I was excited to connect with women who were grappling with the same questions I was—about parenting and family life and career pauses and next steps. After sitting next to them two weeks in a row, I took the lead and asked Suzi and Caroline if they wanted to come over for a coffee playdate later that week. They took me up on it, and the intimacy of being in someone's living room opened us up in a way that the

Babies"R"Us basement never could. We started with the easy topic of in-laws—a universal icebreaker—then moved on to husbands and how we were sharing the parenting load. It was incredibly reassuring to hear that I wasn't the only one who felt like her husband didn't quite "get it," or who was squabbling with her partner about whether naps were necessary.

Before the end of that first playdate we set up another, and another, until we'd formed an informal baby group and text chain, meeting weekly and trading articles about dropping naps or sharing recipes that our kids actually enjoyed. Time worked its magic, and eventually the text thread evolved to conversations about what we wanted out of the moment, if we missed work, ideas we were noodling on, stressors we were struggling with. When I started Mother Untitled, they were among the first friends I pitched the concept to. They read early articles on the blog and liked my posts on social. They made it all feel special—like we were in a graduating class moving through milestones and learning together along the way.

Although we originally bonded over our kids—and that point of connection made it easier to open up more quickly—my friendships with Suzi and Caroline ultimately served me on a personal and professional level. They offered camaraderie at a time when I didn't have coworkers with whom to take a quick break at the proverbial water cooler, and refreshing grown-up conversation on days when I could not recite one more nursery rhyme. At one point we tried to get our husbands together, but that didn't quite work; we didn't become lifelong besties or the unicorn "family friends" of lore. Suzi has since moved to the suburbs, and now that our kids are older it's not so easy for me and Caroline to plop them on a playmat and catch up while we sit back and observe.

Still, I would argue that successful friendships aren't defined by the years they last but the comfort they bring. And when the three of us were in the trenches of early motherhood, there were moments when I needed nothing more than someone who could see what I was going through and say, "I know it's hard, you're doing great, I'm right there with you."

A Lifeline, Not a Luxury

Parenting can be isolating; parenting at home, without the companionship of colleagues or other adults to touch base with throughout the day, even more so. When Bodie was an infant, I absolutely found myself chatting with him about life and the schedule of our upcoming week as if he could engage in small talk. I like to think it was developmentally beneficial for his little brain to hear me yammering on, but I also know the conversations were as much for me as for him. As someone who was used to catching up with coworkers all day, finding myself in a room with no adult conversation was a major adjustment.

Loneliness is a problem in America that is bigger than just parenthood. In 2023, the U.S. Surgeon General issued an advisory entitled *Our Epidemic of Loneliness and Isolation*, citing research that, even before the pandemic, about half of U.S. adults reported experiencing measurable levels of loneliness. This public health concern, according to the report, is "more widespread than many of the other major health issues of our day."

Loneliness in motherhood has been reported on for years. It made headlines long before the lockdowns of 2020, although the pandemic certainly exacerbated the problem: 51 percent of mothers of young children reported "serious loneliness" in the immediate aftermath of the COVID-19 shutdown. But even as we emerged from the fog of pandemic precautions, social connection was still a struggle, as our surgeon general reminded us. And despite the stereotype of stay-at-home moms dishing over yoga mats or at the coffee klatch, in our AMP survey, 44 percent said making friends as a stay-at-home mom is hard, while one in ten said they didn't feel like they had any mom friends at all. "When you become a parent, you become incredibly busy," says Marlo Lyons, a career coach who often works with new parents to envision their next steps. "It might be that you used to talk to your friends weekly, but now you only talk to them once a year. You just don't have time."

And if the friends you used to connect with don't have kids, or if they went right back to work, you might feel disconnected from them in your current situation. "A lot of women in my life are professionals and still working, and when I explained my choice to some of them, they didn't really get it, because they're not feeling the same call to have time at home that I am," says Hannah Bryant, a mom of two in Chicago on a break from her career in wealth management. I'm not here for the so-called mommy wars—the Mother Untitled movement is about empowering parents to make whichever choice works for them without judgment—but sometimes it's nice to connect with someone in your same boat.

As isolating as parenthood, especially stay-at-home parenthood, might be, plenty of mothers I've talked to admit that they still consider friendship a nice-to-have, not a need-to-have. I've been guilty of this myself. When there's a mile-long to-do list, and your kids are tugging at your sleeve for help with homework or even some extra snuggle time on the couch, choosing to be with other adults instead can feel selfish, or at least self-indulgent. "We think we should be more productive, more present, and more viewable for our kids," says friendship coach Danielle Bayard Jackson. "So we worry that pouring into these platonic relationships is somehow taking away from children."

There may also be a cultural component baked into our reluctance to devote time to socializing. Zara Hanawalt, a mom of twins in Pittsburgh, says her parents have put a more concerted effort into building a network than she has. "There's an Indian focus on community, and it's been really nice to watch my parents enjoy the community they've worked really hard to build," she says. "But it's sad for me because I feel like I'll never have that. I just don't think investing in friendships and relationships is considered a productive use of your time in this country." Pop-culture portrayals of ladies who lunch indulging in frivolous neighborhood gossip—even the mere existence of the phrase "ladies who lunch"—only exacerbates the problem. "If you're a mom, especially a mom who works inside the home, and you take some time to have lunch with a friend, you're often shamed for that in this country," Hanawalt says.

But here's what you need to know: connecting with friends might be the single most important thing you can do for your health. Research shows that low levels of social connection can have the same mortality impacts as smoking fifteen cigarettes or drinking six alcoholic drinks a day. It's associated with an increased risk of heart disease and stroke, accelerated cognitive decline, and is worse for your health than obesity or not exercising. On the flip side, social connection is associated with better physical, cognitive, and mental health, and research suggests it increases survival odds by a whopping 50 percent. "We know, intuitively, that friendship is important," says Bayard Jackson. "And the research continues to support that probably the number-one thing that determines our overall well-being and life satisfaction is the quality of our relationships. Nothing else—not being a mother or having a certain income status or being married—is as important as having quality relationships in your life."

For stay-at-home mothers, social connection is particularly important, as studies show that nonemployed women with small children at home are more likely than their employed counterparts to report having felt sadness or anger a lot of the day the day before. And as critical as your connectedness is to your own health, it's also important for your kids. Research shows that a mother's loneliness can negatively impact her child's health, but on the flip side, the benefits you'll get from spending time with friends will reverberate throughout your family. In one study, women who attended an antenatal baby-care class and made friends with the other participants not only saw mental health benefits but also developed greater confidence in their parenting, as they reassured one another that their babies' development was on track. When I spoke to Jennifer Breheny Wallace, author of *Never Enough: When Achievement Culture Becomes Toxic—and What We Can Do About It*, she told me that the one consistent finding in families she dubbed as "healthy strivers" was that the primary caregiver, mostly the mother, spent one hour a week with mom friends, which she believed resulted in an awareness that no one's kids are perfect. By sharing stories and opening up to other parents, she says, moms realize that we are all navigating challenges, which normalizes the struggles and lowers the pressure to get motherhood "right" or push our kids too hard. Plus, by seeing in others that there is no one way to parent, mothers can feel more confident in their own approach. Far from frivolous, investing in strong social support and a confidence in your own parenting will make you 75 percent less likely to be depressed—it's all connected, and it all matters. A lot.

The Time Is Right

It's time for a reframe. What if I told you that there is no period of your life more conducive to making new friends—and forming deep friendships—than during the early stages of motherhood?

I know, I know. But hear me out.

Motherhood and all that comes with it can, if you let it, crack you open so deeply that you have no choice but to just be honest. When I met Caroline and Suzi at our baby movement class, Bodie was six months old. I was truly happy that I was staying at home with him, but I was also tired from the work of navigating a new identity and an entirely unfamiliar existence. I didn't have it in me to pretend that I had it all figured out, even if I'd wanted to. That vulnerability, and the lack of time for or interest in surface-level conversations, is really what fast-tracked our friendship.

When it comes to deepening relationships of any kind, experts agree that vulnerability is key. Parenthood breaks down defenses and can cause lots of uncertainty in its newness—*Am I doing this right? Is this how it's supposed to feel?* As much as you may want to appear like you have it all together, perhaps the best thing you can do for yourself is expose the mess. "Everybody just wants to act like 'I'm doing it. I'm killing it. I've got it under control,' because they think everyone else does," says marriage and family therapist Emily Pardy. "But nobody does. I haven't met a single person who has all their shit together. To make new friends you have to be vulnerable, and we have to give people the opportunity to be vulnerable with us." Pardy suggests starting with something as simple as asking a mom at the playground for advice, or being honest enough about your own struggles that a potential friend feels safe coming to you for help.

Even if the vulnerability piece is hard for you (as it is for many), there's a practical side to stay-at-home parenting that ups your likelihood of making new friends. If you've incorporated a rhythm into your weeks, you probably frequent some of the same spots on repeat—the park you go to on Monday afternoons, the Wednesday-morning story time at your local library. There are probably other moms who have the same idea. "Routine sounds unsexy, I know. But adults are always so nostalgic for their childhood friendships, and a lot of times those friendships were born from the fact that you saw this person all the time," Bayard Jackson says. "This is the mere exposure effect—we just prefer people who are familiar to us." Those exposure opportunities start as soon as you're ready to leave the house with your infant, but they extend throughout parenthood. As your child grows and you enter new communities—daycare, preschool, elementary school, religious school, art classes, soccer teams—you'll continue to encounter opportunities to introduce yourself to people you see repeatedly.

Being new at anything brings people together, whether you're first-year law associates or in the same sorority pledge class. Entering motherhood is no different. A mother with an infant might as well be sporting a sign that says "I'm new here. Please talk to me." Even if they aren't babies, having kids the same age is usually grounds for friendship connections. "That's your in. It's a real advantage to be new in any space or stage," Bayard Jackson says.

"There are other women looking for community, because they want support, too."

WHERE ARE MOMS MEETING?

As part of the AMP survey, we tried to figure out where friendships in motherhood are actually forming. Old friends still reign supreme—there's no reason the people from your before can't fit into your after, whether or not they have kids, and regardless of whether or not they work out of the home. Connections from mutual friends are also reliable, while some of the more common stay-at-home-mom hangout spots . . . not so much. Here's a breakdown of where respondents said they made their mom friends:

- Friends before motherhood: 38 percent
- Mutual friends: 30 percent
- Work: 34 percent
- Daycare/school: 30 percent
- Mom groups: 22 percent
- Social media: 14 percent
- Play groups: 20 percent
- Park: 17 percent

MAKING THE FIRST MOVE

No matter where you meet your potential new mom friends, there will come a moment when someone needs to make the first move. Kids are an easy opening line. "How old?" is usually enough do the trick, just to get conversation going. When you meet someone you think could have potential for broader connection, you may need to take the next step by asking to exchange phone numbers or emails. If that feels weird, like you're trying to pick up a stranger, you might just be doing it right. "It was the most bizarre thing ever," Erin Brown McAlister says of trying to make plans with other moms at the playground. "But I would just say, 'I'd love to meet up for a playdate sometime. Here's my number. Let's try and make this work.'" Be sure to ask for their number, too, since the only person you can absolutely count on to do the reaching out is yourself. But good news: while you may feel uncomfortable, when you touch base, they will likely be happy to hear from you. A study published in the *Journal of Personality and Social Psychology* found that people consistently underestimate how much others appreciate being contacted for a friendly hello.

The Myth of the Mom Squad

As my kids got older and I got more settled into motherhood, I developed what I would describe as a "familiar enough" circuit. There were some intimate friendships and some friendly acquaintanceships, but I did not magically conjure a group of women who were all best friends and took family vacations (or girls' trips) together. Still, that "familiar enough" group—it was, indeed, *enough*. Bayard Jackson says she often talks to clients for whom the myth of the "mom squad" has left them feeling like a failure in the friendship category. "At some point in our conversation, that client will mention to me the gap between how she feels friendship ought to be and what her friendships actually look like," Bayard Jackson says. The expectation, the client says, is that she'll have a group of best friends, like the momfluencers who go apple picking together or the women of *Sex and the City* who gather on Sundays for brunch. "It makes them feel that their friendship landscape is inadequate in some way."

Don't let the illusion of this cohesive group of women keep you from assembling a roster of people who fulfill different needs for companionship. In the early stages of a career transition into a new routine, mostly at home, that list can include someone to go for a walk with, or someone who understands your career considerations. Over time, some of these relationships may expand to something deeper, but those that don't aren't less valuable. Because while you may not be building a mom squad, you're building something else meaningful, something that is very much *not* a fantasy. You're building a network.

The New Networking

If you're a mom on a career pause, building or expanding your network is no small feat. Remember, networking doesn't only refer to meeting new people for the express purpose of getting a new job. It's about building a web of connections. One purpose of that web is to have access to folks you can turn to when you start looking for work. But it's also so that you'll be top of mind for others when they need to make a hire, or so you have thinkers you respect with whom you can volley professional ideas. That's of the utmost importance during a career pause because people in this phase commonly reenvision what their next professional stage might look like. For Godhuli Chatterjee Gupta, the opportunity for career brainstorming and commiseration was the most comforting aspect of the mom friends she made. "My best mom friend is a lawyer who has not worked in the corporate world for several years now. Others are teachers who are taking time off, and a lot of them are going through the same transition of trying to recalibrate and figure out what their next step is," she says. "We all love motherhood, and we chose to take this pause, but we also realize that we have passions and identities of our own. And we're starting to see the light at the end of the early motherhood tunnel."

Prior to my own entry into parenthood, I had a core group of friends composed of women from similar upbringings or similar industries. As a mom, I met women of all races and ages who had worked in everything and anything, from nonprofits to finance to small businesses. These friendships expanded my network infinitely; each friendship connected me to business contacts at companies that had been totally out of my purview when I worked. Of course, I didn't tap into these networks in the thick of stay-at-home motherhood, but it was empowering to know I could when I was ready.

Many women I've spoken to have depended on mom friends to launch themselves back to work. Jaclyn McDonald, of Wayland, Massachusetts, scaled back to part-time hours as a middle school math specialist to spend more time with her kids. She kept working so she could stay connected to the field she'd always known, but was starting to tire of it. One day while sitting on the sidelines at her daughter's swim meet, Jaclyn started chatting with another mom who worked for an education nonprofit. The two became friendly, and months later, Jaclyn took a more fulfilling and enjoyable job at the same organization.

Similarly, Christine Hackett, a mom of two, including one child with special needs, found herself connecting with other moms who were navigating this similar aspect of parenthood. One of the moms, who worked in events, noticed how skillfully Christine managed her own hectic family schedule, especially when unexpected obstacles kept throwing her best-laid plans off track. Now Christine, who used to work in operations and management at start-ups, has a part-time job she loves in the events department at an auction company raising money for nonprofits.

What happened to Jaclyn and Christine wasn't a fluke. In fact, the kind of peripheral social ties that Jaclyn made poolside are the most helpful when looking for a new job. Researchers at MIT, Stanford, Harvard, and LinkedIn found that "moderately weak" ties are more helpful than close ones when the time comes to look for new employment. So, while you cannot expect to trip and fall into the seat next to a mom who will help you find your next gig, you don't need to bend over backward making every mom your new bestie *just in case*, either.

FORMALIZE IT

If want to connect with other moms, but cringe at the thought of approaching an unsuspecting parent at the nursery school open house, you might prefer joining a platform expressly dedicated to connecting mothers. At least this way you know that everyone you connect with is look for the same thing you are. Here are four platforms dedicated entirely to connecting mothers. Yes, they're like dating apps. No, you won't have to endure painful pickup lines.

HeyMama: A membership-based professional networking group for mothers, with an online community platform as well as digital and in-person events across the United States.

Peanut: An app for connecting with women in a similar stage of parenting, from pregnancy through motherhood.

Bumble for Friends: It's Bumble, but for friends. Build a profile, start swiping—when you've both swiped right, you've got a potential pal.

Mother Untitled: Yes, it's my platform, but connecting with like-minded moms is what Mother Untitled is all about. In addition to a digital community, we host seasonal in-person networking events for moms in the various stages between work and stay-at-home motherhood.

Get Strategic About What You Need

When companies assemble boards, they strategically fill roles that complement one another. There's someone who's the cheerleader, someone who is creative, someone with great connections, someone with operating experience. "Build a personal board of directors" has become common advice for those looking to grow in their careers, and I'd suggest taking the same approach to your friendships. No one person can or should check all the boxes. There are the friends who motivate you to stay healthy, or the ones who really relate to your parenting experience, or maybe the ones who understand the exact career transition you're in. There may be those you have deep talks with and those who are fun to go to a rare happy hour with.

Robert Waldinger, director of the Harvard Study of Adult Development, the longest-running study on happiness, emphasizes the importance of friendship as a determinant for longevity in his book *The Good Life,* which he coauthored with the study's associate director, Marc Schulz. His advice to parents who may feel lonely despite all the casual connections at PTA or carpool? Do an audit every so often of what you're craving in your relationships. That may result in seeking out new connections or deepening old ones, but it will help you flex an important personal and professional muscle: identifying what you need and going after it.

What Priscillia de Muizon, a mom of a five-year-old in Napa, California, needed was a friend who could help her think through how to press play on her professional pause. After spending fifteen years as a lawyer, she was toying with the idea of pursuing a writing career, but she was nervous to open up about an idea that still wasn't fully formed. But there was a woman in her mom group who, after battling breast cancer a couple years earlier, was also reconsidering her next career steps. The two ended up having weekly "backyard burrito sessions" where they worked on career goals and acted as accountability buddies. "It started with one of us being vulnerable and admitting, 'Hey I'm working on career stuff, but I'm not feeling super confident.'"

De Muizon met another friend, who filled a different need, at a prenatal swim class. "I have a tendency to be very private, and I'm not especially good at being vulnerable with people at first," she says. "I met a woman who's really good at making friends—she had just moved to town and was pregnant too and she was just persistent. Since she was new to town, she made a really big effort to meet all these different moms. So when she started a baby-mom group, I ended up meeting a great group of mom friends."

Bayard Jackson calls women like de Muizon's friend at swim class "super connectors" and says that if you're not exactly sure who you need in your circle or where to start, these are the moms you should look for. "Super connectors are people who like to ride on making introductions," she says. "We all know that woman who, even if she's not your friend, runs a Facebook group or hosts monthly meetups. Message this woman, even if you're not close, and just say, 'Hey, I'm a new mom. I'm coming out of the newborn phase and I'm looking to get plugged in.'" Super connectors get a rush from pairing up people who would get along and would likely welcome the task of helping you widen your network.

Sometimes what you lack in your network is not someone who can perform a tangible action or join you for a specific activity, but someone who fills an emotional or psychological need. For mothers especially, finding friends who affirm various parts of your identity can be critical. Before having kids, you might have identified as a tennis player, or a chef, or a tech-head, or a great friend. Perhaps your culture or your religion was a big part of how you viewed yourself. These pieces of you still exist after becoming a parent, and yet Motherly's State of Motherhood survey found that more than 70 percent of moms say they are "most strongly defined by their motherhood." Of respondents who were not in the workforce, 87 percent felt this way.

Psychologist Tovah Klein has studied this loss of identity in mothers. "Stay-at-home moms talk about the loss of that piece of themselves who was professional or a striver or career woman," she says. "They wonder what happened to their intellectual side and lament losing it. But we know that when one has multiple identities—I am a mother, a lawyer, someone who likes to bake, go for runs, a reader—those other identities can help buffer when one, in this case the 'career woman,' is on the back burner in some way."

But relying only your mother identity is not enough. "Being dependent on children for your identity is never a good idea," Klein says. "Children are not here to make us happy—they are here for us to love, raise, and guide."

To start finding the friends who might help avert a motherhood identity crisis, Bayard Jackson suggests writing these two words, ten times: "I am . . ." Then fill in each blank with an aspect of your identity. "So for me, for example, I am Black. I am a creative. Then I go through that list and really think, intentionally, about where I can go to find a community of affirmation for each aspect of my identity," Bayard Jackson says. "So, as a Black woman, it's important that I can talk to people who get that experience. They understand my fears as a mother that we share as a culture. As a creative, I need to be able to have conversations that light me up and get me energized with people who get it." It's the first step, she says, of being strategic and asking yourself, "Who am I, and how can I have that identity supported and reflected back to me in my network?"

I was recently reading an article about the one thing that employees value in leaders. It noted that, unequivocally, employees need psychological safety above all else. I've been thinking the same is true in friendships, especially as you get older. As you meet potential friends or people to integrate into your network, notice if they speak poorly about other people often, or if they speak more about other people than they do ideas, or if they make you feel judged or uncomfortable when you leave their company. Surrounding yourself with people is important, but surrounding yourself with the *right* people might be even more so in the vulnerable stages of motherhood.

Gathering and Talking: A Primer

Ultimately, connecting with other people boils down to these two ingredients. They sound simple, and yet the anxiety they provoke in plenty of adults is incredibly complex. One survey, from the on-line language tutor platform Preply, found that 71 percent of respondents would prefer silence to small talk. But despite how much we think we dislike it, research shows that adults pretty much always enjoy small talk more than they expect to. Still, sometimes you need a slight nudge to get going.

In my work building the Mother Untitled community, I've learned some handy tricks for dialing down the awkwardness that can come with gathering and talking. Here are my best tips for getting people together and fostering conversation.

GATHERING:

- If you can, combine forces with one other friend so you can expand your networks together. If you each bring two people to the gathering that the other one doesn't know, you'll widen the network for everyone.
- Create a meeting cadence. Familiarity and recognition rely on regular interaction. For mom groups, with kids or without, biweekly or monthly is a good goal.
- Break the ice with an activity. Maybe you make it a walking group, so there's some self-care built in. If you're gathering at someone's home, making it a book (or, easier still, an article) club is an easy way to give the early conversation focus.

- Be clear on the purpose. In her book *The Art of Gathering*, Priya Parker writes that before any gathering, all participants should be clear on *why* this group is getting together. "A category is not a purpose," she writes. Which is to say, "it's a moms gathering" isn't quite enough. "We hope to connect as moms who could use support from other moms" is.
- Don't be discouraged if not everyone in the group gels or it takes a little bit of extra prompting to make conversation flow. Sometimes everyone dives in and brings their A game, and sometimes people need more familiarity to be at ease.

TALKING:

- Kids make for an easy entry point to any conversation with fellow moms. Offering compliments ("How cute is that diaper bag!") or asking for recommendations ("Have you found a good pediatrician in the neighborhood?") is always low-hanging fruit. If you'd rather be less personal, your location ("This café is so beautiful," "This park is mayhem") is an easy lead-in . . . and at least you're not talking about the weather.
- Ask about a book the other person is reading, a show they're watching, neighborhood restaurants they like, or recent or upcoming travel. Any of these answers can be a jumping off point for conversation, and if you have favorites in common it might be an indication of friendship potential. As you're swapping recommendations, ask specific questions and offer deep details. ("I can't handle stressful shows—I google

the ending before so I don't have to worry while I watch.") Sharing your quirks often invites other people to do the same, laying the groundwork for good conversation.

- The key to transitioning small talk into more authentic talk is listening deeply and offering more information when it's your turn to contribute. In the most basic of examples, if you're on the receiving end of a "How are you?" instead of "I'm fine," try "My parents are visiting this week—so really good!" That quickly leads to questions like, "Where are they in from?" or "Are they helpful with the kids?"

- Take a "yes and . . ." approach. This is often celebrated as the guiding principle of improv comedy—you accept the world your scene partner has built, and then you add to it. But it's a good guiding principle for conversation, too. It doesn't mean you need to agree with everything someone says, but you acknowledge it, and then you add your own information.

- Don't freak out of if you say something "wrong." We usually think much more about whatever awkward thing we said than the person we were talking to does. If you don't think you'll be worrying about it in a year, don't waste time worrying about it tonight!

It Takes Work

I'm bad on text message. You know that meme about the person that either responds in two minutes or two weeks? That's me. I have friends who text back in an instant, but good luck getting them to return a phone call. Or there are those who are all about getting together...in theory. Then, when you try to actually make a plan, coordinating calendars is like playing a game of Tetris.

Whether you are trying to stay in touch with an existing friend or make plans with a new one, it's going to take effort. That's true if you work part-time or full-time or flex time or not at all. When I stayed at home full-time, I would daydream about how if only I worked at an office, I'd be meeting a friend for a lunch or a happy hour while I had childcare. But because my kids weren't even school age, and I was at home without any designated adult-only time, it seemed to take more planning. But now that my kids are at school, and Mother Untitled takes up the hours when they're there, it still feels like there's no time. I have blocks of hours to myself, but they are claimed by the work that will always expand to fit the space available. In short, finding time for socializing is easy for no one.

Ideally, the effort required to connect with friends will be two-sided, but if you're the one feeling short on support, you might be the one carrying more of the workload. That's okay. After I had Lyla, I held myself back from venturing out. I was having a tough time with the juggle of two kids, and I felt shame for not having it all together. I know better now. It's *because* I was struggling that I would have benefited most from connection. Time with female friends builds a reserve of energy to draw from when you need it. Making the effort, even when it's awkward or exhausting, is like adding to that reserve. It may feel difficult in the moment, but it will have big-time value when you're running low.

So what does that effort look like? Marlo Lyons recommends treating the work of reaching out to friends as you would any other commitment, which means you should start by putting it on your calendar. The scheduling piece is important because friendship takes time, and as we already know, free time will never magically appear. One study found that it takes about fifty hours of time together before you will consider someone a casual friend, ninety hours to lose the "casual" qualifier, and two hundred hours before you will consider someone a close friend. If we look at friend making as an extension of networking, then it's worth considering that those who agree with the notion that "networking played a role in my success" spent a little more than six hours a week on networking, on average. In my experience, the vulnerability and camaraderie of motherhood can accelerate the process, perhaps requiring fewer clocked hours overall, but it definitely won't happen without a time investment.

If you, like mom Erin Erenberg, are someone for whom the "schedule it in" advice feels like just another to-do, you might find more success with apps like Marco Polo that allow you to talk to friends on your own time, even if that friend isn't available when you are. Erenberg says when she can't see friends IRL she uses Voxer and WhatsApp voice memos to "hear from my girls in a fluid way." The options are endless, but they all take some degree of effort. Nothing worth having comes easy, as the saying goes.

THE VALUE OF THE GROUP TEXT

While I feel gratitude for the community I've built over my eight years of parenting, it's certainly been a journey. There was a period when my toddler was in the habit of pushing other kids, which made me withdraw from the playdate circuit. There was another phase in which

I was too anxious to see almost anyone. Enter the group text. All else being equal, the best kind of social interaction to combat loneliness is the in-person kind. But when you have children, all else is not always equal. Don't underestimate the value of connecting over text—even a short message of support can go a long way. Friendship is not all or nothing. It's not "get together once a month" or "never see each other at all." Connection is valuable, however you find it.

A Reason, a Season, or a Lifetime

I adored the women I met in early motherhood, but plenty of them are no longer in my life, besides the occasional like on a pumpkin patch photo that appears in my Instagram feed. Some moved away or went back to full-time paid work, which meant we could no longer see one another as often as we once did, or we simply grew apart. That doesn't mean the friendships—however brief—lacked meaning or importance. They opened my eyes to new perspectives and experiences and provided empathy and wisdom when I craved those things most. Many of them helped me grow Mother Untitled into the community it is today.

The average close friendship lasts about ten years, according to sociologist Nicholas Christakis, coauthor of *Connected: The Surprising Power of Our Social Networks and How They Shape Our Lives*. But as a mom, you might have impactful and fulfilling friendships that last only half that time, from the infant years to the time your kids enter kindergarten. The notion that a friendship is only successful if it spans decades is a myth that is hurting relationship satisfaction, Bayard Jackson says. "The word 'failure' is defined as not meeting an intended objective," she says. "So if the objective was for a relationship to never end, then we will internalize that and feel like we failed if a friendship comes to a natural conclusion."

The success of a friendship, she argues, should be measured just like any other endeavor—by whether or not it accomplished its intended goals. "What do you want in a friendship? Are you looking for a space where you can use your gifts and support other people? Are you looking for relationships where you feel like you can express yourself freely?" If that's what you wanted and that's what you got, then count the friendship in the win column, Bayard Jackson says, and let go of any guilt. Instead, pay it forward and offer that same support to the next connection who comes along.

Power Practice: The Connections Challenge

This chapter explored why motherhood can be especially isolating, the necessity of social connections when you're staying at home, and how mom friendships can become critical business relationships. It also offered tools for connecting with other mothers, even when it feels scary. Use this checklist of mini-challenges to help you put yourself out there. Start at the beginning and work your way through the list, doing one a week for ten weeks.

1. Send a text to three friends from your pre-motherhood life to check in and just say hello.

2. Share an article or podcast that a new friend might find interesting.
3. Call a friend during an errand.
4. Invite a friend along on an errand or a planned activity.
5. Research and register for one neighborhood class (with younger kids) or volunteer opportunity (with older kids) where there will be other parents to socialize with.
6. Ask one parent out to coffee to learn about their work.
7. Organize a post-drop-off coffee meet-up (older kids) or a play-date at your home (younger kids).
8. Expand your circle by asking a new friend(s) to help start a TV show/article/podcast club.
9. Ask for a referral or recommendation—of a babysitter, after-school class, anything parent related—from a friend you trust or admire.
10. Calendar a standing night out either weekly, biweekly, or monthly.

8

Let Yourself Pursue New Passions and Find New Strengths

FALSE BELIEF

*My interests and skills are going to
wilt during motherhood.*

NEW NARRATIVE

*I'll have room to grow in new ways and to
try new things that could lead me to where
I'm meant to be—and maybe even where
I'm meant to work next.*

IT WAS EARLY on a Tuesday morning in January 2017. I held my breath, hit send, and then felt my stomach do a couple of flips—a combination of nerves and excitement. Any second now, the email I'd simultaneously been dying to send and *dreading* to send would be in the inboxes of the four-hundred-plus contacts I'd made over a decade-long career. My note announced my new blog, the first iteration of what would eventually become Mother Untitled.

I was eager to send it because I was excited about this project in a way I hadn't felt about anything in a long time. I wanted to share these ideas I was having about stay-at-home motherhood and engage in a dialogue with other parents who were rethinking their careers and family life. But I also felt anxious about broadcasting my endeavor. I worried it would be received with eye rolls, maybe even spark comments about how I'd become some sort of millennial cliché. But now it was out there and there was nothing I could do but wait.

A half hour later, the first reply rolled in. And then the next. And the next. The dozens and dozens of responses to my note—which was both an alert to the existence of my new blog and an invitation to join the conversation—were tender, thoughtful, honest messages from those in my circle about their own experiences with ambition and motherhood. It was enough to make me feel like maybe I was onto something.

Personal development, whether through an experimental passion project like my blog or a professional certification or a continuing-ed class or a hobby you've always wanted to try, can feel risky. It requires a willingness to put yourself out there and do something that maybe isn't the obvious next step. There will be people who don't get what you're doing (like the business school classmate I saw at our five-year reunion who, when I complimented her sunglasses, mumbled something snarky about me blogging about them). But there will also be those who support or encourage or validate you, who volunteer to teach you or share their skills so that you can improve yours. And since you've already made the bold choice to step off the linear career path in favor of doing what feels right for you, you've probably already gotten some practice in valuing what you know will serve you over whatever everyone else thinks you should be doing.

When you take a career pause, one of the most exciting things you have at your disposal is *time*. It may not feel like that in the day-to-day, especially if you're scrambling to fit an hour for yourself into your daily rhythm. But at a high level, when you aren't going to the office every day and you don't have a specific return-to-work date and you aren't under a time crunch to get a new job or climb the ladder, you have freedom to do all the skill building or hobby dabbling you may have been curious about in the past. Yes, your pause is a time to spend with your family and focus on motherhood, but it also affords you a window to expand yourself personally and professionally. In fact, one mom I spoke to called the years she spent on a career break her "creative sabbatical," because one of the goals of her pause was to reevaluate her passions and make sure that if and when she returned to work, it was in a job that fulfilled her.

Pursuing hobbies, interests, and play is brave in a culture that has long emphasized productivity, pay, and profit. But with self-development books and courses aplenty, sewing and pottery classes readily available, and online tools that make it easy to build a website in minutes, it can feel like the options are endless. And that can be exciting, or overwhelming, or both. When you start to feel the itch to do something more, you might find yourself tackling looming questions around what you should do . . . and when . . . and perhaps most importantly, *why*.

What Is Personal Development?

Growth can mean many things and encompass many pursuits. For the purposes of this chapter, when I talk about personal development, I'm referring to activities you might engage in on your own because they are interesting or compelling to *you* and they help you grow personally, expand your interests, and feel engaged. Personal development can fall in any of these buckets—or even a few at once:

Hobbies: An activity done regularly and for enjoyment, not for pay and not necessarily because you want to pursue it professionally. Hobbies usually entail an activity—reading, yoga, knitting, collecting—and are often the closest things adults have to childlike play. Research shows that hobbies can reduce stress and improve mood.

Passion projects: A passion project can be big (Apple started as one!) or a small side gig that simply allows you to experiment with something new. Also known as a "labor of love," a passion project has more of a focused effort than a hobby and may have a more specific end goal. These projects are usually rooted in an idea that you've identified as deeply personal, but they come (at least for now) with limited financial pressure.

Learning/courses: You may want to learn a new skill, hone an old one, or just keep your toolbox sharp for an eventual return to work. In-person options are usually available at local universities or community colleges, while online platforms like MasterClass or Skillshare offer courses in everything from UI/UX design to strategic decision-making, gardening to Texas-style barbecue.

Volunteer work: If there's a cause or organization you're passionate about, and you've already worked out the finances associated with forgoing a salary, volunteering is a great way to stay involved in your community or contribute in a way that feels meaningful while also keeping practical skills sharp.

Self-improvement: Just like "passion project," "self-improvement" is a phrase that might inspire eye rolls, but I use it (and its cousin, "self-help") to refer to personal work—the talk therapy or physical therapy you engage in to feel better; the time you spend reading books about how to parent in ways that feel good or take care of yourself so you can take care of your family. Self-development podcasts and books saw a record boom following the pandemic—in 2020, the self-help book genre was a $10.5 billion business. Self-help podcasts are expected to be a $2.5 billion business by 2028. If this is the area you're most intrigued by, you're clearly not alone.

Your Kid Is Growing, You Can Too

A career pause is not a life pause. You may have put the day-job version of your life on hold (temporarily or otherwise) so that you could lean into motherhood and shift your focus to your family, but as we've discussed in these pages, this phase is for building community and connections, establishing your personal values, and evaluating what you want for your future. When you step into the full power of the pause, it becomes a time of immense growth—both because you learn skills in parenting and household management that can absolutely translate professionally, but also because you may find unexpected skills and talents you never knew you had.

"You have to be nimble and able to think in different ways and wear different hats as a mother because, say you have more than one kid, each of your kids is different. The way you interact with each of them will be different too," says Amri Kibbler, cofounder and CCO of HeyMama, a community for moms building families and careers. She also points out that as your kids adopt passions, you may find yourself discovering new activities whether you want to or not. "You'll end up engaging with the activities they're doing, and putting yourself into social situations where you are suddenly elected, like, treasurer of the Girl Scouts, learning to make spreadsheets because you have to." If you can expand and grow your abilities to accommodate things your kids are interested in, you certainly should do the same for the stuff that *you* are interested in.

Only about 40 percent of the mothers we spoke to for the AMP survey said they participate in an activity outside their role as a stay-at-home mom. Those activities included volunteering at their kids' schools or with a charity, working on a side business or passion project, taking a class to learn a new skill or get a professional certification, or helping a friend with a business endeavor. But of those four in ten mothers, a full 90 percent said that participating in their activity had a positive impact on their mood. Considering that stay-at-home moms have historically reported more depression, sadness, and anger, that's no small thing.

I felt immense satisfaction from launching the Mother Untitled blog, long before I had any sense of its future or career potential. It tapped into a side of myself that didn't get a ton of use during my earliest parenting days, and it provided me an opportunity to utilize my professional skills and apply them to a topic that I was deeply interested in. Research shows that hobbies or creative pursuits improve health and happiness, and the effects can linger for days. In a study of students who pursued creative hobbies, researchers found that even the day after participating in the activity, students showed a significant uptick in happiness. And not only can outside pursuits make you happier, but they can also improve your job performance. Studies have shown that those with creative hobbies are more likely to be considered helpful, collaborative, and creative at work (when rated by co-workers *and* self-rated)—you probably won't sit in on a performance review from your kids (don't they wish!), but if primary parent came with a job description, those might be the exact requirements.

If your hope is to eventually resume work in the same field where you were once employed, your activities might involve taking courses or certifications so you can stay connected to that field. But it's not just about getting back to work one day. Tovah Klein notes that staying engaged in their profession, at some level, can help mothers maintain the professional identity that can suffer during parenthood. "Are you not a doctor just because you're not right now seeing patients? You still have a medical degree, so how do you keep that piece of yourself lit up?" she asks. "Do you read journals? Do you meet with doctor friends? Do you go to some conferences just because it inspires you?" Whatever your field, staying connected to your line of work—through relationships and/or education—can help you hold on to the professional side you worked hard to cultivate, whether or not you decide to seek reemployment in that field down the line.

For Priscillia de Muizon, pursuing her passion helped her establish a *new* identity—one that felt like a better and more fulfilling fit than that of lawyer, her previous profession. During her time at home with her son, she, too, started a blog. "Now when people ask what I do, instead of saying, 'Well, I've left law and I'm trying to figure out what to do next,' I say, 'I'm a freelance writer and my blog is *Innovators of the Valley*,'" she says. "Instantly the conversation is so much more interesting."

Study Yourself

For some parents, there's no question about what passion project or personal development they want to devote time to; it's just a matter of finding the availability. You might have been waiting for the moment your kids start half-day preschool so you could sign up for tennis lessons or take the accounting or Spanish class you've always wanted to try. But sometimes the answer is less obvious—you're antsy to get out there and do something, but the pressure to use the time wisely feels real, and you're not sure what you want to do first. I've talked to plenty of moms who say they feel rusty enough that they can hardly remember what they like to do anymore. For them, the idea of picking up a hobby or "extra-curricular" is totally confounding.

Before you start throwing darts at a wall and hoping something sticks, do a bit of self-reflection. It's possible that you haven't had much opportunity to look inward given all the time you spend focused on your family. For you, "self-reflection" might sound like a self-indulgent woo-woo notion that you don't have time for. If that's the case, take a moment to consider the ways you study your kids. If you have a child who always gravitates toward musical instruments, who loves listening to records or insists on stopping to watch street musicians or scroll guitar performances on

YouTube, it has probably occurred to you that, *Wow, he really loves music. Maybe we should put him in lessons.* Perhaps his interest inspired you to take him to a live concert or buy him a toy guitar or introduce him to new artists. Self-reflection means taking the same lens through which you study your kid and turning it on yourself.

Jill Elliott, a former chief creative officer in Dallas, took a career break to raise her now tweenage daughter, and in that time she pivoted into owning her own creative studio. Her work includes training clients—often mothers—in the art of creativity. Elliott told me that the first step to identifying a hobby or passion is to pay attention to the content you consume. "I often find that what we consume both digitally and in real life is closely related to what inspires us to create," she says. "Start to notice what invites you to linger a bit longer in your day, and know that whatever it is, it might be a clue." For Elliott, the pieces of content she couldn't resist met at the intersection of home design, community, and painting, so she started gathering local adults for sip and paints. Then she decided to turn some of her paintings into custom wallpaper, which she used in her home remodel. Now she's launched her own wallpaper line.

Executive leadership coach Megan Martin Strickland seconds Elliott's advice. "If you find yourself always listening to the same types of podcasts, or reading the same types of news articles, take stock of that," she says. "Those are things that are really interesting to you, so you might want to start looking for opportunities in those areas, whether it's work or volunteering or just exploring." And sure, this could be something creative, like Jill Elliott's wallpaper. Another creative success story is Mimi Chan, a mother of two and serial venture-backed entrepreneur in Oakland, California, who reconnected to her lifelong interest in design and eventually opened a concierge interior design service after a five-year career pause. But it's just as likely that your personal passion will have nothing to do with creativity. Maybe the only way you can unwind at night is by doing a sudoku puzzle. Plenty of people find number crunching maddening—if you relish the logic inherent in identifying patterns in numbers, maybe data analysis would come naturally to you. It's certainly a skill that is endlessly applicable these days. I have a friend who used to work as a web producer and digital writer, but what she loves more than anything is reading. Now, after taking six years off to raise her kids, she's considering a career in library science. For now, she's starting by volunteering at her local public library branch. Baby steps.

There's age-old advice that when it comes to discovering passions in adulthood, we should start by looking at what we loved doing as kids. If you were a student athlete, team sports might still excite you. If you loved school and learning back then, maybe you'd enjoy continuing education classes now—all the joy of education without the pressure of grades. But my experience with Mother Untitled has taught me that for many mothers, raising children has opened their eyes to new talents and interests, whether due to the specific needs of their children or because parenting simply provides a new perspective on the world. A 2022 survey from the distance-learning platform Open Study College found that a third of women change their careers after having kids. Emily Nolan left her career as a plus-sized model when she became a mom to her son, Ollie. When he ended up having severe allergies, Emily noticed how passionate and deeply interested she became in advocating not only for her son, but for all children with similar conditions. Today Emily has followed her passion for advocacy and hosts a podcast, *My Kind of Life*, that offers resources for and interviews with parents of children with food allergies. She has also launched a series of online courses on parenting children with life-threatening allergies. Other mothers I've spoken to have developed a passion for local or national politics where they previously had none, both because they want to improve the world where they are raising their kids and, in the case of local politics, they feel more empowered to enact change.

For Olivia Metzger, mom of four in the Chicago suburbs, a desire to connect with other moms led to a passion she didn't expect. "I felt really isolated in early motherhood," she said. "But I knew there was this online community with babies that were posting pictures and it was kind of fun to get to know people that way." So she started following moms who were posting family-related content online and eventually began posting some of her own. She was surprised to find how much she enjoyed Instagram as a creative outlet. "It was originally motivated by the social aspect, but over time I became even more motivated by the creativity and the art and photos involved. I wanted to have a project that I owned and had full control over," she says.

WHAT ARE YOU UP TO?

Four in ten mothers on pause are engaged in an activity outside the home, according to the AMP survey. There's no one best way to spend your time outside of the home, but here's a look at where the moms we heard from are dedicating their time:

- Volunteering at school: 37 percent
- Working on a side business: 19 percent

- Taking a class to learn a new skill or hobby: 17 percent
- Volunteering for a charity: 16 percent
- Taking a class to receive a certification: 9 percent

A Marathon, Not a Sprint

When I ask women in our community when they make time for their side projects, those with school-aged kids usually say they take advantage of the quiet daytime hours. Those with younger kids say they take advantage of early mornings, nap times, or even after the bedtime hours. I remember those days. I would wait for my kids to fall asleep and then do an hour of writing while also kind of watching *Homeland* with my husband. It can feel like you're doing it all and yet moving *so* slowly. It was frustrating, because I felt like I would never be able to make this thing I truly cared about as big as I wanted it to be at the pace that I was moving. I had limited time allotted for this project, so I couldn't move fast.

In your "before" times, back when you had no kids, you may have gotten used to pouring hours into activities or projects you were passionate about, both personally and professionally. We've been told the story of the tortoise and the hare since childhood— "slow and steady wins the race"—but the reality is that today's work culture often rewards speed and efficiency. And yet, time is a finite resource. If you have intentionally taken a pause to stay at home, your hours for self-development will be limited. You simply do not have many extra moments to dedicate to extracurriculars, and you very likely don't *want* to give these activities more than a small window each day. After all, the AMP survey found that what stay-at-home mothers enjoy most about their pause is spending time with their kids and watching them grow. I wasn't willing to shift gears away from being with my kids when I first had the idea for Mother Untitled, so I had to accept (though somewhat begrudgingly) that planting the seeds would be the first step and it would take a while. I could launch a social media account or create blog content; I couldn't host events or do speaking engagements. At least not yet.

None of this means you shouldn't embark on activities dedicated to self-growth, only that it's important to make peace with the time you can allot to it and to be realistic about what's possible to get done in that time. The good news is that experts say you don't need endless hours of free time to make your self-development time worthwhile. "You don't need to think of it as a huge step like signing up for grad school," says Dara Astmann, a career coach specifically focused on moms figuring out their next step. "You can start by simply having a conversation with someone who's in the industry you're interested in, or by watching a YouTube or Coursera class. Try something that's easier to take on and try out in the limited time you have."

Julie Morgenstern says you should think of your time as twenty-minute units—dedicating one or two units, ideally daily, to whatever self-development you choose. Research backs up the idea of twenty-minute windows. Studies have shown that twenty minutes per day of exercise, meditation, reading, or making art can all have significant positive impacts on health and happiness. There's no harm in taking more time if you have it, but know that it's not three hours or nothing.

Chelsea Weissbaum, an artist and mother of twins, puts her

kids down for a nap each afternoon and then walks straight into her painting studio and sets her kitchen timer for thirty-five minutes. This same approach can be taken for any hobby or self-help. While in-person classes are probably more time-consuming, a single MasterClass lesson (each course is about twenty lessons) is only ten minutes. You'd be surprised how much you can get done in a short window.

If you're still tempted to throw up your hands and forgo the idea of personal growth until you have more time, remember the word that Jill Elliott told me is the secret to self-development: habitualizing. Taking small windows, regularly, will have a more significant payoff than using a big chunk of time only once in a while. "As you start any new habit, beginning in small doses at a consistent time of day helps the habit to stick. For me, that means working in short creative bursts alongside my morning coffee. Ten to fifteen minutes only, before the rest of my house is awake and needing me. Tying my creativity to my morning caffeine ties a new habit to a well-established one, ensuring that I make it happen." Start small, she says, with something doable. "You'll likely find the benefits and fun from this little sliver of time so rewarding that you'll start to sneak in a few extra minutes each day."

Just Do It

Ever since I came across my first Scholastic bookfair catalog and then graduated to *YM* and *Cosmo*, I was hooked on magazines. I stashed clippings and made collages for my teen bedroom wall. Yelp, Pinterest, Tumblr—if there was a platform dedicated to content and creation, I was the first one on. A combination of pictures, words, women, and deep thinking—that was my happy place. I'd gotten some of that from my work in advertising, but oftentimes the joy of play gave way to PowerPoints and data reporting, which didn't exactly fill my cup. For years, I'd wanted to work with content, but I was on the brand marketing path, and no matter how hard I tried to weave content into the job description, it never really happened for me in my professional world. Eventually I accepted that women's lifestyle content might be my leisure interest, but it was never going to be my career calling.

When I stepped into mostly motherhood, I let myself scour the internet and blogs and women-focused communities again. The urge to try my hand at content came back, and this time I had a topic I was eager to write about. And so I went out on that limb and started a blog. I had plenty of nerves and not a small bit of embarrassment (Who did I think I was to be blogging? I didn't have a platform; I wasn't a respected "thinker" on topics about motherhood), and I could have listed about a thousand reasons why I should have stuck to what I knew. Including, but certainly not limited to, the fact that the endeavor didn't come with any clear path to making money. But I was excited again, and that had to be worth *something*.

As I mentioned earlier, some people totally understood my blog. Most did not. When people asked, "So, what is it exactly? How will you make a profit?" I answered honestly: "It's a project right now. It doesn't pay, but I'm enjoying it."

Side projects are quite often diminished. It's all too easy to internalize the cultural narrative that unless something is making money it doesn't have value. But if you've learned one thing in the chapters leading up to this one, I hope it's that some of the most profound and life-altering work can be unpaid. That includes creative projects, volunteering, and hobbies, because they all have long-term potential—professionally *and* personally. So rather than wait until the financial upside is clear or until you can do something all out, make like Nike and, yes, just do it.

Consider Christine Merritt, who took a break from her career in tech after having twins and moved to Austin, Texas, when her kids were eight years old. "When we moved to Austin, I started hearing a lot of country music, and I really took to it; I liked the element of storytelling and the fact that you could hear a complete beginning, middle, and end in a song," she says. Merritt had no musical background—she never played a musical instrument or sang in a choir or performed in any way—but she couldn't help but notice her newfound appreciation for country music. She'd always liked going to concerts, but this felt different. She could tell there was a seed being planted. Then, one evening after kissing her son goodnight, she noticed that he was rubbing his cheek. "It looked like he was rubbing my kiss off because he's too old. And I didn't say anything about it, but I must have had a wistful look in my eye, like 'Oh, sad, he's gotten too old for this,' because when I got up to leave the room he said, 'Mom, I wasn't rubbing it off. I was rubbing it in.'" To Merritt, it was the perfect country lyric.

So, on a whim, she wrote a song, "The next day, I don't even know how it happened, I sat down at my husband's desk and wrote about a child looking backward at his mom on his wedding day," Merritt says. "It just came out and I was like, I can hear this song in my head, but I don't know what to do with it." Had Merritt listened to the myriad of seemingly reasonable doubts she had, she might never have taken pen to paper. First of all, she was a techie, not a songwriter. Then there was the fact that she didn't sing or play an instrument, so she didn't even know what to do with a song once it was written. Not to mention the question of . . . why? There are a zillion songwriters in the world, she knew, and it could have felt presumptuous to think that she could join their ranks or that anyone would be interested in the song she wanted to write. If she had not been on a pause, she might have shooed away the urge to write entirely, if for no other reason than there wasn't time for trying something so brand-new. But rather than succumb to her own insecurities and doubts, or letting the urge pass because there simply wasn't space to try, Merritt wrote lyrics.

As soon as the song was written, Merritt could hear it in her head. A male country vocal, a tune she could hum but not compose. With one quick google, she found a website where you can hire someone to sing a song you write. She connected with a male country vocalist and told him her vision. "A few days later he sent me a recording of him playing guitar and singing the song I wrote, and I had tears streaming down my face," she says. "My life changed forever in that moment."

In the time since, Merritt has immersed herself in getting a songwriting education. She joined an online songwriting community, hired a songwriting coach, took an online course, and even went to a retreat in Nashville to collaborate with other songwriters and vocalists. Today, she is working toward getting a second college degree, this one in songwriting.

Your passion project may not come pouring out of you in some grand, life-altering moment like it did for Merritt. But if you notice an inkling of interest or curiosity around a topic or an activity, or a desire to learn more, do yourself a favor and listen to it. Whether you've always wanted to see if your secret business idea could get off the ground, or you're curious to revisit the instrument you played in high school, or you've always wondered if you'd be any good at speaking a second language, now is the time. There's something about picking up a new skill in your thirties and forties that feels refreshing instead of intimidating—probably because it's easier to see now that no one is really watching or judging, and those who are generally are rooting for your success. You can always second-guess yourself later, or decide it's not for you, but if you don't nurture that tiny flame of curiosity, you'll never find out if it could grow into a fiery passion.

Beware of Imposter Syndrome

Imposter syndrome—that nagging voice in your head that might insist you don't deserve whatever success comes your way—can sow seeds of doubt whenever you start something new. Whether you're a novice nutritionist, coach, artist, writer, consultant, designer, winemaker, or community soccer coach, there is the inevitable question of "Am I trained enough?" You may worry that the answer is no, or that you'll be found out or discounted. If you notice these thoughts, know you're in good company. A study from the consulting firm KPMG found that 75 percent of female executives across various industries have experienced imposter syndrome at some point in their careers. And the truth is that no matter what you take on—especially if it's something relatively new to you—there will always be someone more qualified or more experienced. But as I tell my kids when they're bickering over who got the bigger dessert: only worry about yourself. It doesn't matter if someone else has years of experience on you, as long as you're learning and growing.

Merritt says she was plagued with imposter syndrome when she started songwriting. "I had a self-defeating dialogue in my head when I started," she says. So she decided to hold herself accountable to a learning schedule. That way, no one could claim she wasn't putting in the work. "I just keep chipping away at this, totally on my own time. Sure, there was this initial creative gift that just came out of me, but I work at it constantly and cowrite with someone new every weekday. Education and collaboration are two things that definitely keep me going."

Remember, there's room for more than one success story in any area of personal development. Someone else can be deserving of success, and you can too . . . *at the same time.* If you're showing up and putting in the hours—at whatever your passion—then you belong there. But if you can't shake the feeling that you somehow slipped through the cracks, remember this: recognizing your imposter syndrome is the first step toward eradicating it. "Seeing that the fear is what's holding you back is really helpful in dissolving that fear," says Amri Kibbler.

Make School Volunteering Work for You

I recently declared that I would no longer volunteer at school functions unless my husband does too, and then promptly signed him up to be a tour guide for prospective families at our kids' elementary school. He's a good sport and funny and charismatic, so he was a big hit on the tour circuit, but my point was made nonetheless (at least in my own household): when it comes to volunteering for kid-related activities, women are expected to take on a disproportionate load. This is true even if both parents have plenty of other responsibilities vying for their time. Research bears this out, though if you've ever been to a school function with parent volunteers you probably don't need a study to convince you. But while I absolutely believe that dads are as valuable to the classroom volunteer circuit as moms and are just as equipped to chaperone a museum field trip or lead a craft station at the class Halloween party (and I'll stand on that soapbox for years if I have to), that doesn't mean that moms *shouldn't* volunteer. Contributing your time to your kids' school while on a career pause has significant merit and can be a great launching pad for personal development . . . as long as it's done strategically.

If one of your parenting goals is to model for your kids what it looks like to be a good school or local citizen, volunteering—in the classroom, on a school committee, as a coach, or at an event—is a great way to do it. When I was on a full career pause, I was the school liaison to a charitable organization with whom we partnered on a semiannual basis. On the day I lugged a giant bag of toys three blocks from the school to the neighborhood holiday donation drive, my three-year-old thought I was the most important person on the planet. If you want to strengthen relationships with certain people in the community—administrators, teachers, or specific other parents—scanning the sign-up sheets for those names and volunteering for the same activities can certainly foster those relationships.

Volunteering—at school, but really anywhere—can also be an exercise in experimentation when it comes to personal development. If you are trying to expand your skill set or try out different interests, there are usually opportunities to get involved in various capacities and at different commitment levels. Megan Martin

Strickland told me about a client—a stay-at-home mom for seven years—who spent years trying out different volunteer roles within her children's school. Eventually, she found her way to running the school fundraiser. "She helped with the annual gala, which raised a significant amount of money each year, and she worked with vendors across the board for every part of the event," Strickland says. When this client was ready to return to work, "we helped her position her school experience within her résumé so she got a job as an in-house event planner."

Kristin Rumpf, a mom of two teenagers in El Paso, Texas, and a former NASA engineer, wasn't looking to build a specific new skill set when she joined the school PTA. She just wanted experience working with people who weren't in her NASA world. "I jumped into the PTA so I could get in touch with the community and meet businesses and expand my horizons beyond my little engineering window," she says. Doing work with people with new backgrounds helped her expand her interpersonal skills and think bigger in terms of where she could focus when she was ready to press play on her career.

Almost across the board, schools welcome parent contribution. They need help raising money, facilitating communications, running reading groups, liaising with the school board or other local government organizations, organizing athletic activities, working backstage for the school play, and on and on and on. If there is something you want to try, even if there isn't a pre-existing volunteer opportunity, there's a good chance you can reach out and create one. And because it's free labor, you'll probably need to make a smaller time commitment than work you'd do for pay. Opportunities could be every week, but if all you can promise is once a month or once a quarter, that will probably work too. The important thing is that whatever you've always been curious about—planting the school garden or working the book fair or being a treasurer or secretary of a committee—now's your chance.

While school might be the easiest place to volunteer since you're already sending a child (or children) there, there are endless organizations, online and in person, where you could offer your time. Jacqui Ivey stepped down from her job as a teacher after having her kids, so rather than volunteer at school she chose to give her time to the kid ministry at her church. "I loved feeling a part of something that was bigger than me," she says. She started by volunteering on Sundays, but as time went on, she got invited into leadership roles and eventually into a staff position. Ali Webbinaro paused her full-time career after having kids but wanted to participate in some activity that would give her professional purpose and personal development, so she applied to join the board of her local co-op health food store. The meetings were one Thursday a month, after her kids were asleep. "I thought it would get me into a different frame of mind—that I could use my human resource experience and my organizational management experience and do something good for my community," she says. Webbinaro ended up enjoying it enough that she wanted to get more involved locally. She joined the local planning board, and then the League of Women Voters, and ended up cofounding a market featuring farm-grown or hand-made goods from local vendors in her area. "All those things were a reminder that I'm not just Izzy and Zach's mom. It made me feel like I'm doing something good for my brain and my body, *and* I'm showing my kids that I'm still out there participating in really important stuff."

So why do I say you should volunteer strategically? To start, the hope is that you are doing it out of interest or curiosity, not obligation. Strickland says her clients often admit they give their time to the school because they think they should, not because they want to. "I hear from women, 'Well, I'm not working, and I feel all this guilt to be there for my kids and volunteer,' so they're in the classroom, they're getting their hands dirty, they're on the board with sometimes the most efficient meetings I've ever been a part of, but they feel like they have no time to themselves," she says. This is not the goal! You didn't stop working for pay so that you can work for your kids' school for free, unless that's how you *enjoy* spending your time. "I tell these moms, figure out what you actually like, and do that. If it's volunteering for story time, then maybe when your kids are older you can work at a nonprofit and do literacy training."

Before signing up for anything, you should also consider how much time you have available to you and what you are getting in exchange. Yes, it's volunteering, but you're still trading resources. The school or community organization you're volunteering for is offering you purpose, companionship, or newfound marketable skills, but you are offering them your existing skills and the hours of your day. That is a very valuable resource.

HOW SELF-HELP CAN SERVE YOUR RETURN TO WORK (IF YOU SO CHOOSE)

I mentioned earlier that personal development comes in many forms: hobbies, passion projects, learning and courses, volunteer work, and self-help. It may seem obvious how the first four can help keep you sharp and connected should you choose to unpause your professional life. But the self-help aspect—the therapy or other emotional and physical work you do to stay healthy and feel your best—might not seem as clearly connected. It's important to remember that even if you eventually decide to return to the exact same industry you left, you are a different person after becoming a parent. Your priorities have likely changed, and maybe the way you view the world has changed too.

It can be hard to manage other people's expectations when they've only known you as your pre-child self. Ali Webbinaro says that the self-work she did during her pause helped her set new professional boundaries when she decided to go back to work. "I had done enough work on myself to know that I wasn't going to take the work stress home in the same way anymore," she says. "A big thing I was working on was control of myself and of my body, and now I'm more grounded and I have a lot more confidence in my ability to handle challenging moments and my ability to be in the workforce while still doing what is right for me and my family."

Parenting IS Personal Development

If you're still early in your pause, or even still considering your pause, self-development may be far from your mind. You may want nothing more than time with your kids and a break from the work grind, or maybe you just don't have the capacity for anything more than parenting. Been there. But what I've found is that those low-bandwidth moments actually accelerate growth.

I end up doing deeper inner work in those times because so much is being asked of me. After all, I was never challenged to work on patience in the office. No one was pulling at my emotional heartstrings during our Monday-morning conferences, so I always considered myself pretty calm even in times of office chaos.

When I became a parent, I had to reassess myself. Was I really so calm and patient? Maybe not, but as mom of two Jacqui Ivey reminded me, "When it comes to parenting and the areas where you need to grow . . . well, you will either recognize them and improve, or they'll wreck you. You can't hide because kids bring it all out." The upside is that the parenting moments that demand a lot of us also build a lot *in* us. So before you chastise yourself for not working on yourself more, know that just by showing up for your kids, you are developing a new, stronger self. The work is happening, whether you know it or not.

Today's generation of parents are often referred to as "cycle breakers." It's a term coined by psychologists to refer to the conscious parenting work required to raise a cohort of kids that is softer and safer, and whose feelings are well tended to. Cycle breaking is about changing multigenerational patterns, so that the way you were raised isn't automatically the way your children are raised. It involves rewriting reactive patterns and actively separating your own ego from, say, your child's temper tantrum, so that you can sit there and hold space for their meltdown rather than losing your cool at the irrationality of it all. It's exhausting and it's real work—and it results in skills that will absolutely translate, should you decide to return to work.

During her time navigating the Trump administration, Nancy Pelosi once said that nothing trained her better for handling tantrums than parenting. She has since called motherhood the ultimate leadership training ground. The job search site Indeed even has a bucket for "caregiver skills" that includes effective communication, empathy, flexibility, time management, organization, and observation. I would add patience, creativity, and attunement.

Add to that the fact that today's parents are constantly presented with content encouraging us to get introspective about how we raise our kids. It's been said that millennial parents spend $231.6 million on parenting books and $141 million on parenting apps a year. In our work to grow as parents, we are working to grow as people. So even if you aren't intentionally doing personal development work, if you aren't focused on a specific hobby or passion project, you are still building practical skills and soft skills that will be applicable in your next phase.

Tovah Klein says the skills you develop as a primary parent, both the emotional and practical ones, are a clear result of the management work required to run a family. "Organizing a house, even at the most minimal level, means having enough toilet paper on hand and keeping an eye on the clothes that each child has outgrown," she says. "But then there's the management required when paying attention to, say, what does my child need emotionally? I think we underplay that. Mothers pay such close attention to the developmental trajectory of their kids, and if there's anything that's needed in leadership, it's that level of nuance. If you're leading a team, what each team member needs to be successful is slightly different. There's the common goal of the team, but each person is going to contribute something unique and have different needs at different times. The ability to recognize that is being developed every day when raising children."

And this is true throughout your kids' upbringing, not just when they are babies needing constant care or toddlers who require patience in the face of a tantrum. "You know how when your kids are born, it's as if you are reborn?" Lizzie Assa, founder of the Workspace for Children, asked me. "I feel like now, as a parent of teens, I'm in a whole new realm. I feel like I'm having this rebirth of learning how to show up in parenting and, similarly, how to show up in life."

Power Practice: Getting Personal

This chapter looked at personal development and the various ways we can expand ourselves during a career pause. It offered guidance for finding what type of development is compelling to you, how to get started, and why you shouldn't fret if you can't stomach this additional work right now. Even if you're not yet ready to pursue any hobbies or side projects or learning opportunities, identifying what interests you is a worthwhile endeavor. Use this worksheet to home in on what piques your curiosity and sparks your joy, so you know where to start when the time comes.

What podcasts do you listen to most frequently? What category of nonfiction books do you read? Is there another type of content you particularly enjoy?

_____

_____

_____

What are the social media accounts you tend to linger on?

_____

_____

_____

When you have five to ten minutes to kill, what do you do?

_____

_____

_____

What hobbies did you have as a child or a teenager? Which were you most passionate about?

_____

_____

_____

What, if anything, do your answers to the previous questions have in common? If they seem to have nothing in common, can you imagine a way you could connect them?

_____

_____

_____

What is one project or task you tackled in the past year that you were most excited about or proud of? Was there anything you were surprised to enjoy?

_____

_____

_____

How could you create more of these experiences in the next six months?
The next year?

_____

_____

_____

9

Put Your Pause in Your Career Portfolio and Return to Paid Work (If You Want!)

FALSE BELIEF

*A gap in my résumé is a major red flag
to future employers.*

NEW NARRATIVE

*Primary parenthood is not a résumé gap. It's a
chapter in which I shifted my priorities
to grow and learn in new ways.*

I'M WRITING THIS final chapter in the fall, about a month into the school year. For the first time, my kids are both in school all day, and at the same place. Bodie is in second grade, and Lyla is in pre-K. Getting two kids out of the house each morning and leaving them in the care of their elementary school teachers from eight thirty to three has been a big (exciting! but also nerve-racking!) transition, and it's one that has prompted me, again, to reevaluate my goals, rhythms, and childcare. Because the children are in school, and because I discovered a new professional passion during my pause, I have ramped up my career. Today, I work Monday through Thursday from nine to four thirty (we have an after-school babysitter for ten to fifteen hours a week), and on Fridays until two p.m., at which point I log off and head to school pickup.

Transitioning back to work has felt just as complicated and fraught with emotion as the decision to pause my professional career. I feel simultaneously ready for this next step and grief-ridden that I'm no longer fully present and available for my family. When people ask me what I do, I once again find myself stumbling over my words, but this time it's because I've gotten used to saying, "I'm mostly at home with my kids." Those moments when I'm tongue-tied are a helpful reminder that we can redefine our identities as often as we want, and that we will quickly get used to whatever becomes our new normal. Parents, and humans, are always evolving, and thank goodness for that.

The passage of time is one thing we have no control over. The circumstances that led to your pause will change, because if nothing else, your kids will grow. They say the days are long but the years are short, and it's true—the years when you and your kids are both at home full-time will seem to have come and gone quickly once you're on the other side. If you took your pause at a different time, maybe when your kids were in middle or high school, because that's when you felt an urge to be more present for the family, well, I hear those years fly by too. The impetus for your pause doesn't particularly matter; the point is that parenting situations evolve, and whatever factors led you to take a break will change over time. And whether your kids are going to school for the first time or graduating, none of it means you need to reenter the workforce. But these moments do provide a good opportunity to take stock of how you spend your days and decide if you are as fulfilled as you want to be. They are a chance to consider your next phase, whatever that may look like.

What Do You Want?

Mothers often tell me that when their youngest child heads to kindergarten, they feel an enormous societal pressure to get back to work. There's this sense that without a child by their side from nine to three, they have no "excuse" not to be working. But let's be honest, between the sick days, holidays, the family administration, and all the school emails, being a primary parent with school-age children is still a full-time job with little margin to take care of yourself. And if you do want to return to some version of working outside the home, rushing into it without careful consideration of your new professional life runs counter to all the important self-work you've done during this phase. Pausing your career is not like pausing a Netflix show—the goal is not to eventually press play and pick up right where you left off, as if no time has passed. If you do start again, the goal is to do so with more knowledge about yourself, your values, and your priorities, which will hopefully inform the choices you make about how, where, and when to work.

On the day that you send your child into the big-kid classroom for the first time (and post your obligatory but adorable first-day-of-school photo), you may find that you've been so preoccupied with getting to this moment that you've given no thought to what you'll do next. That's totally fair. And normal. In 2021, I rolled out an offering on Mother Untitled called M.U. Mentors. It was a roster of women who had taken their own career pauses and established themselves in a variety of fields, and now they were offering advice to the stay-at-home moms coming up behind them. I had a range of professionals, from a marketing expert who could speak about freelancing to a nutritionist for interested moms to start learning about careers in dietary health, but the single most booked resource was our return-to-work coach, Megan Martin Strickland, who advises women on navigating careers and motherhood. It became clear to me that when women start thinking about returning to work, many of them still need clarity on what they want to do, or what they want this next iteration to look like.

So, first things first, if you don't feel excited about work and you don't need to jump back in for financial reasons, take the time to explore. Allow yourself a minute to get your bearings. Returning to work is a bold decision, and you need to know what you want to optimize for right now: Is it meaningful work, in which case maybe you need additional time to do the personal exploration required to figure out what lights you up? Or is it getting back to a regular paycheck, in which case you might be willing to trade on the perfect employer to find a gig that fits your lifestyle? Just as you probably didn't jump into a pause overnight, you shouldn't jump back into work without doing so thoughtfully. Anna McKay, founder of Parents Pivot, a training and coaching company that specializes in parents who are reentering the workforce, notes that while we all operate on our own timetables, six months to a year is a reasonable window for identifying the right next steps.

Once you've done that, the odds are that you'll decide to relaunch your professional career in some fashion. Roughly 80 percent of parents currently on career breaks for childcare reasons are interested in returning to work, and companies are eager to meet these candidates. About a third of *Fortune* 50 companies now have return-to-work programs for midcareer professionals, and according to a LinkedIn survey of workers and hiring managers, about half of employers believe candidates with career breaks are an untapped talent pool. But what parents want out of work is often different than what they wanted pre-kids, and pay isn't always the highest priority. The AMP survey revealed that the majority of mothers seeking to return valued flexibility and less stress above all else. Of those who said they were ready to explore reentry, flexibility was the most-cited consideration (a full 85 percent of mothers flagged it), followed by the stress level of the role (74 percent). Only then did salary make the list (71 percent).

One factor that fell toward the bottom of the list: job title. A mere 21 percent of returners ranked job titles as extremely or very important to them, and that stat matters. You might remember from chapter 1 how important titles in the workplace have been, historically, to women in particular. I was absolutely one of those women—reveling in my appointment as a digital strategist at an ad agency, and later, as a brand director at a start-up. I was eager to put the new titles on my résumé as soon as possible. Marissa Mast, a mom of two young children in Phoenix, Arizona, and formerly in marketing at a big tech company, felt similarly. "For so many of us growing up, it was cool to be the 'girl boss' and, thus, a workaholic," she says. "And then you realize, not only is that not sustainable, but that's actually not what you want for your life right now." What she wants now, she says, is a company that will respect her out-of-office message when she's taking days off. "I used to be the person that worked during every 'out of office.' Now I know I was setting a bad standard for my team in doing that. I think once you have kids you realize so much about what's really important, and how to make work be just work, and not your whole identity."

Bettina Cisneros is another mom who figured out what she wanted by realizing, first, what she didn't. "I had spent most of my career in start-ups, and in those jobs you often feel like the whole world is on your shoulders," she says. "I wanted to go to a place where I wouldn't feel like the sky was falling if I went to a parent-teacher conference in the middle of the day." She ended up returning to a large, established organization so she wouldn't feel the singular burden of holding up an entire department.

These culture questions are important, but you should also consider content. What do you actually want to *do*? McKay says the first step is to look at how you spent your time during your break, when you weren't getting paid. "When we make choices about where to spend our time that isn't financially motivated, we gravitate toward things we are naturally interested in," she says. "One of my clients was really interested in operations and logistics—she set up a whole bus schedule in her neighborhood because it didn't have a busing system yet for her kids' school. She really enjoyed navigating those kinds of logistics and she ended up going into a project manager role for a marketing firm. Looking at those seeds of how you choose to spend your time can tell you a lot about what you might want to do for paid work."

If you know you want to return to work but aren't sure in what context, you might want to test the waters with a temporary solution. If you were once a teacher but you're not sure you want to go back full-time, a baby step might be working as a sub, or as a subject specialist, where you aren't necessarily needed five full days a week. Contract, freelance, or consulting projects can be a stepping stone for moms who once worked in corporate America. The marketing consulting work I did early in my pause was helpful in providing income, but it also taught me that I didn't want traditional marketing roles any longer. Starting full-time employment takes a tremendous amount of effort, and once you do you might feel compelled to stick it out for at least a year, so experimenting with shorter-term commitments can uncover valuable information about what you do, and absolutely do not, want.

After all this soul-searching, you may decide that you're not ready to return to work. Or that you simply don't want to. Too many women feel pressure to return to work because their kids are out of the house during the day, but parenting is demanding no matter what stage your kids are in. "My husband and I just recently had a conversation about my returning to work full-time, and we ultimately decided it wasn't right for this moment," says Zara Hanawalt. "I don't know if that's ever going to be something I want to do again. Having ownership over my schedule and my time is really valuable to me, and I think that will be the case even once my kids are in school all day every day . . . even when they are driving themselves to school. I like to have that time to focus on the home."

During my interviews for this book, as well as the countless interviews I've done to help build the Mother Untitled community, I've spoken to women who downshifted their paid work to make space for family life when their children were babies, toddlers, tweens, teens, or applying for college. Every stage is unique, every family is unique. There is no one path or setup that makes sense. And if you've learned anything during your personal pause, I hope it's that your career doesn't need to follow anyone else's timetable. Taking more time to focus on day-to-day caregiving and keeping yourself strong and healthy alongside your family is a modern and ambitious choice. Navigating the onslaught of new experiences as your children grow takes tremendous work and inevitably involves expanding your network, sense of self, and purpose. So if you've gotten to this final chapter only to realize, "Hey, I don't want to return after all," consider that a win. You've zeroed in on what you want, and what's best for your family, and gaining that knowledge is why we're here.

Telling Your Story

Nearly 70 percent of U.S. workers have an employment gap on their résumé. If you're looking for a job and feeling anxious about the years that your résumé doesn't account for, know that you're not alone.

In its survey of employees and managers, LinkedIn found that 56 percent of workers said they acquired new skills and sharpened old ones during their professional break. More than half of the women surveyed said they are better at their jobs now than they were before their pause. Still, we have a ways to go before we can rely on employers to perceive gaps in work history as a training ground for future positions. And that's especially the case when you take your pause for the purpose of raising a family. A survey from job search company Indeed found that nearly three-quarters of stay-at-home moms reported encountering bias in the hiring process as a result of their choice to take a break. The LinkedIn survey found that 20 percent of hiring managers will reject a candidate when they see a career gap.

But your story is yours to tell, and if you have the scripts and the language to speak to your pause with authority and confidence, you can help hiring managers recognize a pause for what it is: a detour off the traditional path that comes with its own set of additive skills, not a mindless vacation where your professional abilities atrophy.

If you've learned anything from these pages, I hope it's that there's no shame in taking a break. It's a source of power, and I hope it's a point of pride for you. If so, communicate that. Address your break head-on, and resist any temptation to brush it under the rug. "When I interviewed for jobs, I told people that every change I've made is intentional," says Nina Lai, a corporate communications professional who took a three-year career break before returning to a full-time C-suite role at consumer electronics company Lenovo. "This was true of every role and every industry I've moved to, and the same applied to when I took time to pause and take care of family. There, I was doing the role of ten different people, so I put it in a business context: I was running from the receptionist all the way up to the CEO, and there were all these decisions I had to make on a daily basis," she says.

There's a reason you paused, and you have new tools as a result, but it's your responsibility to share that in job interviews, just as it would be up to any candidate to explain how their current job has equipped them for the next one. Don't avoid the topic and get angry that a potential employer doesn't see the value in it. If your career path seems nontraditional, "a hiring committee is not going to connect the dots for you, you have to do it for them," says futurist and "change navigator" April Rinne. "When you do that and tell your story, and go to the effort to create what I call your 'portfolio narrative,' you can wow them to such a degree that no person on a ladder is ever going to be able to." By simply giving context to your break, you are already improving your odds. The LinkedIn survey found that 51 percent of employers are more likely to call a candidate back once they know the *why* of their career pause.

But telling your story is not a matter of justifying your time away. It's about positioning those years as the value add they are. Research conducted at the Rutgers Center for Women in Business found that employees who have worked as unpaid caregivers bring meaningful skills to the workplace that "positively impact culture, retention, and ultimately the bottom line," according to the *Harvard Business Review*. These skills include empathy, efficiency, persistence, ability to prioritize tasks, patience, anticipating needs, multitasking, and more. The authors assigned the skills to three buckets: humanity, productivity, and "cognitivity," which describes "the wide range of mental and emotional work necessary for the organization to maintain culture, connect people, and ensure smooth operations." The bottom line of their research: these are the very skills that companies need. When sharing your story of your time at home, don't be modest. Lean into these all-too-rare abilities and how they can positively impact your work performance.

How you craft your story will shift depending on the work you're pursuing. If you're returning to the field in which you previously worked, your work experience is still relevant and didn't evaporate just because you stepped away for a period. Don't shrug off the years you put in as if they were a lifetime ago (even if it feels that way). Your story should also include your efforts to stay on top of changes in your field, as well as the ways in which your newfound skills will enhance the work you did before. If you're pivoting into something new, identify what skills from your previous employment translate well and then identify the experiences you've had, in volunteering, parenting, side projects, or helping friends, that lend themselves to your new pursuit.

I'm not going to lie—heading back into a job search can feel intimidating. When I began to increase my work hours, I periodically found myself in rooms of women who'd never left the workforce. They had the big titles I once dreamed about, and there were times when I wanted to cower in a corner rather than remind people of all the ways my toolbox grew as a stay-at-home mother. But that's going to happen to anyone in the throes of a job search, and I quickly learned that positioning myself with confidence in those spaces required highlighting my clear growth path and the full picture of what my years at home looked like.

That full picture is what April Rinne is referring to when she plugs the "portfolio narrative." You might remember from chapter 1 that she emphasizes having not just a résumé but a full portfolio, which includes the kind of skills that speak to your qualifications and abilities as a worker that might not be included in a traditional CV. "When you zoom out, you see that you're actually a bunch of things that you do and are committed to, like the service or the sports or community engagements you might not typically include. What those things demonstrate is that you show up and practice at something every single week. You've got discipline, you've got commitment, you've got community."

Should You Include Your Pause on Your Résumé?

Yes, and.

Yes, you should account for the years when you were not at a traditional employer and call the break what it was. Chinue Richardson, whose story you heard in chapter 3 and who worked at a law firm before her career break and now works as in-house counsel at a financial services tech company, was advised by an HR professional early in her search to clearly call out her pause. "I wrote 'career sabbatical to care for children,'" she says. "The minute I included that, I got so much more interest in my résumé. I included bullet points just like I did for my other jobs: I was caring for a four-year-old and a six-month-old and I highlighted some of my responsibilities. One hiring manager I spoke to said, 'I was so happy to see that on your résumé.' Putting it on there conveyed a sense of importance of that role . . . because it is very important. It came off as, 'I'm proud to have done this work,' which I was, and I am. I think people respect it if you respect it."

And, you should add all the sub-bullets and details of any projects you did or experience you gained during your pause. If you advised a friend's company, add it. If, for example, you volunteered to chair your kids' school's Family Education Forum (it's me, I did that), then include the full requirements of that experience, including recruiting, communications, and organization. If you did work for the PTA or led a school committee, that should go on the résumé too. And if you're reading this and thinking "But I didn't do any of that," that's fine. Leading a home is work enough, and there's plenty to fill up some sub-bullets when you stop and consider the workload.

Did you run a parent committee at your child's school? If so, consider language like . . .

Lead, Parent Committee | Led committee of 20+ fellow parents dedicated to enhancing student learning outcomes; pitched new classroom technologies, implemented monthly guest speaker program, and streamlined process for receiving special education services.

Did you help your neighborhood association? If so, consider language like . . .

Planning Board Member, ABC Association | Collaborated with local leaders to identify key initiatives to improve the quality of the community, managed budgeting review, led annual planning meeting, researched and presented an implementation plan for series of infrastructure improvements.

Here's how Kristin Rumpf, the former NASA engineer who took a twelve-year pause, accounted for her break on LinkedIn:

STAY-AT-HOME PARENT
Rumpf Household · Full-time

For the past 12 years, I have served as a full time parent and primary caregiver to my 2 children. I have had primary household management responsibilities, including managing family schedules, meal planning and preparation of meals, handling medical issues, household tasks such as cleaning, maintenance and repairs, budgeting and financial management, transportation, and any other duties that arose. During these years, I have also served in a variety of volunteer activities, which have helped me develop a number of skills. I have served as a Girl Scout troop leader, where I was responsible for planning group activities, managing requirements, and group fundraising activities. I also serve [as] membership manager for a Cub Scout pack, where I manage group training requirements and update the troop roster and membership details. I have served in a variety of roles in our local PTA. I have served as communications coordinator where I coordinated the weekly newsletter, PTA website, and Facebook pages. I have served as PTA Secretary, worked on various fundraising activities, and served as special projects chair where I organized a family picnic for 700+ families and managed the fundraising and installation of a sound system for the school cafeteria. I helped to found a new chapter of MOPS (Mothers of Preschoolers), where I served as a group leader, ran fundraisers and served as member care coordinator to provide meals and other services to group members. Through these activities, I have learned a variety of relevant skills, including multitasking, organization, communication, delegating, budgeting, conflict resolution, group management, collaboration, and coordination of multiple variables.

What Might Your Return to Work Look Like?

There are many different ways to shift out of a career pause. Sure, you can return to traditional full-time employment, but today's workforce offers more creative solutions than ever before. You could work part-time or freelance or full-time from home. You could do a job share (where you and another employee split days or workload to account for one full-time job) or launch an entrepreneurial endeavor. Companies are increasingly offering options that may be more appealing than full time to employees who bring a lot to the table. Johnson & Johnson, Costco, JPMorgan

Chase, and Boston Consulting Group are just some of the companies offering benefits, including health insurance, to part-time workers, according to the *Harvard Business Review*. Some companies offer "returnships," two- to six-month internships that offer training and mentorship, usually with a path to full-time employment on the other side.

In polling the Mother Untitled community, I've found that freelance, consulting, contract, and other flexible work are especially popular return options. It makes sense. It's hard to go from being the master of your daily schedule to adhering to a hard-and-fast office clock. But all work options have drawbacks, and it's important to understand what you're giving up if you choose to forgo a full-time gig. It will probably come as no surprise that the biggest draws of salaried work are benefits (health insurance, 401(k), paid time off) and a steady paycheck. If you have a partner who has already been carrying the family on their health insurance, this may not be an issue, but for many workers, good health insurance is crucial. And getting paid even on the days when you're home with a sick kid, or maybe even on spring break, is no small thing.

Even still, the lure of working for yourself, and on your own schedule, can be hard to resist. The U.S. freelance market is growing at a rapid rate—the number of workers who rely exclusively on freelance grew 25 percent in 2021 (to 17 million people!), and about half of the freelancers in the United States are women. But freelance comes with its own set of challenges: if you have a certain income target, freelancing can require a certain amount of hustle to bring in new clients. If you have a strong network of small business owners or a clear skill set like marketing, content, social media, accounting, web development, design, administration, or operational management, you have an advantage in entering freelance and consulting. If you're looking to do independent contract work, like working as a school substitute, you may retain schedule flexibility, but on the flip side you can get called in at a moment's notice. There are pros and cons to any job, at any time in your life—just make sure you aren't glamorizing any option so much that you don't look at the whole picture before making a major life change.

If any single type of work has been glamorized over the past decade, it's entrepreneurship. Owning and running your own business is showcased on social media with hashtags like #NoDaysOff or #BossBabe, and the picture painted often includes fabulous work dinners or conferences, jet-setting, or speaking at exciting panels. You might get these opportunities, but even in the best of cases you will dedicate far more time to the grind work necessary to get a company off the ground. Running a business of any scale, especially one that you're financially or emotionally invested in, is time and headspace intensive. Unlike freelancing or consulting, where you can hold boundaries around the hours you're available, running a business means you are in some ways always on. Not to mention, the decade of unicorn companies—think Uber—has created a false ideal of what a successful business looks like. While the Sara Blakelys of the world are undoubtedly inspiring, you do not need to create the next Spanx to be a successful entrepreneur. Still, if this is a path you choose to pursue, defining what success looks like for you, and identifying how much time and money you have available to give the business in its infancy, is an important first step.

In 2022, women made up nearly half of new business owners, according to research from the online HR platform Gusto. In total, the U.S. Small Business Administration estimates that women own more than 12 million businesses. There isn't clear research on how many of those women are mothers, but 99designs, an online graphic design marketplace, surveyed five hundred "mompreneurs" (a phrase I can't say I love) and found that 80 percent of them started their business *after* having children. The average age of these women's kids when they started their business: six. (Perhaps it's not a surprise that this is about the same age their kids started kindergarten.)

The reasons moms flock to entrepreneurship are the same reasons they take to freelancing. Flexibility is key. I'll reiterate that once your business is off the ground, it can feel like it's always vying for your attention (I speak from experience!), but you do have the power to make your own schedule. And once you've tried your hand at managing the business of your household, steering the ship of a company might not feel so daunting. Amri Kibbler notes that at HeyMama, the networking platform for mothers she founded in 2014, about 70 percent of the members as of 2023 are entrepreneurs. "The rise in entrepreneurship for women, especially mothers, is due to a multitude of reasons," she says. "As a mother a lot of times you need to redesign what you want your life to look like, and the corporate construct doesn't fit that anymore. There's also this phenomenon that occurs: we're really great at fixing things because we're fixing things constantly for the people in our lives, and we get really passionate about solutions when we see a problem. Many of these businesses start out as a mom who is solving a problem for her own family or her children. She sees them in some way struggling and so she finds a great solution that other people would like access to and then she turns that into a business."

To make entrepreneurship work, you'll probably need to revisit your North Star from chapter 4. Let's say it's to prioritize your family even as you wade back into work. "You might then start to look at 'What are my top four priorities?' and you may juggle them around a bit but hopefully you'll always come back to 'Am I still prioritizing my family?'" Kibbler says. "It's important to track yourself. If you allocated yourself ten hours a week to work on your project and you're noticing that you're repeatedly going over your time budget, be mindful of that." It can be tricky, she points out, because it gets exciting when a business is taking off, but it's the only way to sustain the home *and* job piece with any real satisfaction.

Holly Blakey, the founder of Breathing Room Home we met in chapter 4, wrote a three-year road map before diving headfirst into her home organizing business. The business plan included her budget, expenses, and personal goals. Once she launched, she started a company social media account as a marketing channel, but it ended up becoming a central part of her revenue stream, helping her secure partnerships with the Container Store and Home Depot. When a book deal landed in her lap, she surprised even herself when she turned it down, but her three kids were still young and she knew working on a book would steal from the time she still wanted to preserve for home. Entrepreneurship, freelancing, consulting, and independent work all demand the same clarity, boundaries, and, ultimately, the same degree of prioritization that we've talked about throughout this book.

CULTURE MATTERS

Interviewing is stressful, especially if you're out of practice, so it's easy to forget that while the company is evaluating you, you're evaluating them right back. One thing to look for is a culture of people who get it. During those early interview conversations, pay attention to how employees talk about parenthood and how they bring up or respond to topics of flexibility for sick days or doctor's appointments. That's something you can't negotiate—respect for parental responsibilities either exists in an organization or it doesn't, and it will make your transition back to the workforce a whole lot easier if you don't have to hide who and what you care about, or where your priorities are.

You might also seek out current employees who are not involved with your hiring process to speak to more candidly. "If I have a good rapport with the recruiter or the hiring manager, I might ask if they mind if I reach out to a couple of employees to ask about the company," Nina Lai says. "I also try to find connections through friends or people who used to work there, to get a better understanding of a company. Ultimately I think this is not science, but more about trusting your gut."

Where to Look for Your Next Big Thing

In our AMP survey, 58 percent of stay-at-home moms said they find the prospect of applying to jobs intimidating. But it doesn't have to be! There are a growing number of resources for job searching these days, including platforms that are specific to moms and those returning to work. Still, networking, that old mainstay, is always the easiest place to start. And *that* starts by speaking your goals aloud.

If you've been on an extended career break, it can feel vulnerable to tell people you're ready to go back to work. Just as you might have worried about how your pause would be received, you might be nervous that those who haven't taken a break might make snarky comments or judge your choices. But sharing with friends and family will make your search feel more definitive, and that alone can help build confidence. It also adds a level of accountability (some might call it pressure, but let's be positive). Anna McKay says moms are often shy about their search and try to keep it to themselves until they have something to show for it, but that behavior can be counterproductive: networks are always the best job-search resource, especially in the case of returning from a career break, because your connections are the people who can attest to your character and skills. And don't limit this to your close contacts. If you've volunteered at school and worked with other parents, these are people who can speak not only to your personality but your work ethic.

Once you've spread the word personally, consider return-to-work resources that specialize in placing candidates in your exact position: The Mother Untitled flex jobs board, yes, but there's also the Mom Project, ReBoot Accel, and Freelancing Females, all of which partner directly with corporations to bring women back into the workforce on flexible terms. Bigger sites like LinkedIn and Indeed might have more listings, and that can be helpful, but return-to-work platforms usually vet the organizations or jobs that post on their boards, so you can be confident the roles listed will be returner friendly. They also list flexible roles with which you can build up your résumé and experience while you consider returning to a more traditional employer.

Jessica Ponchak, a mother of two, was following Mother Untitled closely during her career break. Jessica, who is deaf, had worked in People at Apple (this is what tech companies often call their HR departments), and while she was interested in returning to work she was especially nervous about the job search. She'd had a supportive community at Apple, and she knew she would have to overcome bias about her five-year career break on top of bias regarding her disability. Jessica found a contract administrator position at Bugaboo North America on the Mother Untitled flex jobs board. The role was temporary and more junior than Jessica's previous role, but it ended up being a stepping stone to a full-time position in a caring community. Jessica now leads HR at Bugaboo and has advocated for the bereavement, maternity, and parental leave that has earned the company the highest happiness scores globally.

Job boards and the like are productive places to find a wide range of listings, but if you desire a specific business culture in your next job opportunity, you might start by seeking out the companies that are already known to offer these environments. The Flex Report, which looks at data from four thousand companies globally, found that workplace flexibility varies largely based on an organization's industry, location, and size. Smaller companies—in this case defined by fewer than five hundred employees—are more likely to be flexible, while the biggest organizations (fifty thousand employees or more) generally offer less flexibility. Amri Kibbler suggests that small businesses might be especially receptive to applicants looking for part-time or independent contract work. "I see small businesses being very interested in flexible employees, because these businesses are growing and may not be at a place where they can hire full-time employees. If you were, say, a marketing expert or you worked in finance in your previous career, you're able to contribute to these businesses and lend your expertise, but maybe they are happy to only pay for five hours a week. Or maybe they only need five hours a month," she says. She also notes that female-owned businesses seem more inclined to hire women. The research bears this out: in 2018, a survey of entrepreneurs conducted by *Inc.* and *Fast Company* found that female founders are "disproportionately likely to hire other women."

Career coaches are another option that can be especially helpful to those who have years of experience but are looking to make a shift after an extended pause. "I work with a lot of stay-at-home moms," says career coach Marlo Lyons. "I've worked with moms who have been home for fifteen, eighteen years and are getting back into the workforce. You need somebody who can draw out of you what you've done in that period of time. I promise you that you have skills and capabilities that you don't even realize."

Nailing the Interview

I'm not going to pretend that interviewers and hiring committees don't still have biases about career gaps. We've covered some of the research already—the one in five hiring managers who say they reject candidates with gaps, the 75 percent of moms who report experiencing bias about their break. A U.K. study found that rewriting a résumé to highlight the number of years worked at a job rather than the dates you worked there increases callbacks from employers by 15 percent. These dated attitudes are certainly improving, but until every employer can be educated on how to meaningfully approach and ask about career breaks with genuine curiosity (not impossible!), having productive conversations about your break can be a challenge—and it might be on you to ease any of the awkwardness. Anna McKay says that employers want to hear you acknowledge your break, but more importantly, to acknowledge your readiness to return. "The three C's that employers are looking for are commitment, competence, and connection—as in connection with the team members, the company, and the mission of the organization," she says. "When you address your career pause, the biggest question on an employer's mind is, 'Will she be committed to the work that we're doing?' So you want to express and acknowledge that: 'Yes, I did have a career pause for caregiving, and now I'm excited to get back and I bring all of this value and I've brushed up on my skills by doing X, Y, and Z.'"

Remember, interviewers are human. A lot of your success in these conversations is based on comfort with small talk and feeling confident in your choices and expressing that. It's not always easy to speak to how you grew through your time away, so this is something you should practice. If I was returning to a traditional employer in a brand or marketing role, I might talk about developing a clarity of communication and a deeper sense of patience in the home and using the time to sharpen my skills in digital marketing with additional training. I might mention my volunteer roles and my deeper understanding of the parenting audience now that I am a part of that demographic. You might say that as an interviewee, you should have three C's of your own: confidence, clarity, and creativity.

The Traps and Pitfalls of the Return

It would be nice if, once you landed your next career opportunity, the hard work was done and the shift in your family dynamic came easily to all. If only it were so simple! As is the case with any change, transitioning into outside work comes with its own set of obstacles—the kind that can be navigated if you know what to look for, but can really trip you up if you're flying blind. Consider the following common pitfalls in advance of starting your next gig. It's a lot easier to prepare for them before you've got the added stress of work responsibilities hanging over your head.

Pitfall 1: Not adjusting the distribution of household labor

My husband, Dan, started building his own technology company during the years that we had small kids at home. He was able to throw himself into work because he had a mostly stay-at-home partner. As I've increased my Mother Untitled work schedule, I haven't had that same privilege. Since my husband and I both work out of the home these days, I thought we would both share the work *in* the home. And to some extent that has been the case—Dan's job allows him to make his own schedule, which makes our household labor split a bit easier. But research shows that even when both parents work out of the home, mothers disproportionately handle the domestic chores. In fact, the 2017 Modern Family Index, a survey from the childcare provider Bright Horizons, found that working mothers are twice as likely to manage the household, and three times as likely to manage the children's schedules.

When stay-at-home mothers return to work, they often get

stuck shouldering the same amount of family responsibility they had as the primary caretaker because their family doesn't update their expectations. For Dan and me, it takes Sunday check-ins, calendaring *everything*, and clear asks regarding household chores to make sure we're sharing the load in a way that feels fair. But it took a good amount of miscommunication (and one forgotten pickup) to get there.

Pitfall 2: Blurring the lines of work and family

Starting a job can come with a desire to prove your commitment to your new employer, which can often be mistaken for showing that you'll work at all hours. I am constantly reminding myself that I was too intentional for too many years to fall into the trap of being a martyr to work. But there are some days when work commitments mean I miss something at home. This happens, and I find that everyone in my house is happier when I'm all in on one thing or another, rather than trying to do two things at once. If I'm at home with the kids, I try to really be with the kids and accept that work isn't going to get my attention. If it's a day that I've committed to meetings and I won't be home until dinner, I have to very consciously accept that today will not be a big mother-child bonding day.

Child development psychologist Tovah Klein says that what kids need from parents is presence. "The 'home office'—that rectangle in our hands—doesn't actually help us be a career person one moment and a parent the next," she says. "The transitions need so much intention." Trying to figure out the balance as you go, or attempting to pop back and forth between your two roles, can backfire on everyone. "These very fluid boundaries are too fluid for children, for sure, but I think they're too fluid for the moms as well," Klein says.

Pitfall 3: Not asking for help

As we discussed in chapter 6, support is a crucial element of any phase of parenting. When your family routine changes, the type or amount of help you need will likely change too. You might, for example, need to extend your hours of childcare, or pay for help with household chores. Productivity expert Julie Morgenstern told me that many of her clients who are working mothers book their childcare to leave the second they arrive home, which once again cuts out any time parents have for themselves. She encourages parents to build in some breathing room so they don't have to always rush home from work to immediately dive into, well, other work.

You might also have days where, say, your kid needs to be picked up early from school and you can't necessarily make it. If you have a partner, perhaps they can jump in, but you should have conversations ahead of time with anyone you might rely on as a contingency plan. "Even though I'm now working, I am still the 'default' parent," Ponchak says. "Whenever my daughter is home sick, the responsibility still falls to me to care for her. It's challenging at times because I still want to protect my time at work, so learning how to ask for help and set boundaries as far as what I can realistically do has been a key thing for me." Sometimes the boundary is, "I need to stay at work, would you mind please picking up my kid?" But other times it might be, "I have to pick up my kid, do you mind covering for me at work?" Setting up support systems at work that you can rely on for help (knowing that you can offer help in return) is equally as important as establishing them at home.

Pitfall 4: Feeling like you have something to prove

Yes, you may need to account for your résumé gap during your job interviews. But once you've been hired, you are just as entitled to be on the payroll as any other employee. Let go of any urge to explain yourself or justify your decisions or prove that you can keep up. "I remember explaining something that had to do with my work history and all the male executives said, 'We don't need you to prove anything. You're here. And we're glad you're here. That's it,'" Lai says. "It was such an eye-opener. It really made me think about how to approach future talent, but also other women who are trying to get back into work."

Remember: You were hired for a reason. You deserve to be there. You don't owe anybody anything and certainly shouldn't apologize for your choices.

The Kids Are All Right

Stay-at-home mothers aren't "better" for kids. Working mothers aren't "better" for kids. Research shows that a parent's career status has no bearing on the happiness levels of their children. What *is* best for kids, notes Tovah Klein, is to have a parent who's generally happy with their life. "A more centered mother who feels good about herself in all of her identities is a better parent," she says. "No matter how you cut the data, any work-family setup that supports a woman in her confidence and her sense of self and meaningfulness will make her a better parent."

If you're worried that your return to work will create chaos for your children, now's the time to breathe a sigh of relief. Kids can handle change, and they will follow your lead. If you seem anxious, they will pick up on that. If you feel confident in everyone's ability to make tricky transitions, they will too. Set the stage for the upcoming shift by talking to your family about it directly. "Children really do respond to adults when they pave a way that says, 'This may be hard initially, I'm here to help you. We're going to all get used to it,'" Klein says. "It's what builds a child's strength."

How you address your return with your family will depend on a number of factors. How different will their day-to-day be? How old are your kids? How much information do they need? "I had a neighbor who went back to work when her kids were in high school. So that's a really different conversation—you can talk about why you're going back and what lights you up about work and what feels exciting and what you're scared about and how you need your kids' help," says clinical psychologist Anne Welsh. "If you've got a two-year-old, it might just be saying, 'I'm going back to work. I am going to miss seeing you and I'm really excited to do this thing for myself or our family. And it may be hard, because you don't get to see mom as much every day, and that's okay.' Recognize that your kid might have feelings about this, but it doesn't mean you're being a bad mom. It means it's something different."

Pressing Play

Rebecca Finkel is a mother of two in Seattle who took a pause, then returned to work part-time, and eventually transitioned back to full-time. Having experienced these various combinations of work and motherhood, what she's realized is that mothers—no matter our career phase—have more in common than we don't. "Never in my whole life did I think that I'd be a stay-at-home parent, even for a little while. I think that's why it was so important for me to do it," she says. "I'm grateful now to have been a part-time working parent, a stay-at-home parent, a full-time working parent. Each version is challenging. They each have their own costs and benefits. And I get to see that full picture—everyone's working really hard."

Power Practice:
Own Your Narrative—Starting
with Your Résumé

This chapter explored how to position your pause for employers, how and where to look for work, and how to avoid the pitfalls of diving back in. As you consider applying to jobs, the first step is updating your résumé. Use the blank space below to do a brain dump of all your experiences—volunteering for schools, helping a friend, fundraising—and then extract the elements of each experience that generate the most pride.

_____

_____

_____

_____

_____

_____

_____

Now it's time to formalize this brain dump. It can be tempting to slap on a "consultant" title and call it a day—and that might be a good solution during the time of your pause—but now that you're actively looking for work, take a cue from Chinue Richardson or Kristin Rumpf and own your time away with clarity. Honesty is always the best policy. However, two things can be true: you can be focused on family life and away from the traditional work-force, *and* you may have grown in many nontraditional ways. Even if you're not considering reentry to traditional fields, this exercise is a confidence-boosting approach to reflecting on how you have grown, sharpened your skills outside of the workforce, and contributed in a meaningful way.

Use this collection of words and catchphrases in any sub-bullets to your lead parent or primary caregiver section on your résumé.

Sample Headlines

Career Sabbatical for Caregiving

Career Break for Family/Health/Special Projects

Lead Parent

Self-Employed

Professional Development

Sample Sub-Bullets

Managed family systems and schedules

Led fundraising committee

Implemented new programs

Orchestrated family relocation

Identified key community initiatives

Managed complex budgeting review

Collaborated with parent leaders

Pitched local initiatives

Researched improvements

Earned certification

Advised local business marketing efforts

Consulted for local organizations

Coordinated logistics for local youth programs and teams

Conclusion

IT WAS THE privilege of my lifetime to pause my career to make room for family life. Being home with my kids was what I wanted, and it was the most challenging and rewarding way I could have spent my last eight years. As happens at the end of any significant time period, I look back on my stay-at-home phase with deep gratitude and also some wistfulness. I wish I had felt more at ease sometimes, and not so self-conscious about not having an income, or how other people were viewing me. I often felt that I wasn't doing enough, or contributing enough—monetarily and also to society as whole—and I wish I hadn't put that pressure on myself. But I also made a point of appreciating the small moments of silliness or connection that were the reason I made this choice. I learned so much—about myself, my children, my partner and extended family, my values. I discovered a new passion, and a new career.

At the start of the school year, I showed my daughter, Lyla, a picture book I made that detailed our new routine. When she saw the image of her beloved babysitter at school pickup, I could tell she was confused. "Mommy, why do you have to work, why can't you get it done while I'm at school?" she asked. I couldn't decide whether to laugh or cry—I really wanted to do a little bit of both. But it's my daughter's job to push and my job to be clear, and to love her whether I'm at pickup or not. And here's what I know: if I do my work well, and we change this cultural conversation, one day when someone asks her whether her mother was a "working" or "stay-at-home" mom, she won't know how to respond. She'll just know I was whole, and I was there. Even when I wasn't.

Parenting can be humbling, but it's equally as empowering. If there's anything I've learned as a mother and new business owner, it's that we are all so much more capable than we thought. But navigating motherhood and your ambitions requires a certain amount of trust—trust in the long game and, mostly, trust in yourself.

It's time to write your next chapter. I know you will make it your own.

Acknowledgments

THIS BOOK WAS the culmination of years of living in a career pause and going through professional shifts and building a community of women doing the same. Each of those women lent to the collective narrative. Thank you to every member of the Mother Untitled community who helped amplify this message.

Kristin van Ogtrop, having you in my corner meant the world. Julia Edelstein, you are so sharp, and your fine-tuning of my ideas helped put this book on its path. Rachel Bertsche, I would write a dozen more books with your help—thank you for making it a joy. Michelle Howry, you are the best—a caring and careful editor who took a chance on me and this message, and I will be forever grateful. You rallied an incredible roster of women at Putnam and Penguin Random House around this work to bring it to the world: Sally Kim, Alexis Welby, Ashley McClay, Ashley Di Dio, Ashley Hewlett, and Molly Pieper. Alison Rich, Rachael Perriello, Zehra

Kayi, and Stephanie Bowen, thank you for lending your talent to building our community. Emily Mileham, Maija Baldauf, Anthony Ramondo, Vi-An Nguyen, Brittany Bergman, Katy Riegel, and Amy Ryan, I appreciate all you did in the details that make this book unique. Hilary McClellen, you rounded out a dream team with your diligence in ensuring we all feel confident in the research and data that makes this work solid.

Amanda Schumacher, Eugenia Cassidy, Kaitlyn King, Lizzie Goodman, Victoria O'May, Megan Wai, and Elisa Hayden, thank you for investing your precious time into building this movement with me.

My girlfriends who checked in, texted, forgave me when I didn't text back, and sent flowers and hugs—I won't list you because I'll leave someone out, but I look forward to celebrating.

To my generous in-laws, babysitters, and helpers who have been the "village" I wish for everyone. For helping care for my family so I could do this work, Joshua, Julia, Lina, and Lauren, there's not enough credit I could give you.

Mama and Papa, I hope I do a fraction of the good in the world that you do. Thank you—for everything. Dan, you raise the bar for every dad in the game. I can't wait to see what we do next together.

Bodie and Lyla, this book is because of you. Thank you for letting me grow up with you. I love you.

Notes

Chapter 1: Discover Who You Are Without a Job Title

9   **high-quality daycare:** Jorge Luis García et al., "Quantifying the Life-Cycle Benefits of an Influential Early-Childhood Program," *Journal of Political Economy* 128, no. 7 (July 1, 2020): 2502–41, https://doi.org/10.1086/705718.

12 **"Although 95 percent":** Stephanie Coontz, *The Way We Never Were: American Families and the Nostalgia Trap* (New York: Basic Books, 2016), 28.

12 **"Nineteenth-century middle-class women":** Coontz, *The Way We Never Were*, 27.

13 **The 1960s and 1970s brought:** Martha Weinman Lear, "The Second Feminist Wave," *The New York Times*, March 10, 1968, https://www.nytimes.com/1968/03/10/archives/the-second-feminist-wave.html.

14 **"Our failure was":** Betty Friedan, *The Second Stage* (Cambridge, MA: Harvard University Press, 1998), 171.

14 **"a boring, limited woman":** Susan J. Douglas and Meredith W. Michaels, *The Mommy Myth: The Idealization of Motherhood and How It Has Undermined All Women* (New York: Free Press, 2004), 204.

17   **The *New York Times* first used:** Jessica Grose, "Can't We Think of a Better Term Than 'Stay-at-Home Moms'?," *Slate Magazine*, March 26, 2013, https://slate.com/human-interest/2013/03/housewife -homemaker-or-stay-at-home-mom-what-should-we-call -women-who-don-t-do-paid-work.html.

18   **In a 2023 Pew Research survey:** Juliana Menasce Horowitz and Kim Parker, "How Americans View Their Jobs," Pew Research Center, March 30, 2023, https://www.pewresearch.org/social-trends/2023 /03/30/how-americans-view-their-jobs/.

19   **story that encouraged professionals:** Rachel Feintzeig, "Stop Telling Everyone What You Do for a Living," *The Wall Street Journal*, April 10, 2023, https://www.wsj.com/articles/stop-telling-everyone-what-you -do-for-a-living-5daa8fc9.

Chapter 2: Work Out the Finances and Feel Empowered

39   **half of opposite-sex marriages:** Richard Fry, Carolina Aragão, Kiley Hurst, and Kim Parker, "In a Growing Share of U.S. Marriages, Husbands and Wives Earn About the Same," Pew Research Center, April 13, 2023, https://www.pewresearch.org/social-trends/ wp-content/uploads/sites/3/2023/04/Breadwinner-wives-full -report-FINAL.pdf.

40   **About half of the mothers:** Charlie Joughin, "Economic Data Underscores the Need for Significant, Sustained Investment in Child Care and Early Learning," First Five Years Fund, December 20, 2021, https://www.ffyf.org/latest-economic-data-underscores-the-need -for-significant-sustained-investment-in-child-care-and-early -learning/.

40   **Women who have paused:** Amy Stewart, "2023 Gender Pay Gap Report (GPGR)," Payscale, May 17, 2023, https://www.payscale.com /research-and-insights/gender-pay-gap/.

41   **The change was a response:** Julianne McShane, "How LinkedIn's 'Career Break' Feature Could Help Normalize Caregiving," *The Washington Post*, April 6, 2022, https://www.washingtonpost.com /business/2022/04/06/linkedin-career-break-caregiving/.

41   **"The pandemic made the career break":** Carol Fishman Cohen, "From Hire to Retire 6: Taking a Break Without Breaking Your Career," June 21, 2022, in *As We Work*, https://www.wsj.com/podcasts

/as-we-work/from-hire-to-retire-6-taking-a-break-without-breaking
-your-career/579128bc-fdc6-42fd-9024-46502ae709bc.

43   **Retirement planning received:** Emily Oster, "Retire Inequality:
TIAA White Paper," ParentData.com, 2023, accessed September 4,
2023, https://retireinequality.com/assets/oster/TIAA-White
-Paper.pdf.

56   **More than two-thirds of couples:** Alyson F. Shapiro, John M. Gottman,
and Sybil Carrère, "The Baby and the Marriage: Identifying Factors
That Buffer Against Decline in Marital Satisfaction After the First
Baby Arrives," *Journal of Family Psychology* 14, no. 1 (January 1, 2000):
59–70, https://doi.org/10.1037/0893-3200.14.1.59.

56   **when their kids are toddlers:** "Beyond Parental Leave: Supporting the
Marathon of Working Parenthood," Vivvi.com, January 2023,
accessed September 4, 2023, https://7061949.fs1.hubspotusercontent
-na1.net/hubfs/7061949/Beyond%20Parental%20Leave_Werklabs
%20x%20Vivvi%20FINAL.pdf?__hstc=111372315.f95718782
072b8a6c1979e9c8380f4a3.1693851265646.1693851265646
.1693851265646.1&__hssc=111372315.1.1693851265646&__
hsfp=399449310.

Chapter 3: Trust That Your Career Isn't Over and Resign Strategically

65   **93 percent had experienced:** Jocelyne Gafner, "Report: 93% of Stay at
Home Moms Have Experienced or Anticipate Experiencing
Challenges When Reentering the Workforce," Indeed.com, updated
August 10, 2023, https://www.indeed.com/career-advice/news
/stay-at-home-mom-valuable-transferable-skills.

65   **résumés that listed a career pause:** Katherine Weisshaar, "From Opt
Out to Blocked Out: The Challenges for Labor Market Re-Entry after
Family-Related Employment Lapses," *American Sociological Review*
83, no. 1 (January 10, 2018): 34–60, https://doi.org/10.1177
/0003122417752355.

66   **mothers viewed their experience:** Gafner, "Report: 93% of Stay at Home
Moms Have Experienced or Anticipate Experiencing Challenges
When Reentering the Workforce."

66   **84 percent of them foresee:** *Millennial Careers: 2020 Vision, Facts,
Figures and Practical Advice from Workforce Experts*, 2020,
ManpowerGroup.com, accessed April 18, 2024, https://www

.manpowergroup.co.uk/wp-content/uploads/2016/05/Millennials Paper1_2020Vision.pdf.

69   **the first Baby Einstein video:** Ruth Graham, "The Rise and Fall of Baby Einstein," *Slate*, December 19, 2017, https://slate.com/technology/2017/12/the-rise-and-fall-of-baby-einstein.html.

69   **"Nothing prepared me":** Susan Page, "'You Play Rough, You Get Hurt': How Nancy Pelosi's Family Life Prepared Her to Make Political History," *Vanity Fair*, April 16, 2021, https://www.vanityfair.com/news/2021/04/how-nancy-pelosis-family-life-prepared-her-to-make-political-history.

69   **women succeeded in returning to work:** Pamela Stone and Meg Lovejoy, *Opting Back In: What Really Happens When Mothers Go Back to Work* (Oakland, CA: University of California Press, 2019), 108.

70   **More than two million women:** "Women Are Back in the Workforce After Leaving to Caretake During the Pandemic," NPR, September 27, 2022, https://www.npr.org/2022/09/27/1125478595/women-are-back-in-the-workforce-after-leaving-to-caretake-during-the-pandemic.

75   **the "in the loop" resignation method:** Anthony C. Klotz and Mark C. Bolino, "Saying Goodbye: The Nature, Causes, and Consequences of Employee Resignation Styles," *Journal of Applied Psychology* 101, no. 10 (October 1, 2016): 1386–404, https://doi.org/10.1037/apl0000135.

77   **Burned-out, resentful employees:** Anthony C. Klotz and Mark C. Bolino, "7 Ways People Quit Their Jobs," *Harvard Business Review*, September 15, 2016, https://hbr.org/2016/09/7-ways-people-quit-their-jobs.

79   **mothers who work part-time:** Cheryl Buehler and Marion O'Brien, "Mothers' Part-Time Employment: Associations with Mother and Family Well-Being," *Journal of Family Psychology* 25, no. 6 (January 1, 2011): 895–906, https://doi.org/10.1037/a0025993.

87   **LinkedIn now even includes:** Kim Elsesser, "LinkedIn Adds 'Stay-At-Home Parent' to Job Titles—Research Says Don't Use It," *Forbes*, April 15, 2021, https://www.forbes.com/sites/kimelsesser/2021/04/15/linkedin-adds-stay-at-home-parent-to-job-titles---research-says-dont-use-it/?sh=817e768459b1.

96   **"higher motivation, self-esteem":** Gary P. Latham and Edwin A. Locke, "New Directions in Goal-Setting Theory," *Current Directions in Psychological Science,* 15, no. 5 (October 2006): 265–268, https://doi.org/10.1111/j.1467-8721.2006.00449.x.

Chapter 5: Create a Daily Rhythm to Maximize Joy

124   **"social media has drastically increased":** Ciera E. Kirkpatrick and
Sungkyoung Lee, "Comparisons to Picture-Perfect Motherhood: How
Instagram's Idealized Portrayals of Motherhood Affect New Mothers'
Well-Being," *Computers in Human Behavior* 137 (December 2022),
https://doi.org/10.1016/j.chb.2022.107417.

126   **24 percent of American women:** United Nations Department of
Economic and Social Affairs, *The World's Women 2015: Trends and
Statistics,* accessed December 13, 2023, https://unstats.un.org/unsd
/gender/downloads/worldswomen2015_report.pdf.

126   **a paper in the** *Journal of Global Health***:** Elizabeth Hyde, Margaret E.
Greene, and Gary L. Darmstadt, "Time Poverty: Obstacle to Women's
Human Rights, Health and Sustainable Development," *Journal of
Global Health* 10, no. 2 (December 2020), DOI: 10.7189/jogh.10.020313.

127   **fourteen hours per week:** U.K. Office for National Statistics, "Men
Enjoy Five Hours More Leisure Time Per Week Than Women,"
January 9, 2018, https://www.ons.gov.uk/people
populationandcommunity/wellbeing/articles/menenjoyfive
hoursmoreleisuretimeperweekthanwomen/2018-01-09.

127   **a general mental-health term:** World Health Organization, International
Classification of Diseases, 11th revision, January 2023, https://icd
.who.int/browse11/l-m/en#/http://id.who.int/icd/entity/129180281.

127   **job burnout can lead to excessive stress:** Mayo Clinic, "Job Burnout:
How to Spot It and Take Action," June 5, 2021, https://www
.mayoclinic.org/healthy-lifestyle/adult-health/in-depth/burnout
/art-20046642.

127   **the term "caregiver burnout":** Cleveland Clinic, "Caregiver Burnout,"
August 16, 2023, https://my.clevelandclinic.org/health/diseases
/9225-caregiver-burnout; Tara Parker-Pope, "How to Be a Caregiver,"
The New York Times, December 1, 2020, https://www.nytimes.com
/interactive/2020/well/family/well-caregiver-guide.html.

127   **55 percent of the stay-at-home mothers:** Motherly, "State of
Motherhood: 2022 Survey Results," https://www.mother.ly/state
-of-motherhood.

128   **"feeling pressure to be a perfect mother":** Loes Meeussen and Colete
Van Laar, "Feeling Pressure to Be a Perfect Mother Relates to Parental
Burnout and Career Ambitions," *Frontiers in Psychology* 9 (November
2018), doi:10.3389/fpsyg.2018.02113.

128 **"Those first weeks":** Thao Thai, "My Partner Was the Stay-At-Home Parent—Now I Am. Here's the Difference," Mother Untitled, October 5, 2022, https://www.motheruntitled.com/blog/2022/10/5/how -stay-at-home-parenthood-differs-for-men.

129 **Parents who say they always feel rushed:** Pew Research Center, "Parenting in America," December 17, 2015, https://www .pewresearch.org/social-trends/2015/12/17/2-satisfaction-time -and-support/#feeling-rushed.

129 **A 2020 study found:** Sara F. Waters et al., "Keep It to Yourself? Parent Emotion Suppression Influences Physiological Linkage and Interaction Behavior," *Journal of Family Psychology* 34, no. 7 (2020): 784–93, http://dx.doi.org/10.1037/fam0000664.

130 **boost cognitive function, reduce stress, and improve productivity:** Katherine R. Arlinghaus and Craig A. Johnston, "The Importance of Creating Habits and Routine," *American Journal of Lifestyle Medicine* 13, no. 2 (March–April 2019): 142–44, doi:10.1177/1559827618818044; "Health Benefits of Having a Routine," Northwestern Medicine, December 2022, https://www.nm.org/healthbeat/healthy-tips /health-benefits-of-having-a-routine.

130 **kids with routines:** Elisa Muñiz, Ellen J. Silver, and Ruth E. K. Stein, "Family Routines and Social-Emotional School Readiness Among Preschool-Age Children," *Journal of Developmental and Behavioral Pediatrics* 35, no. 2 (February–March 2014): 93–99, https://doi.org /10.1097/DBP.0000000000000021.

134 **the average American's 6.8 hours:** Jeffrey M. Jones, "In U.S., 40% Get Less Than Recommended Amount of Sleep," Gallup, December 19, 2013, https://news.gallup.com/poll/166553/less-recommended -amount-sleep.aspx.

135 **It's when we feel stagnant:** Corey L. M. Keyes, "The Mental Health Continuum: From Languishing to Flourishing in Life," *Journal of Health and Social Behavior* 43, no. 2 (June 2002): 207–22, https:// doi.org/10.2307/3090197; Corey L. M. Keyes, "Complete Mental Health: An Agenda for the 21st Century," in *Flourishing: Positive Psychology and the Life Well-Lived,* ed. Corey L. M. Keyes and Jonathan Haidt (Washington, DC: American Psychological Association, 2003), 293–312.

139 **kids who are assigned chores:** Marty Rossman, "Involving Children in Household Tasks: Is It Worth the Effort?," University of Minnesota

College of Education and Human Development, September 2002, https://ww1.prweb.com/prfiles/2014/02/22/11608927/children -with-chores-at-home-University-of-Minnesota.pdf; "Harvard Second Generation Study," Harvard Medical School, https://www .adultdevelopmentstudy.org; Julie Lythcott-Haims, "How to Raise Successful Kids—Without Over-Parenting," TED Talks Live, November 2015, https://www.ted.com/talks/julie_lythcott_haims _how_to_raise_successful_kids_without_over_parenting; George E. Vaillant, Charles C. McArthur, and Arlie Bock, "Grant Study of Adult Development, 1938–2000," Harvard Dataverse, 2022, doi: 10.7910 /DVN/48WRX9.

141   **A 2018 survey of two thousand parents:** "Study: Parents Get About 30 Minutes of 'Me Time' Every Day," CBS News, October 9, 2018, https://www.cbsnews.com/minnesota/news/study-parents-get -about-30-minutes-of-me-time-every-day/.

141   **leisure time is harder:** Wendy Wang, "The 'Leisure Gap' Between Mothers and Fathers," Pew Research Center, October 17, 2013, https://www.pewresearch.org/short-reads/2013/10/17/the-leisure -gap-between-mothers-and-fathers.

141   **four in ten women develop:** Mother Untitled, American Mothers on Pause (AMP) survey, slide 85, https://www.motheruntitled.com /americanmothersonpause.

143   **the American Academy of Child and Adolescent Psychiatry recommends:** "Screen Time and Children," American Academy of Child and Adolescent Psychiatry, updated February 2020, https://www.aacap.org/AACAP/Families_and_Youth/Facts _for_Families/FFF-Guide/Children-And-Watching-TV-054 .aspx.

149   **employees spend 10.5 hours per week:** "Wake-Up Call: Survey: Workers Report Being Bored More Than 10 Hours a Week," PR Newswire, October 19, 2017, https://www.prnewswire.com/news-releases /wake-up-call-survey-workers-report-being-bored-more-than -10-hours-a-week-300539272.html.

149   **more than 60 percent of U.S. adults:** Cynthia Weiss, "Mayo Clinic Q and A: Boost Your Brain with Boredom," Mayo Clinic, January 13, 2023, https://newsnetwork.mayoclinic.org/discussion/mayo-clinic -q-and-a-boost-your-brain-with-boredom/; Alycia Chin, Amanda Markey, Saurabh Bhargava, et al., "Bored in the USA: Experience

Sampling and Boredom in Everyday Life," *Emotion* 17, no. 2 (2016): 359–68, doi.org/10.1037/emo0000232.

Chapter 6: Get Help Without Guilt

157   **we are the only rich country:** Anna Gromada and Dominic Richardson, "Where Do Rich Countries Stand on Childcare?," United Nations Children's Fund, 2021, https://www.unicef-irc.org/publications/pdf /where-do-rich-countries-stand-on-childcare.pdf.

157   **Rich countries across the globe:** Claire Cain Miller, "How Other Nations Pay for Child Care. The U.S. Is an Outlier," *The New York Times*, October 6, 2021, https://www.nytimes.com/2021/10/06 /upshot/child-care-biden.html.

157   **"Weak investments in leave and childcare":** Gromada and Richardson, "Where Do Rich Countries Stand on Childcare?"

158   **29 percent of stay-at-home mothers:** AMP survey slide 15.

158   **42 percent of stay-at-home moms:** Motherly, "State of Motherhood: 2022 Survey Results," https://www.mother.ly/state-of-motherhood.

159   **the average cost:** "Babysitting Rates—2023 Average Rates by State," UrbanSitter, accessed November 29, 2023, https://blog.urbansitter .com/babysitting-rates.

159   **In New York City:** Jacob Zinkula, "The Typical NYC Family Is Spending More Than 25% of Its Income on Childcare—Triple What's Deemed Affordable," *Business Insider*, September 12, 2023, https://www.businessinsider.com/childcare-daycare-cost-new-york -city-crisis-housing-2023-9; "Childcare Prices as a Share of Median Family Income by Age of Children and Care Setting," Women's Bureau, U.S. Department of Labor, accessed December 19, 2023, https://www.dol.gov/agencies/wb/topics/childcare/median-family -income-by-age-care-setting.

159   **Stay-at-home moms cited:** AMP survey, slide 15.

159   **babysitters ran parents:** "Babysitting Rates," UrbanSitter.

162   **39 percent of parents feel guilty:** "PR Study with Birchbox Fuels 'You-Time' Campaign," Kelton Global, August 5, 2019, https://www .keltonglobal.com/recognition/pr-study-birchbox-you-time-report.

162   **"don't acknowledge there's a caregiver":** Lauren Smith Brody, "The Invisible Nannies of Instagram," *Harper's Bazaar*, April 17, 2019, https://www.harpersbazaar.com/culture/features/a27074175 /nannies-instagram.

164 **62 percent of parents polled:** Rachel Minkin and Juliana Menasce
Horowitz, "Parenting in America Today," Pew Research Center,
January 24, 2023, https://www.pewresearch.org/social-trends
/2023/01/24/parenting-in-america-today.

165 **valued the work:** "How Much Is a Mom Really Worth? The Amount
May Surprise You," Annual Mom Salary Survey, Salary.com, May
2021, https://www.salary.com/articles/how-much-is-a-mom
-really-worth-the-amount-may-surprise-you.

171 **she resisted this conversation:** Neha Leela Ruch, "A Lawyer on Identity
Crisis, Maintaining Friendships & Reality of Solo Entrepreneurship,"
Mother Untitled, February 18, 2021, https://www.motheruntitled
.com/blog/2021/2/18/erin-a-former-lawyer-on-identity-crisis
-maintainig-freindships-reality-of-solo-entrepreneurship.

173 **bringing in help involved:** "This Is How Much Child Care Costs in
2023," Care.com, November 28, 2023, https://www.care.com/c
/how-much-does-child-care-cost/#key-findings; "2023 Cost of Care
Report," Care.com, accessed November 29, 2023, https://www.care
.com/business/resources/ebooks-and-reports/2023-cost-of
-care-report.

Chapter 7: Discover the Limitless Value of Mom Friends

192 **the U.S. Surgeon General:** U.S. Surgeon General, "Our Epidemic of
Loneliness and Isolation," U.S. Surgeon General's Advisory on
the Healing Effects of Social Connection and Community, 2023,
https://www.hhs.gov/sites/default/files/surgeon-general-social
-connection-advisory.pdf.

192 **51 percent of mothers:** Richard Weissbourd et al., "Loneliness in
America: How the Pandemic Has Deepened an Epidemic of Loneliness
and What We Can Do About It," Making Caring Common
Project, Harvard Graduate School of Education, February 2021,
https://mcc.gse.harvard.edu/reports/loneliness-in-america.

194 **low levels of social connection:** U.S. Surgeon General, "Our Epidemic
of Loneliness and Isolation."

195 **nonemployed women with small children:** Elizabeth Mendes, Lydia
Saad, and Kyley McGeeney, "Stay-at-Home Moms Report More
Depression, Sadness, Anger," Gallup, May 18, 2012, https://news
.gallup.com/poll/154685/stay-home-moms-report-depression
-sadness-anger.aspx.

195   **a mother's loneliness:** Marie Mandai et al., "Loneliness Among Mothers Raising Children Under the Age of 3 Years and Predictors with Special Reference to the Use of SNS: A Community-Based Cross-Sectional Study," *BMC Women's Health* 18, no. 131 (2018), doi.org 10.1186/s12905-018-0625-x.

195   **an antenatal baby-care class:** Mary L. Nolan et al., "Making Friends at Antenatal Classes: A Qualitative Exploration of Friendship Across the Transition to Motherhood," *The Journal of Perinatal Education*, 21, no. 3 (Summer 2012): 178–85, doi: 10.1891/1058-1243.21.3.178.

196   **investing in strong social support:** Esther Hsieh, "Motherhood Can Be a Lonely Place," *Scientific American*, September 1, 2015, https://www.scientificamerican.com/article/motherhood-can -be-a-lonely-place.

199   **people consistently underestimate:** Peggy J. Liu et al., "The Surprise of Reaching Out: Appreciated More Than We Think," *Journal of Personality and Social Psychology: Interpersonal Relations and Group Processes,* 124, no. 4 (2023): 754–71, doi.org/10.1037/pspi0000402.

202   **"moderately weak" ties:** Karthik Rajkumar et al., "A Causal Test of the Strength of Weak Ties," *Science* 377, no. 6612 (September 15, 2022): 1304–10, doi: 10.1126/science.abl4476; "A Team of MIT, Harvard and Stanford Scientists Finds 'Weaker Ties' Are More Beneficial for Job Seekers on LinkedIn," MIT Sloan School of Management, September 15, 2022, https://mitsloan.mit.edu/press/a-team-mit-harvard-and -stanford-scientists-finds-weaker-ties-are-more-beneficial-job -seekers-linkedin.

205   **more than 70 percent of moms say:** Motherly, "State of Motherhood: 2020 Survey Results," https://www.mother.ly/news/state-of -motherhood-survey.

206   **employees need psychological safety:** Ross Brooks, "Why Psychological Safety Is the Key to High Performing Teams," *Workday* (blog), August 17, 2018, https://blog.workday.com/en-us/2018/why-psychological -safety-the-key-to-high-performing-teams.html.

207   **71 percent of respondents:** Matt Zajechowski, "Survey Reveals Most Americans Would Rather Sit in Silence Than Make Small Talk," Preply, October 13, 2023, https://preply.com/en/blog/small-talk.

211   **fifty hours of time together:** Jeffrey A. Hall, "How Many Hours Does It Take to Make a Friend?," *Journal of Social and Personal Relationships* 36, no. 4 (2018): 1278–96, doi.org/10.1177/0265407518761225; Cari Romm, "This Is How Many Hours It Takes to Make a Friend," *The*

Cut, April 6, 2018, https://www.thecut.com/2018/04/this-is-how
-many-hours-it-takes-to-make-a-friend.html.

211   **"networking played a role":** Ivan Misner, "How Much Time Should You
Spend Networking?," Dr. Ivan Misner (website), https://ivanmisner
.com/time-spend-networking; Ivan Misner, "NetTime: How Much
Time Should You Devote to Networking?," *Fox Business,* updated
March 23, 2016, https://www.foxbusiness.com/features/nettime
-how-much-time-should-you-devote-to-networking.

Chapter 8: Let Yourself Pursue New Passions and Find New Strengths

219   **Self-development podcasts and books:** Marshall Sinclair, "Why the
Self-Help Industry Is Dominating the U.S.," Medium, February 24,
2019, https://medium.com/s/story/no-please-help-yourself
-981058f3b7cf.

219   **Self-help podcasts are expected:** Stewart Townsend, "Podcasting and
Self-Improvement: Spreading Inspiration Through Audio," Podcast
Hawk, August 22, 2023, https://podcasthawk.com/podcasting-and
-self-improvement-spreading-inspiration-through-audio/.

220   **stay-at-home moms have historically reported:** Mendes, Saad, and
McGeeney, "Stay-at-Home Moms Report More Depression, Sadness,
Anger."

220   **Research shows that hobbies:** Jill Suttie, "Doing Something Creative
Can Boost Your Well-Being," *Greater Good Magazine,* March 21, 2017,
https://greatergood.berkeley.edu/article/item/doing_something
_creative_can_boost_your_well_being; Tamlin S. Conner, Colin G.
DeYoung, and Paul J. Silva, "Everyday Creative Activity as a Path to
Flourishing," *Journal of Positive Psychology* 13, no. 2 (2018): 181–89,
doi.org/10.1080/17439760.2016.1257049.

221   **outside pursuits make you happier:** Alexandra Sifferlin, "Being
Creative Outside of Work Makes You Better at Your Job," *Time,*
April 16, 2014, https://time.com/65487/being-creative-outside-of
-work-makes-you-better-at-your-job/; Jeremy Dean, "The Positive
Effect of Creative Hobbies on Performance at Work," PsyBlog,
April 28, 2014, https://www.spring.org.uk/2014/04/the-positive
-effect-of-creative-hobbies-on-performance-at-work.php?ref=buffer
.com; Kevin J. Eschleman et al., "Benefiting from Creative Activity:
The Positive Relationships Between Creative Activity, Recovery
Experiences, and Performance-Related Outcomes," *Journal of*

Occupational and Organization Psychology 87, no. 3 (September 2014): 579–98, doi.org/10.1111/joop.12064.

224 **a third of women change their careers:** "A Third of Women Change Career After Having Children," Open Study College, September 30, 2022, https://www.openstudycollege.com/blog/career-changing -mothers.

232 **75 percent of female executives:** KPMG International, *Mind the Gap*, 2022, https://assets.kpmg.com/content/dam/kpmg/xx/pdf/2022/12 /mind-the-gap.pdf.

234 **Research bears this out:** Soraya Chemaly, "School Volunteering and Parental Pressure: One Mom's Unapologetic No," *Time*, January 21, 2014, https://time.com/1313/school-volunteering-and-parental -pressure-one-moms-unapologetic-no/; "Volunteering in the United States, 2015," U.S. Bureau of Labor Statistics, February 25, 2016, https://www.bls.gov/news.release/volun.nr0.htm.

240 **millennial parents spend:** "The Avg Amount Millennial Parents Spend on Parenting Books and Apps," Wonder, August 7, 2017, https://askwonder.com/research/avg-amount-millennial-parents -spend-parenting-books-apps-field-great-break-down-xjjsxbcdl; Marcella Hines, "How Millennials Learn: Check What They're Reading," Deloitte, September 26, 2023, https://action.deloitte .com/insight/3552/how-millennials-learn-check-what-theyre -reading.

Chapter 9: Put Your Pause in Your Career Portfolio and Return to Paid Work (If You Want!)

247 **parents currently on career breaks:** Kathy Gurchiek, "Don't Overlook Job Applicants Returning from Career Breaks," SHRM, March 17, 2022, https://www.shrm.org/resourcesandtools/hr-topics /organizational-and-employee-development/pages/dont -overlook-job-applicants-returning-from-career-breaks.aspx.

247 **About a third of *Fortune* 50 companies:** Carol Fishman Cohen, "Return-to-Work Programs Come of Age," *Harvard Business Review*, September–October 2021, https://hbr.org/2021/09/return-to -work-programs-come-of-age.

247 **according to a LinkedIn survey:** Jennifer Shappley, "LinkedIn Members Can Now Spotlight Career Breaks on Their Profiles," LinkedIn, March 1, 2022, https://www.linkedin.com/business

/talent/blog/product-tips/linkedin-members-spotlight-career
-breaks-on-profiles.

251   **Nearly 70 percent:** "Amid Economic Uncertainty, Indeed Flex Survey
Finds Two in Three Workers Have Experienced Gaps in Employment,"
Indeed Flex, March 16, 2023, https://indeedflex.com/about-us
/press-releases/amid-economic-uncertainty-indeed-flex-survey-finds
-two-in-three-workers-have-experienced-gaps-in-employment/.

251   **56 percent of workers:** Shappley, "LinkedIn Members Can Now
Spotlight Career Breaks on Their Profiles."

251   **More than half of the women:** Shappley, "LinkedIn Members Can Now
Spotlight Career Breaks on Their Profiles."

251   **three-quarters of stay-at-home moms:** Jocelyne Gafner, "Report: 93%
of Stay at Home Moms Have Experienced or Anticipate Experiencing
Challenges When Reentering the Workforce," Indeed.com, August
2023, https://www.indeed.com/career-advice/news/stay-at-home
-mom-valuable-transferable-skills.

251   **20 percent of hiring managers:** Shappley, "LinkedIn Members Can
Now Spotlight Career Breaks on Their Profiles."

252   **51 percent of employers:** Shappley, "LinkedIn Members Can Now
Spotlight Career Breaks on Their Profiles."

253   **Rutgers Center for Women in Business:** Lisa S. Kaplowitz and Kate
Mangino, "Research: Caregiver Employees Bring Unique Value
to Companies," *Harvard Business Review*, August 10, 2023,
https://hbr.org/2023/08/research-caregiver-employees-bring
-unique-value-to-companies.

257   **Johnson & Johnson, Costco:** Joanne Lipman, "Helping Stay-at-Home
Parents Reenter the Workforce," *Harvard Business Review*, June 7,
2019, https://hbr.org/2019/06/helping-stay-at-home-parents
-reenter-the-workforce.

258   **the number of workers:** "Stronger Together: The State of
Independence in America 2023," MBO Partners, October 2023,
https://www.mbopartners.com/state-of-independence; Bradley
Little, "The Growing Popularity of Freelance Work," WeWork,
January 18, 2022, https://www.wework.com/ideas/research-insights
/research-studies/the-growing-popularity-of-freelance-work.

258   **about half of the freelancers:** Gabriella Hoffman, "Freelance
Workforce Grows to 64.6M Participants," Independent Women's
Forum, December 5, 2022, https://www.iwf.org/2022/12/05
/freelance-workforce-grows-to-64-6m-participants.

260   **women made up nearly half:** Luke Pardue, "The Rise of Women Entrepreneurs," Gusto, October 2, 2023, https://gusto.com/company-news/the-rise-of-women-entrepreneurs.

260   **women own more than 12 million businesses:** "Facts About Small Business: Women Ownership Statistics," U.S. Small Business Administration, March 21, 2023, https://advocacy.sba.gov/2023/03/21/facts-about-small-business-women-ownership-statistics/.

260   **80 percent of them started their business:** "How Mompreneurs Balance Business and Family," 99designs, 2016, https://99designs.com/blog/business/mom-entrepreneur-infographic/.

264   **workplace flexibility varies:** "The Flex Report," The Flex Index, 2023, accessed December 13, 2023, https://www.canva.com/design/DAFwaFvbYas/1_Maguz8DmUAPGkfYS4wxg/view?utm_content=DAFwaFvbYas&utm_campaign=designshare&utm_medium=link&utm_source=publishsharelink; Alana Semuels, "Return-to-Office Full Time Is Losing. Hybrid Work Is on the Rise," *Time*, May 19, 2023, https://time.com/6281252/return-to-office-hybrid-work.

265   **a survey of entrepreneurs:** Kristin Lenz and Maria Aspan, "Exclusive Report: Hundreds of Female Founders Speak Out on Ambition, Politics, and #MeToo," *Inc.*, September 18, 2018, https://www.inc.com/women-entrepreneurship-report/index.html; Kimberly Weisul, "Report: Female Entrepreneurs Much More Likely to Employ Women," *Inc.*, December 18, 2018, https://www.inc.com/kimberly-weisul/these-entrepreneurs-hired-very-few-men.html.

265   **rewriting a résumé:** Ariella S. Kristal et al., "Reducing Discrimination Against Job Seekers with and Without Employment Gaps," *Nature Human Behaviour* 7 (February 2023): 211–18, doi.org/10.1038/s41562-022-01485-6.

267   **working mothers are twice as likely:** "Modern Family Index 2017," Bright Horizons, 2017, accessed December 13, 2023, https://www.brighthorizons.com/-/media/BH-New/Newsroom/Media-Kit/MFI_2017_Report_FINAL.ashx.

Index